Inequality and the Global Economic Crisis

Inequality and the Global Economic Crisis

DOUGLAS DOWD

PLUTO PRESS
www.plutobooks.com

First published 2009 by Pluto Press
345 Archway Road, London N6 5AA and
175 Fifth Avenue, New York, NY 10010

www.plutobooks.com

Distributed in the United States of America exclusively by
Palgrave Macmillan, a division of St. Martin's Press LLC,
175 Fifth Avenue, New York, NY 10010

British Library Cataloguing in Publication Data
A catalogue record for this book is available from the British Library

ISBN   978 0 7453 2944 4   Hardback
ISBN   978 0 7453 2943 7   Paperback

Library of Congress Cataloging in Publication Data applied for

This book is printed on paper suitable for recycling and made from
fully managed and sustained forest sources. Logging, pulping and
manufacturing processes are expected to conform to the environmental
standards of the country of origin. The paper may contain up to
70 per cent post-consumer waste.

10 9 8 7 6 5 4 3 2 1

Designed and produced for Pluto Press by
Chase Publishing Services Ltd, Sidmouth, England
Typeset from disk by Stanford DTP Services, Northampton, England
Printed and bound in the European Union by
CPI Antony Rowe, Chippenham and Eastbourne

CONTENTS

PREFACE

Inequality began when our species began. Since then its dimensions and its harmful consequences have both multiplied. This work is concerned mostly with its meanings for our era: the decades from the end of World War II to the present. Soon after that war's end, there seemed a promise of a significant diminution of inequalities and a movement toward a safer and saner world. Instead, taking hold in the 1970s were the beginnings of an increase in the inequalities of income, wealth and, in a mutually strengthening set of policies, of socio-economic *power*. As the moderately equalizing policies of post-1945 were stifled, the door was opened for always more of the same. Now, within and between all societies, the inequalities of income, wealth and power are worse than ever; dangerously so. Their whys and wherefore are the focus of the book.

This Preface was written in July, 2009, as a last-minute attempt to "update" the spreading, deepening, and multi-faceted global *crisis* now threatening to become the worst in history. Below we will comment upon ongoing and related political, military, and environmental developments. First, what is meant here by "crisis"?

It is a medical term signifying a body's dangerous condition from which it will move toward either better or worse. Given the strong roots, dynamics, and complexities of today's troubles (discussed throughout the text) it is virtually certain that by the time this is read all of what is relevant will be worsening, not improving. As you read, note that, as with our bodies, the several parts of society are interdependent: for better and for worse.

The Economy

The "globalization" and "financialization" that began to dominate as the 1970s ended were initially vital in bringing buoyancy to most national economies and to the world economy (see Chapters 6 and 7). But they also made virtually all national economies – European, African, Asian, and Latin American – importantly or critically dependent upon what was happening in the US economy. What those nations were "depending" upon was (1) a nation in which hyped-up consumerism was financed by reckless buying at home; (2) whose always rising imports were made feasible by endless borrowing of capital by the US from Europe and, mostly, from China and Japan (who, together, were already owed two *trillion* dollars by 2007); (3) which in turn fed the move toward record-breaking financial *speculation* within the US and in its global providers of money and goods; as there ensued (4) an ever-accelerating *destruction* of the financial regulations created after the 1930s, created specifically to prevent a repeat of the madness of the 1920s. The destruction of those rules began in the Reagan presidency of the 1980s and was pushed further in the Clinton administration of the 1990s. Nor is it encouraging to note that Clinton's financial advisor for *de*-regulation, Lawrence Summers, is now President Obama's financial advisor; and that his Treasury Secretary, Timothy Geithner, was head of the NY Federal Reserve Office in the wildest years of Wall Street's monkey biz.

The entire world is now locked in a recession that lurches toward depression. Nonetheless, in a worrisome repeat of the 1930s, the news intermittently announces that "the tide has turned"; that, as the saying went from 1930 on, "prosperity is just around the corner." But 1930s unemployment never went below 10 percent until 1942, a year *after* Pearl Harbor. By the time you read this, *official* US unemployment will be over 10 percent, but that official measure is understated: if the US were to measure unemployment as it is measured in Europe, to include those who were working full-time but are now on part-time and/or have given up looking, that number would be 15–16 percent. (See Chapters 10 and 11.) China and India are the only major economies still expanding, but because their growth depends critically upon their exports to the US, their rates of expansion are steadily falling. Why this and much more that is worrisome is under way is examined at length in Chapters 6 and 7. A disgusting part of the answer has to do with the fully corrupted politics of the US, to which I now turn.

Poisoned Government

To be "corrupted" is to act in ways you *know* are wrong, dangerous, illegal, etc. Perhaps nobody is innocent of such behavior, whether as regards "little white lies," peeking over the shoulder of a fellow student in an exam, or perhaps more underhand actions. Such corruption may or may not harm others; the corruption discussed in this book does. It includes doctors, for example, some of whose income comes from drug companies (see Chapter 9); or, more to the point, it includes elected politicians who vote the way they were bribed to by a business group (or gun lover group, etc.) with money and threats to finance a rival in the next election. (See Chapters 5 and 11.) Today's widespread corruption is by no means new to history, but it is surely deeper and broader than ever before. It has to be, because today we live in "democracies."

Why the quote marks around "democracies"? Because, especially in the US, our democracy is partial, only a *political* democracy, not a full socio-economic democracy. It is almost entirely confined to voting for politicians who should be named Tweedledee or Tweedledum, and who give their OK to whatever their financial supporters wish. For a decade or more after World War II, whether in the US, UK or Western Europe, there was a meaningful movement toward a fuller democracy. Not only were legal limits passed as to what business could, or could not, do as regards wages and hours, safety conditions, etc., but also (minimally in the US) there were provisions for strong unions, governmental health care and housing projects, education, and so on. Then, in the 1970s, especially but not only in the US, the business community consciously "re-politicized" itself so as to regain the political strength it had disgracefully abused in the interwar period (most clearly as regards the secretive support of fascism in four of the six leading capitalist countries: France, Germany, Italy, and Japan). From the 1970s corruption became and remains king, with big business financing tens of thousands of lobbyists and "research institutes" devoted to the wholesale corruption of national, state, and local governments. (See Chapters 4 and 5.)

When today's economic crisis erupted in the US, it was greatly facilitated by the years of congressional corruption which had closed the door on regulation and opened another of feverish speculation – symbolized by "derivatives," "credit default swaps," and other swinging doors of financial hocus-pocus. The players made billions; we are now on the decades-long road of paying the bill for their greed, and in more ways than one – not least by the millions who have lost their homes and/or jobs already, with more on the way.

The "bailouts" initiated by the Bush administration and continued and expanded by the Obama government are more likely than not to increase associated economic problems. Up to now these "cures" have been a gift to the highly paid instigators of the problem. Badly needed is a significant popular movement whose main policy criteria are to meet basic needs of the people rather than the playboy desires of well-dressed criminals and the politicians they have bribed and threatened. Pleased though I was by Obama's victory (I did a pre-election turn for him on TV), his continued bowing to the financial giants is more than disappointing; it is frightening. Also frightening are his policies regarding US involvement in the Middle East and Central Asia (see below).

Obama has made it clear that he wants to see at least the beginnings of a decent health care system, and evidently he thinks he has support from insurance companies and health care organizations (e.g., Blue Cross). Wrong. As I write, "the insurance industry is busily lobbying to block health care reform, and Blue Cross of North Carolina is preparing a series of ads attacking the public health care option" (Paul Krugman, "Calling Obama's Bluff," *New York Times*, May 23, 2009). In short, if the best side of Obama is to have a chance, we must put *our* political best side to work. Which is also what we must do as regards war and peace.

Wars

The Obama presidency inherited a seriously sick economy, but at least those troubles can be dealt with even though they involve an uphill fight against Congress: its GOP members want Obama to fail, as do all too many Democrats who have entered the corruption gate and may be stuck there. That's bad enough, but the resolution of those problems requires "only" the coming to life of a drugged public. Unfortunately, the resolution of our military struggles is more demanding, more difficult, more dangerous.

Our ongoing wars in Iraq and Afghanistan and the all too strong possibilities of a war with Iran will not be resolved unless and until the people of the US and its European allies shake off the militant attitudes to which we became accustomed in the Cold War and that were reborn and intensified in "the war on terrorism"; attitudes which Obama appears to share. As argued in Chapter 8, the origins of the Cold War had more to do with anti-communism and modernized imperialism than with a Soviet military threat. Note that World War II caused more deaths and economic and military weakness to the USSR than to any other combatant, and that although there have been, are, and increasingly will be "terrorists," their origins and always increasing strength are a consequence of a long and continuing history in which the Western powers (and, especially since World War II, the US) have sought to use and exploit their rich resources and to corrupt their leaders. Now "the chickens have come home to roost." The bases for the foregoing can be found in Chapter 8; but here is a summary of the major threats or problems the US is exacerbating with all too much popular support or acquiescence, and all too little popular resistance.

First: Iran. A major and justifiable basis for Iran's muscled anger against the US has its origins in the 1950s. Iran's first free election was in 1951. Mohammed Mossadegh was elected. His announced goal was the nationalization of Iran's rich oil resources. Soon after, in1953, with the now known support of the CIA, a military coup led to the arrest and jailing of Mossadegh. His office was taken by the young son of the earlier Shah (who had supported Hitler).

Then, in 1979, as with his father, the young Shah was overthrown by a popular revolt. There is much more to be said (see Chapter 8); suffice it to say here that it should be no surprise to learn that in 2009, the government of Iran has taken the position that, apart from much else, without an apology from the US, there can be no conciliatory talks. That "much else" includes, not least, the decades of very cozy relationships between the US and Israel. Not only has Israel been the largest recipient of US financial aid, but the US looked the other way when Israel bombed Iraq in 1981, and has never said a word about Israel's threats to attack Iran from the air or admitted that Israel possesses nuclear bombs, at the same time that it threatens Iran for its nuclear research.

Iran's June 2009 election was very probably fixed. The ensuing turmoil and repression make it more difficult for Obama to improve US relationships with Iran and make it more tempting for Israel to do what it has long wished to do – to attack Iran from the air. Whether or not the US can prevent that is moot; if it cannot, the door will be thrown open to an endless war.

Next: Afghanistan. As the Shah was being kicked out of Iran in 1979, the US took its first suicidal steps in Afghanistan. It was then – 30 years ago – that President Carter's National Security Advisor Zbigniew Brzezinski persuaded him to sign a directive for the CIA to provide weaponry to a small and then weak group in Afghanistan called the Taliban. Why? Because Brzezinski accurately believed that a newly-armed Taliban would draw bordering USSR into a trap what would, as he put it, "become the USSR's Vietnam." He was right: the Soviets charged in and, three years later, left in defeat. But what they left behind was a strong, ambitious, and respected Taliban. Since then, the ruthless and heartless Taliban has had an always spreading control of Afghanistan and with significant penetrations into an unstable Pakistan (a nuclear power). So it is that Afghanistan may become the *second Vietnam* for the US.

Much more needs saying and some of it may be found in Chapters 8 and 11. Suffice it to say here that the time has come – is indeed overdue – for the US to recognize that its arrogant military behavior has become self-destructive; perhaps globally-destructive. That recognition must first find its way into "the hearts and minds" of the US citizenry and make itself felt in the White House. Soon. Which takes us to still another emerging disaster that cannot be avoided without substantial popular and political effort...

Environmental Dangers

Already in 1950 it had become clear to a few scientists that the modern world and its ways and means were committing suicide. (See Chapter 5 and the reference to Kapp.) Since then, with the US in the lead, the world has become increasingly wasteful of a growing list of exhaustible natural resources. But there is more: in addition to what must be seen as "institutionalized *waste*" there has been associated "institutionalized *destruction*." The waste and destruction march always more damagingly in step, in tune with an insanely consumerist economy that presses us "to want what we don't need, and not to want what we do" (Baran, 1969). What is being destroyed are the bases of life: "earth, air, and water." The damage has been and is being done by the processes intrinsic to the "successful" functioning of capitalism and the infantile nationalism, racism, and greed underlying the ceaseless wars of our era. We are on a path that will either destroy us because we have misused the elements of life and/or because we have not learned how to stop killing each other. Time is running out.

The fault is not in our stars; it is in our having allowed ourselves to be taken for a fool's ride. It may too late to get off and "save ourselves alive" but it's not too late to try.

ACKNOWLEDGMENTS

First I wish to thank the staff at Pluto Press and Chase Publishing Services. When, without asking, I sent the manuscript to Pluto's chairman, Roger van Zwanenberg, his response was not to say yes, no, or maybe, but to suggest that I do a fair amount of this or that. Those suggestions and many that followed were such that I took them with pleasure. After many interchanges I found that, without saying so, he had decided to publish the book. Then I was placed in the hands of Pluto's Managing Editor, Robert Webb, who, after welcome comments, handed me and my manuscript over to Ray Addicott and Oliver Howard at Chase Publishing Services. Olly and I worked together meticulously for many weeks. His spirit and his numberless suggestions of form and substance were invaluable. Olly, you should write a book of your own.

For much else in another realm I also wish to thank Michael Slaughter. Michael, now a good friend, happened to wander into my free night classes in and near San Francisco. They began in the 1970s, along with my university teaching, and continued until a few years ago when my Italian wife Anna and I made a permanent move to Italy (where I have taught for many years, alternating with semesters with the US). Michael is a whiz with computers (inter alia), and years ago he set up a still functioning website for our classes: www.dougdowd.org

Now, last and most, I lovingly thank Anna. She has made my life truly wondrous; despite the hell going on outside. She is everything: in intelligence, in politically applied anger at a cruel and insane world; she is beautiful, has a marvelous sense of humor, and a long and undying commitment to decency and wellbeing for all, be they friends in Bologna or strangers in Africa; me included. Call me Lucky Louie.

PROLOGUE

Introduction

Inequality has been universal throughout humans' existence, varying over time and place in its form, intensity, and consequences. In the main capitalist nations life has always been difficult for a significant percentage of their working class, and horrible for almost all in the poor countries. Inequality has always tended to deepen in "hard times" and to lessen in "good times" in the rich countries, often at the expense of the poor countries.

Since World War II, the US has been the most influential of all nations. Its "influence" has been both positive and negative as to one degree or another most other countries have become "Americanized": economically, politically, socially, militarily. In becoming so, their patterns of inequality could not help but be affected; if neither in the same ways nor degrees.

From the 1970s on, the world entered a new era: the global economy became always more integrated and interdependent; there have been substantial periods of both expansion and contraction, and simultaneous inflation and deflation. The effects were most marked in the US but not unique to the US. Whether during expansion or contraction, the always substantial inequalities of income, wealth, and power worsened from the 1970s to the present.

This book was begun in 2006 and completed a few months after the US election won by Barack Obama. It is hoped that his presidency will not only halt but reverse the ugly tendencies that took root in the 1970s. Evidently, the election itself signified a marked lessening of racism against blacks. That said, it is also generally understood that the election took place just as it became clear (1) that a serious economic crisis had begun and, (2) that the Bush administration was not only critically responsible but that its emergency policies of "bailout" were favoring the very companies

1

and executives which had contributed to and profited from the causes of that crisis. It may be hoped that a considerably different direction, one concerning all the people rather than financial bigwigs, will be undertaken by the new administration.

Financial wildness is not unique to the present; a reading of economic history shows that as far back as the seventeenth and eighteenth centuries, the early years of capitalism, the two leading economies created *their* financial crises (first the Dutch "Tulip Mania," then the English "South Sea Bubble"). Their causes were centered on the greed aped in the US "Crash of 1929" and again in today's collapse. However, it must be understood that as capitalism moved from the seventeenth century to the present, always more complex economies and technologies have multiplied and deepened the consequences of greed-driven speculation. There is much to be understood and read about those developments: see Boxer (1965) for the Dutch, Bowden (1937) for England, and, for the US, Zinn (2000), Mitchell (1947), Soule (1947), and Phillips (2008).

The focus of ensuing chapters is mostly upon the US: its capitalism, its class structure, and its related inequalities of income, wealth, and power. It emerged as the most powerful of all capitalist societies during World War I, and its power greatly accelerated because of the enormous damages done to others by World War II. In the ensuing years, US policies have brought almost all other nations toward "Americanization" to a significant degree.

Capitalism's inherent *class* structure carries with it related income and wealth inequalities. But substantial attention must also be given to the ways in which economic and political inequalities have been supported and worsened by long-standing realms of discrimination and prejudice based on gender, color, religion, and national origin; not least in the US.

Capitalist Paradise: the US

Uniquely in the capitalist world, the US did not have a *pre*-capitalist existence; its inequalities have been stamped "American," from its Constitution to the present. That its "all men were created equal…" and that it omits all women and non-white men was doubtless unconscious: after all, Jefferson and most of the other drafters had slaves and, of course, all were men, were also landowners or commodity traders (most profitably of slaves), and were incipient capitalists. Without knowing it, they were paving the way for industrial capitalism and its institutionalized inequality between those who own the means of production and those who do not. As the historian George Fredrickson has put it, "Rather than being an exception to the grand themes of liberty and democracy, slavery and the racism it engendered have exposed the shallowness and narrowness of the national commitment to these ideals" (Fredrickson, 2009).

Thus it was that from the US's "birth as a nation," inequality ruled; as it had for most of history for all others. After World War II, inequality was noticeably reduced in many European nations and, in lesser degree, in the US, but only for a while. Since the 1970s, through an always more concentrated and decreasingly challenged capitalist system, the pre- and postwar social reforms have been smothered or abandoned by an even tighter, more reckless, and more ruthless "Americanized/globalized" capitalism; whether in the major industrial capitalist or in once-imperialized now-industrialized countries: for example, in India, Vietnam, and "Communist-capitalist" China (Wang Hui, 2003).

Those controversial generalizations will be discussed at length in ensuing chapters; but here we begin with the "birth of the nation." As it took hold, Tom Paine famously wrote "These are the times that try men's souls." It was too soon for anyone to see that the basis for such "times" was the dawning transformation of colonialism into imperialism, the stirring of the industrial revolution and an ever hungrier, more demanding capitalism. The nature of that new social system was seen simultaneously in 1848: by Marx and Engels in their *Manifesto* seeking to overthrow it, by John Stuart Mill in his *Principles* hoping to cleanse it.

Because the US became a nation in the early evolution of capitalism meant that it was not encumbered by non-capitalist habits and values; only one of its many advantages. Among the others were:

- its easy access to the vast and vital resources it would soon control
- its protection against enemies by two giant oceans
- an open door to the profitable slave trade and gainful exploitation of its victims
- a militarily weak native population
- an always rising flow of eager workers from elsewhere.

Meanwhile, other capitalist nations had to struggle against each other for even a portion of the thievery. Those struggles ultimately took them to their mutual defeat by the two world wars as, perversely, they carried the US to unheard of heights of wealth and power. The gods of capitalism and imperialism had selected Uncle Sam as their favorite son. Thus began the US history of militaristic imperialism and of treating "non-whites" as being "non-human" and which have since served all too well as a training school for the habit of "blaming the victim" (Ryan, 1976).

It was in those early years that the US came to view its endless aggressions both within and beyond North America as a blessing for those conquered while, in 1823, blandly announcing the "Monroe Doctrine": "Keep out of *our* hemisphere!" (W. Williams, 1980). Since then, the US has made many wars. (See Chapter 8.)

Only in its Civil War, if then, did the US seem to live up to its stated ideals of "the land of the free and the home of the brave," where "all 'men' are created equal." But 600,000 died in its Civil War; was not that to rid the US of slavery? Part of the answer is that at least half of those dead soldiers died to *maintain* slavery; nor is there reason to believe that a majority of the Northern troops were fighting to end it. As to the equality of men and women, it was not until the twentieth century that women were allowed to vote, let alone to be seen as "equal"; and many more decades passed before blacks would be seen as being among the "free and the brave"; by a few, now and then. Consider this: General MacArthur became a hero as the US Commanding General in the Pacific war. Early on, he issued an order that black soldiers were not to carry weapons: no matter what, no matter where; in or out of combat areas. (Some of that dirty history is found in Killens, 1969, who was a black soldier in the Pacific war.)

That was in the past. The chapters to follow discuss and analyze the details concerning the many realms of contemporary inequality, the anti-democratic ways and means to which the US has become accustomed, and their revival since the 1970s.

Slouching Toward Hell

Since the 1970s the dominant socio-economic tendencies in the US and, increasingly, elsewhere, have pushed us to the political right, reversing the moderate left-leaning reforms after World War II. It should go without saying that inequalities are harmful to their victims in many ways, including daily misery and shortened lives. That may change with Obama if there is popular pressure and support. Less obvious, however, is that those same inequalities wreak great economic, political, and social harm upon the society as a whole, including those who create or permit them. That will be elaborated upon in Chapters 8–11; Chapter 7 will show how post-1970s "let the devil take the hindmost" as financial policies allowed Wall Street to become a free-for-all playground for gambling. In those same years economies were increasingly transformed from being centered upon industrial production to being dominated by the free-for-all standards of high finance; and thrust into today's financial collapse. In Chapter 12, US inequalities and their treatment are compared with those in Western Europe. There it will be seen that although capitalism *requires* class inequality and inequalities of gender, color, are universal, that after the horrors of interwar fascism in most of Western Europe, their capitalist countries were led by popular movements to be less inhumane and reckless than the US's. Today almost all countries in the globalized world have adopted much of the politics and economics of the US. It has become all too possible that, unless interrupted and reversed, today's centralized socio-economic power and consumption crazed populations could open the door for the emergence of what Bertram Gross called "friendly fascism" (Gross, 1980).

That possibility will be examined in the Epilogue, where it will be shown that the term "friendly" as used by Gross was ironic. His argument is that as fascism looms again the relevant populations will resist so little that the violence and concentration camps of (say) German and Italian fascism would not be needed. A better term could be "acquiescent fascism." Whether or not the 2008 election of Obama will eliminate that possibility in the US will be determined by whether or not its people rise from their TVs and shopping and become politically involved in building a decent world. In that regard, it is disturbing to have to add that the US record regarding both the pre- and post-World War II fascisms is not encouraging, to note that until attacked by Japan and Germany declared war against the US, it stood aside, even cooperated with European fascist nations (Italy, Germany, Spain). Moreover, since World War II, the US helped the fascist Pinochet to depose the Chilean democratic government in 1973 (Uribe, 1975; and see Chapter 8).

It is both conceivable and essential that the political apathy accompanying consumerism will be altered substantially if, or when, the ongoing financial crisis spreads and deepens into a global depression. In the US, the presidency of Obama could quite possibly generate a move toward social sanity. If it does not? Such a worrisome matter has also come to apply to Western European capitalist societies. After World War II moderately left-leaning policies took firm hold in most of Europe. More recently, their socio-economic policies have given way to those resembling the US's; as they also "shop 'til they drop." (See Chapters 5–6.)

What is it about current developments that is especially worrisome, and why? The main theme of this book is that the always deep and wide inequalities of the capitalist world, although lessened significantly after the war, have since the 1970s been given an always stronger life. The US business world has consciously and effectively deepened its power to achieve its ends as giant corporations have created or strengthened a many-sided rightwing political movement and were determined to go back to the "good old days" of unchallenged prejudice, discrimination, and poverty. Along the way they have created an anti-democratic, happily militaristic many-sided rightwing movement. (See Chapter 4 for the US.) The rightist movement was and is fed and supported not only by the all too indifferent, even cooperative media and generously subsidized "research" organizations, but (especially in the US) by numerous politically-geared gun lovers, passionate racists and sexists, and a string of zealous religious groups; despite that the activists of one or more of such groups are themselves among the victims of one or more other groups.

The above holds mostly for the US; unfortunately, but not inexplicably, such developments have emerged in Europe as well, most obviously in Italy (where I now live and teach), with the third electoral triumph of Silvio Berlusconi. He is the richest man in Italy, at once fierce and jovial, a passionate businessman and sportsman. He controls several companies in the communications world (radio, TV, newspapers, etc.) and owns one of Italy's major soccer teams. As liberal and left politics have become paralyzed, Berlusconi has become always more powerful and always more arrogant. He is meaningfully seen as "Mussolini in a business suit."

One may dislike and fear all of that greatly and still ask: What is to be feared? Is not today's lurch to the right just another bump in the road? Perhaps. But it should never be forgotten that early in the twentieth century, Italy and Germany were generally seen as the most civilized of nations because of the beauty of their art, literature, music, and science; nonetheless as the 1920s became the 1930s they had become the first and most murderous of fascist nations. If a repetition of that horrible fate is to be avoided in the US or elsewhere, "we the people" must activate ourselves and become the leaders of a genuinely democratic society. Time is running out.

1

INEQUALITY: AN INTRODUCTION

These opening chapters will examine the many ways in which inequality's persistence and deepening have always and everywhere prevented our species from achieving decent and safe societies. Inequality may or may not be "the root of *all* evil," but it surely sits at the causal center of a world now rife with poverty, misery, economic crisis, wars, and environmental self-destruction. A major element of economic inequality was usefully noted in the *Wall Street Journal* in its "Boom in Financial Markets Parallels Rise in Share for Wealthiest Americans" (December 10, 2007):

> The richest Americans' share of the national income has hit a new record since World War II: The wealthiest *one* percent of Americans earned 21.2% of *all* income in 2005, according to new data from the Internal Revenue Service, up sharply from the previous high... The bottom *fifty* percent earned 12.8% of all income, down from 2004... The nation's top 400 taxpayers reported a total of $85.6 *billion* – an average of $213.9 million each...twice as large as it was a decade earlier... Until this summer [2007], soaring stock prices and buoyant credit markets had produced spectacular payouts for private equity and hedge fund managers and investment bankers. A University of Chicago study shows that in 2004 there were more than twice as many such Wall Street professionals in the top half of one percent of all earners as there are executives from *non*-financial companies... The top 25 hedge-fund managers earned more in 2004 than the chief executives of *all* the companies in the Standard & Poor's 500-stock index...

In 2004, both the US House and Senate passed a health care bill providing care for about *10 million children* without health care. Bush vetoed the bill; then, a few days later he provided an extra $200 billion for the Iraq war, whose total costs already exceed $3 *trillion*.

In capitalist societies, such data are "the facts of life." As will be seen in what follows, there are all too many such facts in other areas (health, housing, poverty, etc.), all ranking high in the world of inequality's injustices and its social criminality. The focus here will be mostly but not only on the US; later, in Chapter 12, US conditions will be compared with those of the major capitalist nations of Europe; there it will be seen that although capitalism's intrinsic inequalities of income, wealth and power function in Europe, until recently they have been less severe than in the US. But before proceeding further about *inequality* it is important to indicate what here *is* and is *not* meant by *equality*. What follows is very much dependent upon the reasoning of R.H. Tawney's classic book *Equality* (1931).

Inequality of Whom, Regarding What?

We live in a world in which the many kinds of inequality are normal, pervasive, taken for granted, usually seen as proper, and where arguments for lessening inequality are likely to be mocked: "You mean you want everyone to have the same education? Have the same way of life? Eat the same food and wear the same clothes? Listen to the same music? Do the same work?" Or, more to the point, and what would irk most: "To be viewed with the same respect?" The answers to some of those questions should be "yes"; to others, "of course not." But that's not the problem. Mockery might be expected from those who oppose any and all arguments for a genuinely democratic society; but even many who see themselves as open-minded and decent also raise such questions: we have become all too accustomed to acquiesce in a deeply unequal society.

So, what in this work is or is not meant by the "equality" seen as desirable? A starting-point is that "from womb to tomb" all human beings are equal in their *basic needs*: adequate nutrition, shelter, education, and health care, the need of equal *opportunity* for *all* to work toward the fulfillment of their diverse possibilities.

Those basic needs will be discussed at length later on, a fine treatment of which can be found in the analyses of Sen (1981) and Streeten (1984).

Basic needs are not fully met anywhere on earth; least of all in the dozens of once colonized/imperialized and now "globalized" societies of Africa, Asia, Latin America, and the Middle East. There the overwhelming majority of people live in desperation and poverty from birth to what is usually a premature death. It is rarely understood that their lives were both more bountiful and more dignified before they were taken over by colonization and imperialism: the critical bases for the world's rich nations' ability to *become* so rich (Wright, 1992).

However, having stolen the resources and potential riches of the poor countries, the thieving countries nevertheless have failed to meet the basic needs of the peoples of their own countries: notably, especially, and most disgracefully in the US, the richest country in history where, however, tens of millions live in poverty. This work seeks to show that when compared with the other *rich* countries, the unmet basic needs of the majority of the US are the broadest, deepest, and most damaging while, adding insult to injury, the US power structure and ideology have allowed and caused those unmet needs to be widely accepted as "natural."

Those US realities are a product of still another problem; namely, that it is the most "rugged capitalist" of all nations. In being so, it has led Americans to accept ugly social realities and to "blame their victims" (Ryan, 1976). More than all others, the people of the US have "learned" to take the ideology of capitalism as a "given"; to believe, as Britain's Prime Minister Margaret Thatcher put it when she was in power: "There is no alternative."

Inequalities have always existed, everywhere, beginning with those between men and women. Even assuming that inequality is timeless and ubiquitous, what's the fuss? The "fuss" is because although contemporary industrial capitalist societies are by far the most abundant in all of history, that abundance and the meeting of "basic needs" are available only to some of their people. The "some" may be a strong majority, as in Scandinavia, but it is a small minority in the US and elsewhere. (See Chapters 9–10.)

Although pre-modern societies were blotched by inequality, it was neither as pervasive nor as *essential* to their existence as for ours. Capitalist societies require the meeting of one inequality in particular as essential: the inequality of power between workers and owners – *class* inequality. In the next two chapters, where the inequality of economic and social power will be the focus, as will be seen, that class inequality is fed and strengthened by the other realms of inequality: those between men and women, and those between "races," nationalities, and religions. (Quotation marks are placed around "race" for reasons explained in Chapter 3.) In the preceding pages, "capitalism" has been accused of social wrongdoings; before proceeding further it seems important to support that by examining its "nature."

Capitalism's Nature and Nurture

Capitalism is, and must be, not only an economic but also a political and social system whose processes go well beyond production and trade for profit. From the seventeenth century on, Britain was first to seek and achieve the necessary depth and breadth of the processes *systemic* to capitalism: (1) expansion, (2) exploitation, and (3) oligarchic rule (Mantoux, 1906). In turn, those essentials of capitalist "health" could only be met within the larger processes that characterize "the modern world": *capitalism* itself, and three interacting and interdependent developments: *colonialism* (which became *imperialism*, which has become *globalization*), *nationalism*, and *industrialism*. Taken together, they provided capitalism's vitality and have become the leading characteristics of modern society (even, it is revealing to note, for the capitalism of Communist China).

However, the interaction of capitalism's "imperatives" has inexorably produced intermittent crises and threats to its very survival, most destructively the socio-economic upheavals and wars of the twentieth century. First, we examine the "imperatives" of exploitation and expansion; then the critical relationships between them and "oligarchic rule."

Exploitation and Expansion

Capitalist profitability requires and capitalist rule has provided ever-changing areas of exploitation, both geographic and social as well as economic; all made possible by minority ownership and control of the means of production (land and its resources, factories and machinery, etc.); combined with a supply of powerless workers eager for any wages they can get; no matter how sordid or dangerous the conditions (Hobsbawm, 1968; Mantoux, 1906).

Given those socio-economic relationships, the strengths of each capitalist enterprise and its nation vary with the volume, scope, and rate of *capital accumulation*; that is, the expansion of the capitalist's "capital," the "accumulation" of which is the driving force of capitalist development: profits are "plowed back" to be converted into more capital, and more profits, *ad infinitum*. Capitalists' personal consumption is well above the average, but that is not their main drive; that is provided by their endless passion for wealth: more and more, always more. Marx put it succinctly in this famous passage:

> [The capitalist] shares with the miser the passion for wealth *as* wealth. But that which in the miser is a mere idiosyncrasy is, in the capitalist, the effect of the social mechanism of which he is but one of the wheels...
> [And, a few pages later, Marx concludes:] Accumulate, accumulate! That is Moses and the prophets! Accumulation for accumulation's sake... (1867)

Capital accumulation is the basis for economic growth, itself interwoven with and dependent upon geographic expansion; most recently by today's "globalization." Taken together, economic and geographic expansion are capitalism's "heartbeat." They in turn depend upon the "muscles" that enable them to exploit labor and whatever it takes to gain governmental cooperation in geographic expansion: *plus* what follows...

Oligarchic Rule

Capitalism and political democracy came into existence at roughly the same time (if also with varying intervals and selectivity). But political democracy in itself, whatever its virtues, is a *limited* democracy, providing only the formal right of the citizenry to install and/or remove those allowed to govern by the electoral process. Political democracy has always been contaminated and diluted by its coexistence with capitalism's inherent inequalities of income, wealth, and power. Taken together the latter enable those "at the top" not only to remain there, but to always increase the gaps between themselves and all others, to sustain policies that favor and strengthen them, and to obstruct those which do not.

Capitalism benefits from having a formally democratic system, but it has worked best when, as in the US, the general public is *de*-politicized, made so by the combination of consumerism, the media, the subtle consequences of our socialized prejudices, discrimination and capital's associated ideological triumph. (See Chapters 2 and 4; and McChesney, 1999.)

Capitalism's Ideology of Inequality

To view inequality as "the cause and consequence of what's wrong in the world" might be seen as foolish or at least as a serious exaggeration. Of course there are other "wrongs." Even so, the many inequalities to be examined in this work intensify whatever else is socially harmful:

> The equality of civil and political rights is of the essence of democracy; the *inequality* of economic and social opportunities is of the essence of capitalism... Democracy is unstable as a political system as long as it remains a political system and nothing more; instead, democracy should be not only a form of government, but a type of society and a manner of life which is in harmony with that type. (Tawney, 1931)

Capitalist democracy *has* remained only "a political system and nothing more." Its main beneficiaries have sought seriously to keep it that way, up to and including wiping out democracy with the ferocities of fascism, if necessary. (See Epilogue.) In doing so, capitalism's normal functioning has intensified the inequalities of the deep past, modified and extended them, and, with the support of its ideology, fortified and strengthened them.

To repeat, for millennia inequalities have existed everywhere. With the coming of a settled agriculture and its superior productivity, it became possible (and necessary) for non-agricultural centers – cities and "civilization" – to come into being. What also came into being as they did so were *class* societies, ruled over by priests and/or warriors (with women doing the work both "at home" and in the fields) (Childe, 1951). With that evolution there soon developed what is now called "ideology"; a set of cultivated beliefs, principles, and values within which people live, usually unconsciously (Mannheim, 1936). Ideologies have always served to justify inequalities in income and wealth, in status and prestige, in opportunity, and diverse levels of wellbeing.

Insisting that they are "natural" or "normal" or "necessary" serves the purposes of inequality's main beneficiaries as both victimizers and their victims come to believe that they "deserve" their conditions. Tawney again:

> One of the regrettable, if diverting, effects of widespread inequality is its tendency to weaken the capacity for impartial judgment. It pads the lives of its beneficiaries with a soft down of consideration, while relieving them of the vulgar necessity of justifying their pretensions, and insures that, if they fall, they fall on cushions...; causes them to apply different standards to different sections of the community, as if it were uncertain whether all of them are human in the same sense as themselves... It seems natural to those who slip into that mood of tranquil inhumanity that working-class children should go to the mill at an age when the children of the well-to-do are just beginning the serious business of education; and that employers, as the history of coal reveals, should be the sole judges of the manner of conducting an industry on which the welfare of several hundred thousand families depend...; and that different sections of the community should be distinguished not merely by differences of income, but by different standards of security, of culture, and even of health. (1931)

Today the disdainful attitudes of the fortunate toward the poor, given the richness of modern economies, are at least as damaging as those in Tawney's time; and as globalization has its ways, the numbers of poor in both the rich and the poor areas have increased, and the "blame" continues to fall upon "the victims." (See Chapters 6 and 10.) Such opinions may be seen as a major component of the functional relationship between inequality and ideology, a relationship made all the more evident when it is realized that those harmed, as often as not, develop the same attitudes:

> Capitalism is maintained, not only by capitalists, but by those who would *be* capitalists if they could; and the injustices survive, not merely because the rich exploit the poor, but because, in their hearts, too many of the poor admire the rich. They know and complain that they are tyrannized over by the power of money; they do not yet see that what makes money the tyrant of society is largely their [socialized] reverence for it. (Tawney, 1931)

Tawney's focus was principally upon early twentieth-century Britain. As time went on, Britain and other rich countries developed a substantial labor movement aimed toward democratic socialism, and for which Tawney's ideas were pivotal. It was such efforts in Western Europe which, after World War II, went much further to decrease their inequalities than did the US labor unions in America. In recent decades, however, such political efforts "from the bottom up" have weakened or disappeared, as the US "social disease" of consumerism has come to "bewitch, bother and bewilder" always more, here, there, and elsewhere. Since World War II, consumerism, the media and globalization have had the US as pacemaker: as all have "learned to want what they don't need and not to want what they do" (Baran, 1969, and see Chapters 4–6).

The Dangers of Inequality

The existence, causes, dimensions, functions, and consequences of inequality must be the first and most enduring question asked about our socio-economic processes; they and the means and ends of those responsible and supportive are "the heart of the matter" for understanding the social problems of our time.

In all societies inequalities have been and remain the key obstacles facing people as they seek to meet their needs and possibilities;

but reaching their true potential is virtually impossible for most people because of:

- where and when they were born
- their gender and what is unscientifically called their "race"
- the income and wealth of their parents
- "the laws of the land"

Where "laws" are involved, they were provided by and for the powerful and the privileged at the cost of all others. That is most clearly so in the US, whose powerful and privileged are and always have been overwhelmingly "rich white men" and their inheritors. In the US even the bare idea of a fully democratic nation has only rarely been discussed. That said, it is worth adding that since World War II several other societies – the Scandinavians and Dutch, most clearly – have rightly seen their *political* democracies as more to be admired than ours. Those societies are also capitalist and also have economic and social inequalities, but their capitalism had been "softened" by socialist movements for a century or more. (See Osberg, 1991, and Chapter 12.)

Political democracy is of course essential and desirable; but when democracy is *limited* to the political realm, inequalities are not only allowed to persist and flourish but are assisted and sheltered by the presumptions accorded political democracy itself. In consequence, as time goes on, political democracy is thus itself corrupted and perverted. By whom? How and why? With what consequences? At whose costs and for whose benefits? The answers to those questions are among the aims of this book. It will be argued in later chapters that the limited political democracy of the US has long served the function of obscuring the non- and anti-democratic realities of a society that principally serves the wishes of its most powerful corporations. Understandably, the business world has generally gone along with or encouraged racism and militarism: racism because it divides and weakens workers; militarism because it is assists economic and geographic expansion and high profits. (See Chapter 8.)

Such realities and dangers will be explored at length as we proceed; here let it be said that if even political democracy is to endure, we must consciously seek to move it toward becoming also social and economic democracy; as with our bodies, gaining or at least maintaining strength is vital to prevent illness. Instead, the substantial and numerous inequalities of capitalist society have produced an always more concentrated system of power that must be *de*-concentrated and replaced by truly democratic societies that enable the basic needs of *all* to be met in an environmentally safe and peaceful world; despite which, led by the US in recent years, almost all nations have turned in the opposite direction, at an always accelerating rate. The surprising election of Barack Obama as US President is a hopeful sign that a vital change could be underway.

The goals of a society dedicated to equality would of course include the right to vote for all, but it would also include equal access to power; the *right* for everyone to be an effective part of the decision-making processes that determine what will – and will not – be done. It is of course unrealistic for the foreseeable future to expect to achieve an equal distribution of power; but it is not unrealistic for that to be the *goal* of those working for a more democratic society. Only as that goal is striven for can it be expected that all people's basic needs and possibilities could receive serious consideration. However, and despite its great importance, power is seldom discussed or analyzed in our schools, in the press, or, publicly, by politicians. For that reason, the nature and bases of power will be treated at length in the ensuing chapters, as equality is also given further attention. (See Mills, 1956, and Chapter 2.)

2

CLASS INEQUALITY AND THE INEQUALITY OF POLITICAL AND SOCIAL POWER

Inequalities of many kinds have existed always and everywhere. Not only has each form been harmful in itself but the inherent *class* inequality of capitalism has been supported and increased by its ability over time to exploit the long-standing inequalities of race, gender, religion, and nationalism. (See next chapter.) Thus, as capitalism spread and strengthened, its *class power* has become the most dangerous and harmful ever; feeding and being fed by imperialism and its wars.

Capitalism could not exist without class inequality. Its birth and functioning have required and achieved the unequal distributions of income, wealth and associated power. That essential was first made clear by David Ricardo. Writing as industrial capitalism was birthing, and inspired by Adam Smith's *Wealth of Nations* (1776), Ricardo became the "voice" of economics when he originated what ever since has been the methodology and the focus of economic theory. Note his opening paragraph:

> The produce of the earth – all that is derived from its surface by the united application of labor, machinery, and capital – is divided among three *classes* of the community, namely, the proprietor of the land, the owner of the capital necessary for its cultivation, and the laborers by whose industry it is cultivated. But in different stages of society, the proportions of the whole produce of the earth which will be allotted to each of these *classes*, under the names of rent, profit, and wages, will be essentially different. To determine the laws which regulate this distribution is the *principal* problem of Political Economy. (Ricardo, 1817)

That became *the* method of modern economics. In doing so, what Ricardo called "political economy" and his emphasis on "class" was dropped like a hot potato by economists as the class struggles of the late nineteenth century took hold. Those who have studied "economics" in US schools will seldom if ever have heard even a whisper of that reasoning of Ricardo. At the center of Ricardo's attempts to determine the "laws which regulate this distribution" was his refinement of what Smith had earlier called "the labor theory of value." Marx, asking different questions from capital's to workers' point of view, shifted Ricardo's argument and logic into capitalism's enemy territory. Using Ricardo's own assumptions, he transformed the labor theory of value into a theory of exploitation:

> Marx argued that embedded in capital...is an antagonistic relationship between workers and their employers, the essence of [which] is the exploitation of workers; the extraction of a surplus by the employers from their labor, necessary to funnel the accumulation of capital in a milieu of intense competition. Unlike other modes of production such as slavery or feudalism, this exploitation is hidden by the market; it takes place behind the workers' backs, so to speak. They sell their ability to work in the impersonal market, and it *appears* that the *market* dictates their pay...; but once they sell their labor power to the employer, it belongs to the boss just as surely as does the machinery. (Yates, 1994)

The first volume of Marx's *Capital* was published in 1867. The already stuffy economics profession, as though breathless from a punch in the stomach, rather than responding to the Marxian critique, buried or circumvented the labor theory of value and flew up to the sweet clouds of "marginal utility" (Rogin, 1956). Marx showed that Ricardo's theory of value can and should be put to work as a theory of *power*: Those who own the means of production (land and equipment) therefore also control the means of life itself; and they would naturally be those who determine how "the produce of the earth" would be distributed among the three "classes." Given that workers have nothing to offer but their labor, their share would not be proportionate to their contribution but to their weakness (Marx, 1867).

In what follows, the emphasis will be on human and social "needs"; but in economic theory the focus is on cultivated "wants" and market demands; "needs" are *never* discussed in economic analysis. That concentration upon "wants" suits the business world nicely. In the US we pride ourselves on the principle of "one man, one vote," but the structure and functioning of power ensure that the votes are almost entirely for those directly or indirectly selected by the powerful. A society dedicated to equality would make every effort to see that in addition to the vote, all would have an equal access to power. When, as now, that is not so, it is unlikely that our human and social needs will ever be met; not least because we have been socialized to think otherwise.

Inequalities are the capitalist norm for income, wealth, and power. Needs and possibilities are met or *not* met dependent upon where and when we are born, our gender and "color," and the income and wealth of our parents; that is, the structure of power is triangular in varying degrees of steepness (Albelda et al., 2001). In the following examination of inequality as both a condition and a consequence of capitalism, the latter will be temporarily treated as principally an *economic*, rather than as a *socio*-economic system; that is, the impact of all the other inequalities – those of color, gender, etc. – will be taken as "givens." (See Chapter 3.) The multiple meanings of *power* will be given special attention in the last part of the present chapter. I now continue the discussion of the *quantitative* aspects of class inequality in the US with a probing quote from US Senator Jim Webb (*Wall Street Journal*, November 15, 2006):

The most important – and unfortunately the least debated issue – in politics today is our society's steady drift toward a class-based system, the likes of which we haven't seen since the nineteenth century. America's top tier has grown infinitely richer and more removed over the past 25 years; they are living in a different country. Few of them send their children to public schools; fewer still send their loved ones to fight our wars. They own most of our stocks, making the stock market an unreliable indicator of the economic health of working people. The top 1% now takes in an astounding 16% of national income, up from 8% in 1980. The tax codes protect them, just as they protect corporate America, through a vast system of loopholes... The average CEO of a sizeable corporation makes more than $10 million a year, while the minimum wage for workers amounts to about $10,000 a year, and has not been raised for a decade. When I graduated in the 1960s, the average CEO made 20 times what the average worker made. Today, the CEO makes 400 times as much.

Inequality and US Capitalism

Capitalism depends upon the structural inequality of economic *classes*, not individuals; and, as will be seen in Chapter 12, it varies over time and place. It is notably worse in the US than all other rich capitalist societies (Osberg, 1991). The *economic* inequality referred to here is that regarding two phenomena closely related to class; namely, *wealth* and *income*. Their differences are often visualized by seeing wealth as a lake and income as a stream that flows into and out of that lake; that is, "wealth is a stock, income a flow." But wealth both results from and creates income, and income can both come from and create wealth; moreover, those from wealthy families need not inherit their families' wealth to have adult lives providing them with high incomes made easier by a privileged education and good jobs *because of* family and contacts, etc.

There have been many studies of wealth and income, and they will be cited as we go along. Among those are several by Kevin Phillips. In his *Wealth and Democracy* (2002) he pays the greatest attention to *inheritance* in the US, the most unearned wealth of all. His tables and charts from the eighteenth century to the present dramatically illustrate how the wealthiest families gained and used their wealth from oil, railroads, cars, chemicals, etc., at seven points in time: 1901–14, 1928, the 1930s, 1957, 1968, 1982, and 1992. The US was never a full-fledged democracy, but it did flirt with that possibility late in the nineteenth century and then again after the 1930s. But since the 1970s, giant business has created the tightest "plutocracy" of US history. Wealth creates wealth and protects the virtually permanent members of its privileged club. Now we examine some of that history.

From Capitalism's Youth to the Present

Foreign trade was the critical early source of wealth: trade in slaves, rum, "spices," sugar, cloth, etc. Taken together they provided the "seed corn" of capitalist development. As noted earlier, a hallmark of capitalism was the making of both land and labor into commodities to be bought and sold. Human beings had long been bought and sold and enslaved; but when land also became a "thing" to be bought and sold, "commodification" took on a new meaning. Before then, previously "free people" could not survive except to work the land as though enslaved, often under conditions worse than slaves who, after all, were "property" to be preserved (Hammond, 1924).

Given the accumulating gains from centuries of trade, what enabled young industrial capitalism in Britain to function and to expand rapidly was the exploitation of workers whose farming land had been commodified by "the enclosure movement." Those who had worked the land, free but far from rich, were swept off the land as though by a hurricane and were transformed into desperate and powerless laborers. Earlier, they had worked "for themselves" on their own and nature's terms. When their lands were "legally" stolen from them, they had to labor for others, under conditions entirely decided by the "thieves" and their allies (Mantoux, 1906).

Today, we no longer distinguish between "worker" and "laborer"; 'twas not always thus. In the pre-capitalist world of the ancient Greeks, those who "labored" for others were called slaves; those who "worked" by and for themselves were free; as capitalism moved toward industrialization, workers came accurately to be called "wage slaves."

The equipment of a cotton factory must be created; for which "capital" is required. The first mill in England depended upon steam engines for spinning and weaving and, of course, a building in which the work could be done. The essential "productive capital" did not fall from the skies; it had to be "produced," and financed. How, and by whom? As industrial capitalism began, it came directly or indirectly from the merchant class; the traders of slaves, spices, cotton sugar, etc.

Then, as the "industrial revolution" began and matured, the capital needs of always enlarging companies led to the first stages of modern banking and (in the 1850s) the modern industrial corporation. Companies came to be owned by shareholders and controlled by executives; profits went partially to shareholders and partly as interest to lending banks. What was moving back and forth between industrialists, financiers, and investors was "the economic surplus"; it was controlled and used by the capitalist class, but extracted from the working class; from those who "earn" more than they receive, and who want and need more than they can pay for. How that "surplus" will or won't be used is decided by the capitalists who own and control the means of production; for present purposes more usefully seen as "the means of life." In the days of the emerging industrial revolution, the wealthy were the big landowners, merchants, and financiers of Britain's economy. Their wealth had accrued from colonialism abroad and the land at home; the latter, as noted earlier, from the profitable agriculture associated with the enclosures of the eighteenth century, including that from their Irish colony. (See Chapter 1.)

When the first factory was built there were no "corporations" as that term is now used. Would-be industrial companies could not sell shares in their projects; the first factories were financed by their own and/or a partner's savings. The modern corporation was brought into being simultaneously in Britain and the US in the 1850s, as mass-production became common. Given that as a beginning, the always more rapidly accumulating wealth of *industrial* capitalism came from the "unpaid labor" of the working class; from the income they earned but did not receive; from their exploitation. Some elaboration is in order:

The production process has two kinds of personnel: owners and workers. The owners have the "capital" to "invest" in the engines, etc.; the workers do the production. *If* workers do the production, and *if* they were paid in terms of the value of what they had produced, whence the profits, and whence capital "accumulation"? The answer was first provided by Smith and Ricardo in the above-noted "labor theory of value." That theory would be turned on its head and subverted by Marx's *Capital* (1867). Smith, Ricardo, and Marx all agreed that the workers do *not* receive a return equal to the value of their production (their "use value"). Instead they received a money wage equal to their "*subsistence needs*" (their "exchange value"). That is, their wages were just enough to keep them alive; if only for a while. Note that, in the early decades of industrial capitalism (1821–50), that "while" *decreased* markedly, because workers' wages were *less* than subsistence. In consequence, in the first decades of industrial capitalism, the life span of the average worker decreased notably (Hobsbawm, 1968). Marx carried the logic of the labor theory of value to its full meaning: the profits of business were equal to the "surplus value" of workers; that is, the difference between the value of what they produced and what they received. That cruelly created "difference" became the main source of capitalist wealth and of the capital for use in further investment; it was the fount of capital accumulation. "Accumulate, Accumulate! That is Moses and the Prophets!" wrote Marx (1867). But didn't all of that change when industrialization deepened and spread and carried with it political democracy, and…so on? Things did indeed change, for better *and* for worse; what also changed was what we have been taught to *mean* by "better" and "worse." Question: "who and what belongs in which category; and why?" We look at "the better" first.

Possibilities versus Realities

If only in the past century, industrial capitalist societies have been *able* to furnish to most of their people what earlier was available to few or none: that is, satisfaction of the basic needs of health care, housing, education, and nutrition, along with democratic politics and what might be called a democratized culture. That became possible, but it did not become the reality. Instead, access to all of the above has been grossly unequal, both within and, even more, outside the rich nations, and the riches of rich people and rich nations *depend* upon that limited access: "It is precisely the relationships between the poor and the rich peoples of the world that keeps both the poor *and* the rich that way" (Baran, 1957).

That was written in 1957, responding to the horrible history of what capitalism and imperialism had already done to most of the people of both the rich and the poor countries, and what was on its way as the post-World War II era unfolded. Baran expected all hell to break loose; but, if anything, he underestimated what troubles the next 50 years would bring both in the US and elsewhere. The remainder of this chapter will focus on the US and the impact of the lopsided distributions of income and wealth upon the basis for living well or badly. As we proceed, keep in mind that however disturbing the intrinsic inequalities of income and wealth of capitalism are in themselves, they are intensified and solidified by the discrimination and prejudices targeting gender, color, national origin, and/or religion, discussed in the next chapter.

The Distribution of Wealth

The distribution of wealth naturally affects the distribution of income. Were wealth less unequal, income distribution would be considerably less unequal than now. The realities are of course that both wealth and income are highly unequal and, as will be discussed later, since the 1970s both have become distinctly *more* unequal and disgustingly so, with equally disgusting "side-effects." In the year 2000 in the US the top 1 percent of wealth holders owned more than 40 percent of *all* assets (including homes and financial investments) – the most unequal distribution of wealth since the 1920s (Phillips, 2002). Also, the bottom *80* percent held only 17 percent of US wealth. The ownership of stocks, much touted as being "democratic," is anything but: the top 1 percent of stock owners hold almost half (47.7 percent) of *all* stocks, while the bottom 80 percent hold only 4.1 percent (Mishel, 2007–08). In addition, note this excerpt from the article "The Super Wealthy" from the *Wall Street Journal* (December 14, 2004): "About 250,000 US households already had a net worth of five *million* or more in 1983; by 2001 there were five times that many. The wealth controlled by individuals in North America with more than $30 million in personal financial assets (not including real estate) in 2002 had jumped 45% by 2003; that is, in one year from $2.1 *trillion* to over $3 trillion."

So what do they do with all that money? One common and very costly thing they do is to work real hard at letting other very rich men know who's in the lead, by buying *really* expensive things, from Patek Philippe watches at more than $200,000 each, to cars costing more than $450,000 (the Mercedes "Maybach") and/or, ever-larger yachts. Take, for example, this spoiled baby game of Paul Allen of Microsoft:

> He first went real big with his "354-foot Le Grand Bleu" (which has its own 72-foot sailboat on board). When others outdid him, "he commissioned the largest yacht-builder to produce the 414-foot Octopus…; price tag, $200 million." [Plus]: A builder of large yachts recounts that one of his clients "ordered a yacht and saw one of his business competitors with a larger boat. "He asked us to make his one yard larger…" (Mishel, 2007–08)

As you laugh (or snort), keep in mind that these are the men who run "our" country. When Veblen coined the phrases "conspicuous consumption" and "conspicuous display" in 1899 he was describing people who were seen as very rich then; today they wouldn't be able to get in the party. So much for *wealth*; now we turn to the increasingly unequal US distribution of *income*.

The Distribution of Income

The data provide answers to a long list of different but overlapping questions concerning various groups, time periods, and processes. First we look at the inequality of the levels and movement of US family incomes, wages, and jobs. Unless otherwise indicated, all data are from Mishel (2007–08). US Census data show that since the mid 1980s the share of the national income going to the top 20 percent of families has risen; note also the "inequality" *within* that 20 percent:

It's not simply that the top 20 percent of families had bigger percentage gains than families near the middle; the top 5 percent have done better than the next 15, the top 1 percent better than the next 4, and so on up to Bill Gates. In turn, 60 percent of the gains of that top 1 percent went to 0.1 percent [that is, the top *ten* percent of the top *one* percent: those with incomes of more than $790,000 (in 1998)]. Almost half of those gains went to a mere 13,000 taxpayers, the top 0.01 [one-hundredth of *one*] percent, who had an income of at least $3.6 million and an average income of $17 million. (Krugman, "For Richer," *New York Times* [*NYT*], October 20, 2002)

To which, add this from Krugman's 2007 book:

The wealthiest 0.01 percent of Americans are seven times *richer* than they were 30 years ago, while the inflation-adjusted income of most American households has barely edged upward. CEOs who typically earned 30 times more than their average employee in the 1970s now take home more than *300* times as much.

OK, it might be said; even though the other 80 percent aren't getting as big a slice of the pie as the rich, still, the 1990s gave more jobs, higher wages, and a higher income than ever, no? Yes and no. Yes, but only for a while; but both the absolute and the relative amounts (for those still fully-employed) are always shrinking; a trend that began in the 1970s and very much worsened by today's financial crisis. (See Chapter 7.) But what about what was called the "roaring 90s" a decade or so ago? They were not a reversal of that trend, but a hiccough:

Between 1947and 1973 real median family income grew 2.8 percent annually, then dropped to 0.4 percent from 1973 to 1995. In the boom of late 1990s, it sped up again to 2.2 percent annually. But when recession took hold in 2001, the median family income decreased at an annual rate of 1.4 percent (equal to $741 in 2001 dollars); a decrease which has accelerated tragically since 2007, as unemployment has risen in the hundreds of millions: and rising. (Mishel, 2007–08)

Two further comments: Among the bottom 80 percent, those who gained relatively most in the US in those years – blacks,

Hispanics, and women – are normally objects of discrimination. The 1990s "boom" meant a temporary sharp drop in unemployment. A main key to workers' incomes is the level of unemployment. However in those same years there was another element, not entirely positive; namely, a step-up in the employment not only of more women, but of more *married* women with children. That was a consequence more of need than of opportunity. The need arose from the mountains of debt incurred by the average family, which, since the 1990s, has faced a monthly debt charge (credit cards + mortgage debt) well *exceeding* their monthly average household income. (See Chapter 7.)

As the long-term convergence of wages for men and women stalled, the gap between them at the end of the 1990s was as wide as at the beginning. Also, as health care and pension benefits declined and wages fell for the typical worker, the incomes of US executives soared: "From 1980 to 2000, the salary of the median chief executive grew 79 percent, and their average compensation grew *342* percent. In 1965, CEOs made 26 times more than a typical worker; this ratio had risen to 72-to-1 by 1989 and to 310-to-1 by 2000. US CEOs make about three times as much as their counterparts abroad" (Mishel, 2007–08).

As will be seen in later chapters, what was getting worse in those years has since become considerably more so. A recurring theme in Phillips (2002) was the similarity between the 1920s and the years since the 1990s:

- the ongoing control over the economy by an always smaller and always hungrier bunch of CEOs and financiers
- the swooning cooperation of governments at all levels
- the fragility of the US (and the global) economy, due to recent and ongoing financial madness, much worse than in the 1920s
- the evolving weakness of a good majority of the rest of the economy both at home and abroad
- troubles in the agricultural sector, in much of industry and construction
- and, not least, spreading and deepening poverty.

The 1920s ended with the biggest "crash" ever; however, as will be seen in Chapter 7, what seems now to be well on its way (initiated by the "subprime" housing madness) is likely to become much more explosive economically, as does all too much else, especially if, as seems likely, we are moving toward a rerun of the past.

Item: 1929 was the first step toward the Great Depression. The US economy continued to contract for four years, in every one of which there were several moments during which it became common to hear that "prosperity is just around the corner." In fact, the economy did not even *begin* to recover until strong governmental job-creating programs were put into effect *after* 1935. Full employment was not reached until 1942, a year after the US entered World War II (Baran and Sweezy, 1966).

Even using today's (disgracefully understated) definition of poverty in the US (see Chapter 9), over half of the US population already lived in poverty in the 1920s (as was also true in Britain). Little help was expected from the government in the 1920s, nor was any received; unions were few and weak and the US government was controlled by Harding, Coolidge, and Hoover; all beholden to the business world, as would be the case even more in the Bush years.

A major difference between then and now in terms of US inequality is that from the 1930s on, unions multiplied and gained strength. As they did, so did Roosevelt's "New Deal." Its policies (and those up through the 1960s) reduced inequalities: real wages increased, working conditions improved, at least some social security and some public housing were provided, there was improved access to education on all levels, and at least some access to health care for the aged, disabled, and poor came into being. However, from the 1970s on, all such reforms have been weakened or abolished, alongside always increasing inequalities. As of early 2009, in what ways and degrees the ongoing economic crisis will be dealt with can only be guessed at. As will be noted later, however, the policies submitted to Congress have been inadequate for anything but a serious recession, and even they have been watered down by the GOP (Republican) opposition. Further discussion of these matters will be offered in Chapter 7.

The numerous economic and social reforms from the mid 1930s through the 1960s, taken together with the consumerism they allowed and encouraged also meant that the politics took a back seat for workers and political liberals. Among the many disturbing consequences of that "de-politicization" was an open door for the return of "rugged individualism." Here a few numbers already in 2005 confirmed that observation; numbers which have worsened since then. In an article headlined "Chasm Widens between Rich and Poor" (*NYT*, December 17, 2007) we were told:

> The *increase* in incomes of the top *one* percent of Americans from 2003 to 2005 exceeded the total income of the poorest 20 percent of Americans (in a new report by the Congressional Budget Office). The poorest 20 percent of households had a total income of $383 billion in 2005; just the *increase* in income for the top *one* percent was $525 billion, 37 percent higher than of the bottom 20 percent. The total income of the top 1.1 million households was $1.8 *trillion* = 18.1 percent of the total income of the nation's income, up from 14.3 percent two years earlier.
>
> Reports based on tax returns for 2005 showed that the top 10 percent, top 1 percent and *fractions* of the top 1 percent enjoyed their greatest share of income since 1928–29. About half of the top 1 percent comes from investments and business profits.

As will be seen in Chapter 12, other rich nations have considerably less inequality in terms of income and wealth and the meeting of basic needs. However, as globalization and "Americanization" took hold, those countries have become all too like the US, becoming increasingly unequal and also reducing the degrees to which they meet the basic needs of their people. Along the way, they were sucked into the US financial crisis and its consequences.

Inequality and Social Power

Power is the ability to act effectively, to cause things to go one's way and to remain so; and, equally often more important, to keep others from having *their* way regarding, for example, health care and drug prices. (See Chapters 4 and 9.) The Latin root for the noun *power* and the verb *to be able* is the same. What decides who has or does not have power, and how much? What are its sources, who are its possessors? The short answer is that social power is held by those who control what is, has been, and is coming to be most valued in their society; it may be something tangible (productive assets or weapons), or intangible (the ability to formulate or represent cherished beliefs or hopes). Control over the means of material survival has placed its possessors at the center of power in all societies. In the modern world the key has been private ownership and control over the means of production; the very definition of capitalism. That control and its use also explain the extraordinary dynamism of capitalist development: for better and for worse.

The survival and strengthening over time of capitalist socio-economic power has depended upon more than its mere ownership and control of the means of life; its economic power also needs to be seen as the peak of a pyramid of social power. The metaphor of "pyramid" is a simplification, but it is a useful way to begin as we seek to *understand* the nature and meanings of *inequality*. In one form or another, inequality is brought about, maintained, and deepened by and for those with power. A most insightful and readable modern analysis and discussion of the structure and behavior of power in the US is found in C. Wright Mills' *The Power Elite* (1956). When he wrote, a decade or so after World War II, big business was well on its way to becoming *very* big business, especially in the US.

As that was becoming evident, a new social concept became necessary to analyze it. This was provided in 1966 by Baran and Sweezy. As their book's title reveals, like Mills they saw the need to be concerned with more than just the economy: *Monopoly Capital: An Essay on the American Economic and Social Order*. However, what they described and analyzed in 1966 now applies to *global* capitalism and "Monopoly Capitalism *II*." Why *II*? Because the relationships and processes taken up in the 1960s have altered greatly and swiftly: from the 1970s to the 1980s and 1990s, and even more since 2000, the power and practices of giant business have picked up both their reach and speed, and in doing so have greatly deepened their dangerous consequences. As will be seen in ensuing chapters, the nature and rapidity of contemporary socio-economic change is now taking us to "Monopoly Capitalism *III*"; if we can survive Number II.

Now, back to "*I*." From the mid 1930s until the 1960s, the political life of the US was altered enormously from what it was when Roosevelt was first elected to the presidency. FDR was a traditional "conservative" in 1932, but by the time he died in 1945 he had fathered the New Deal's badly-needed reforms and had become a "liberal." The reforms were angrily resisted by the business world, but this resistance was weakened by the depression and temporarily shoved aside by the newly-muscled and organized labor. Then, as the 1950s began, business – re-muscled by its enormous profits from war production – increasingly turned the political clock back. That change was symbolized by the anti-union Taft–Hartley Act and assisted by politically repressive McCarthyism. As the 1960s ended, the business community had entirely recovered its nerve and embarked upon a sustained effort to politicize itself and to reach out to other conservative groups (most importantly, fervent religious groups, racists, gun lovers, and militarists). Meanwhile, consumerism stuffed the minds of those who had earlier worked for reforms.

Taken together, since the 1970s the right-leaning group has become an increasingly powerful team, getting its way increasingly; culminating in the Bush–Cheney White House, a conservatively dominated Congress and Supreme Court. Separately and jointly, all three main elements of US government bowed to Big Business and to giving a free hand to anti-union, anti-reform, and pro-war interests. (See Krugman, 2007, and Chapter 4.) Whether or not, and to what degree, any of that will be reversed by the Democratic victory in the 2008 elections is yet to be seen. Such a badly-needed reversal will take hold if and only if there is a "democratization" of the power structure. To that problem we now turn.

Concentrated Power

The US power elite analyzed by Mills resided in three sectors: business, politics, and the military. Within that triad are supporting structures, each with its own "pyramid": for example, industry, trade, finance, agriculture, and the media, all with their own functioning power structures. The evolution of the three "sectors" of power will be the focus of Chapters 4–7. There it will be seen that since Mills wrote in the 1950s the role of big business has deepened and spread so as to dominate politics and the military considerably always more. Implicit in that evolution has been capitalism's need and ability to create and to function in processes of constant change, within and between the three power dimensions. Here is an astute characterization of their "whys and "wherefores":

> Capitalism cannot exist without constantly revolutionizing the instruments of production, and thereby the relations of production, and with them the whole relations of society. Conservation of the old modes of production in unaltered form was, on the contrary, the first condition of existence for all earlier industrial classes. Constant revolutionizing of production, uninterrupted disturbance of all social conditions, everlasting uncertainty and agitation distinguish the capitalist epoch from all earlier ones. All fixed, fast-frozen relations, with their train of ancient and venerable prejudices and opinions, are swept away, all new-formed ones become antiquated before they can ossify. All that is solid melts into air, all that is holy is profaned, and man is at last compelled to face with sober senses, his real conditions of life, and his relations with his kind. The need of a constantly expanding market for its products chases capitalists over the whole surface of the globe. It must nestle everywhere, settle everywhere, establish connections everywhere.

That reads as though it were written yesterday, but it is found in *The Communist Manifesto* written in 1848 by Marx and Engels, when industrial capitalism was just learning to strut. Central to the existence and behavior of power structures are the dynamic interdependencies and interactions of their members. In contemporary capitalism, the unquestionable driving force that sits at the pyramid's apex is the strength of giant corporations. A clear example of that is found in the relationships between big business and the military. Taken together with the always cooperative media (whose giant companies also sit at the table of power) they persuade Congress and the public to accept a set of aggressive foreign policies and conservative domestic policies that come to be just what Dr. Capitalism ordered. Or is it Dr. Strangelove? Or have they become one and the same? (See Chapters 6–8.)

Power relationships are important not only at society's top, but at all levels, and in all nooks and crannies: in local, state, and national governments, in the classroom, in the office, in every social setting; and, of course, in the realms of racism and sexism. Still, whatever the complexities and however constructive or destructive the impact of all power relationships may be, what ultimately sets the rules and determines the rewards and punishments within which the social process takes place is "the power elite," which, in turn, is ruled over firmly by *big business* (see Chapter 4).

What has been true for all modern societies has been especially so for the US, the most capitalist of all nations. From its beginnings the US has been unconstrained by the long-established traditions common to all others. Such traditions drowned in the fabled US "melting pot." In Chapter 12 important differences between the US and all other rich industrial capitalist societies as regards the socio-economy will be noted at length, and it will be seen that what has been most devastating are the degrees to which "the basic needs" of nutrition, education, health care, housing, and opportunity have not been met.

The differences are many and substantial, in favor of all of the other rich countries, and for at least three reasons:

- As just noted; other countries have had long periods of *non-*capitalist history.
- The absence in the US of anything approaching the "class consciousness" of, say, Western European workers, symbolized as US workers usually call their unions "business

unions," dealing with a given company; in contrast with the more powerful *labor* movements elsewhere; and, although US unions have achieved higher wages and better working conditions for their members, elsewhere workers have also had their own political parties with politics that significantly transformed the socio-economy.

- The substantial and common social role of the family and organized religion in Western Europe, has had a dampening effect on the "rugged individualism" of the US.

Given those considerations, it is understandable that it was in the US that "consumerism" (if only for the top 20 percent) would be invented in the 1920s. To the Europeans' undoing, that particular "Americanism" has all too eagerly been adopted by European workers in recent years. In doing so, they have also crippled their politics. (See Chapter 5.)

Long ago, Britain's Lord Acton remarked that "power corrupts, and absolute power corrupts absolutely." Especially since the 1970s, that has been most obviously shown in the US, along with its always stronger concentration of business power and the related deepening of inequalities. Chapters 9–10 underline what that has meant for the "quality of life," as measured by the worsening of the majority's health care, education, housing, nutrition, and opportunities to realize their potentialities. Then, Chapter 11 will examine the larger and unintended consequences of that concentrated power for the US economy and politics.

It may be hoped, but cannot be taken for granted, that the Obama presidency will change the domestic and global directions of US politics, whether as regards a healthier people, a more sensible economy, less war, and/or lowered environmental dangers. At this moment in early 2009, we cannot know; but it is a certainty that without substantial efforts and support for a better world from the now powerless, nothing will change for the better.

3

INEQUALITY BASED ON GENDER, "RACE," NATIONALISM, AND RELIGION

The most pervasive and ancient of all inequalities is that of gender. All inequality is finally harmful to both victimizers and victims, but gender inequality wins the prize for self-harming. I begin with a brief discussion of the often misleading language of gender and "race" inequality as regards prejudice and discrimination. (Why "race" is in quotation marks will be explained below.)

Discriminatory behavior is usually attributed to the personal prejudices and resulting behavior of those thinking and behaving in that way; much more often, however, prejudices and discrimination have been "institutionalized" (as with which side of the road one drives upon). Living that way we come to see such attitudes and behavior as not only "the way things are," but, consciously or not, as "the way things ought to be." Thus, when the women's movement took hold over a century ago in the US, those who led and supported it were treated as combining insanity with arrogance (Feagin and Feagin, 1978).

Sexism and racism are both "institutionalized" and have many similarities, but there are also important differences. We are "prejudiced" when we make judgments about others without knowing them. Because such prejudices are created by merely living in a society where such attitudes are common; they lead to various forms of harmfully discriminatory behavior toward a person or group, often without conscious intent: they have been "institutionalized." Not all of participation in discriminatory behavior depends upon the participants' attitudes. For example, when one works in a company where blacks are not hired, eats in a restaurant where blacks are not served, or attends an all-white school in an all-white neighborhood, the discrimination has also been "institutionalized" in the sense that those allowed to work, eat, etc. are unconscious of the discrimination that favors "their own kind"; usually they won't "give it a thought" (unless, or until, someone of color *is* hired).

Whether personal or institutionalized, the prejudices of men against women have all too often led to wife-beating, rape, and murder; as has also been true in the realm of racism. After slaves were freed by the Civil War in the US "race" prejudice encouraged the lynching of many thousands of blacks in the South (and, as will be discussed later, of Chinese in San Francisco, Mexicans in Texas, etc.). Such killings must be seen as "legalized murder," especially when, as has been frequent in the US, sheriffs participated. Gender and "race" prejudice also have in common that both are forms of "biological discrimination," even when "biology" is not involved. (See below.) As such prejudices persist and even increase, and as the US and other countries stride into militaristic conservatism against, especially, Muslims, it is pertinent to consider the warning of biologist Stephen Gould (1981): "Resurgences of biological determinism correlate with episodes of political retrenchment..., and reduced governmental spending on social programs, and increasing military spending."

"Race" prejudice and discrimination have diverse histories and actions, discussed later at some length. Here are a few examples, beginning with a major difference between gender and "race" discrimination, due mostly to how, when, and why the discrimination began. This is how one social psychologist put it:

> Prehistoric man, living in bands as hunter and food gatherer, was characterized by a minimum of destructiveness and an optimum of cooperation and sharing; and only with the increasing productivity and division of labor, the formation of a large surplus, and the building of states with hierarchies and elites, did large-scale destructiveness and cruelty come into existence, and grew as civilization and the role of power grew. Because man has less instinctive equipment than any other animal and does not identify his own species as easily as do [other] animals...he experiences

the stranger as if he belonged to another species; in other words, it is man's humanity that makes him so inhuman. (Fromm, 1997)

Modern Racism

Few of us would prefer to live in the pre-modern world; still, it has often depended upon developments which have facilitated negative as well as positive activities. Here we examine two of those:

1. The abilities of nations through improved modes of transportation to bring whole peoples of different colors and cultures within easy reach also enabled them to take control of the lands of the relatively "backward" peoples and to enslave large numbers of their inhabitants. In the sixteenth to seventeenth centuries virtually all of those enslaved were dark-skinned; but in that era so were many of those who enslaved and sold them. That had changed by the eighteenth century; then North America became the major buyer and exploiter of black people and the leader in racist discrimination against all black people and the hemisphere's "Indians" (a name given to them by Columbus). From the first, those enslaved and the people of the native tribes were seen as "inferior"; although, by any reasonable standard for being fully "human" the enslavers and other enriched whites were disgracefully inferior (Wright, 1992).
2. Another major contribution to modern racism (especially in the US) was stimulated by the evolution of industrialism from the latter decades of the nineteenth century to the present and the always increasing sources and numbers of immigrants to the US (initially from Europe, and later from Mexico and China). More recently, emigration has been from the poorest countries to the richest: from Africa to Western Europe, from Latin America to the US and, within Europe, Turks to Germany, Rumanians to Italy, etc. (Handlin, 1981).

Taken together those emigrations stimulated new waves and kinds of "racism": those directed at national origin, not "color" as such. That kind of "racism" was fired by the job competition of white workers vs. white workers; for example, English vs. Irish, using racist language (discussed later). Tragically, nowadays we confront at least two other forms of "racism": that of well-off blacks vs. poor blacks; and against Muslims (who are "brown," "yellow," and "white").

However, neither the "racial" nor the gender discriminatory practices now common are "unconscious discrimination" excusable in self-styled democratic societies. This is not a matter merely of abstract principles. The pervasive and life-distorting damages of both gender and "racial" discrimination have meant lives marked by danger and mistreatment for a majority of the world's people for many centuries. Perpetrated by the small minority that has had "a good life" owed much of that to the destruction of others' lives. Now we turn to some details, beginning with the oldest and most pervasive discrimination.

Gender Inequality

The initial focus will be on the US. The abuse with which women have been and are still treated in the US has had much in common with the atrocities of US racism and slavery; but there are also many differences:

1. They are similar in that neither of them are confined to one country; different in that the oppressions of racism and slavery in the US have been more severe than the oppression of women, harsh though women's oppression has been.
2. They are similar in that however serious *class* inequality has been and remains in the US, it is considerably more so for the victims who are also harmed by racist and gender oppression (and the victims of class, "race," *and* gender are of course the most damaged of all).
3. However, as noted in the preceding chapter and will be discussed again later, *all* workers have lost and their employers gained from the poisoning of worker solidarity resulting from both gender and "race" discrimination.

4. In addition and even more damaging, though impossible to measure, all concerned suffer from the linked diminution of their humanity. The damage done to women is beyond measure in all of social existence; but men have paid little or no attention to the ways in which they have diminished their own lives in forcing their mothers, lovers, daughters, and sisters into that mold.

5. A basic similarity for both forms of oppression is that the relevant attitudes of disdain, fear, scorn, and hatred are deeply ingrained in us by the socialization "taught" to us from our species' beginnings.

6. Added importance must be given to women's oppression: experience has conditioned men to see the female *half* of all human beings as being inferior in one way and another to the *male* half. In consequence, all men (and many women), in becoming habituated to thinking prejudicially, have become unthinkingly open to accepting other prejudicial views as well; just as one disease makes us vulnerable to many others.

7. The results of women's enduring mistreatment neither begins nor ends there; it has found its way into every nook and cranny of our lives, allowing men's predilections to shape and set the standards for almost all social institutions: We live in "a man's world." It has been a nasty world for most, most of the time – cruelly for many, dangerously for all.

Now a closer look:

What hath men wrought?
Among the many appalling effects of human history has been the systematic and lifelong disadvantaging of girls and women. It begins in the life at home as children, continues as adults, works its way through educational levels from K-12 (ages 5–18) to PhD, and manifests itself in all other walks of life: on the job (and *which* jobs are granted), in entertainment, in…everything, everywhere. The resulting corruption and distortion of both human and social needs and possibilities is mind boggling; especially if we concentrate upon what has thus been lost, what life could have

been and could be, as contrasted with what it has been and is. Women's lives have by far been more damaged than men's, but, as will be noted below, men have seriously harmed themselves as they have wrought that damage.

How to explain this folly, these crimes and tragedies? The deeply-rooted tendencies of men result from the combination of our genetic makeup (which usually makes the male more muscular) and, more important, the prehistoric social processes of survival in the initial natural environment that endured for a time period which makes "historic" time seem like a few seconds compared with a month.

The basic instinct for all species is, of course, survival. Its elements are reproduction and adaptation to the natural/social environment by *production*, in order to eat sufficiently and to be protected against the weather and surrounding enemies. Men and women both participated in those processes, but in different ways. In comparison with women, men's involvement in "reproduction" diminishes sharply soon after children are born (or sooner). Put bluntly, were women to have behaved similarly, our species would not have survived its "accidental" beginnings. Whether or not we term "maternal" behavior as "instinctive," it is clear that there is nothing comparable for all but a small minority of men; except their economic production that supports life. In the numberless prehistoric years, men's "production" was that of the production, protection, and the aggression of hunters and warriors. In the pre-agricultural epoch, women searched for and gathered food. Then, and importantly, once a settled agriculture had become possible, it was the women who did most of the farming (as they still do in the non-rich world).

The nature and meaning of what is called "the maternal bent," does not usually end with the activities of mothers with their own children; it extends also to the general tendency of women to be "motherly" whether or not they themselves have children. It isn't that men never behave in similar ways, but those who do are "the exception that proves the rule."

Implicit in the foregoing is that the main functions of men in the deep past entailed prowess in the realms of aggressive or protective violence, in contrast with the relatively peaceful realms of home and field. By the time that technology and production had improved sufficiently to allow "civilization" (that is, "cities" in addition to "farms") to develop, those who ruled over them and, subsequently, over nations and empires were those who had mastered the arts of violence (Veblen, 1899; Childe, 1951).

That limited sketch of millennia of change perforce neglects substantial exceptions; but the basic processes are generally agreed upon. Thus, here and there a Cleopatra ruled, but the list of rulers was and remains denominated by a Julius, a George, a Louis, until modern times. In recent times, of course there have been the Margaret Thatchers and Hillary Clintons, but they have been more "macho" than womanly.

When ancient and medieval developments were shoved aside by the emergence of nation-states and industrial capitalism, men continued to rule, in "suits" instead of robes and uniforms, not only in business but in almost everything except kindergartens and nursing. Recently that has begun to change for the better, but only slowly, only here and there. Where such change has taken hold, women have increasingly come to take up "man's work" as a distinct minority, whether as doctors, lawyers, professors, politicians..., or soldiers.

But in doing so, and often *in order* to do so, as noted above, women frequently do and often must "act like men": in dress and manner, to be like "one of the boys." The desirable changes achieved so far amount to a bare beginning of what is just and desirable. But even for those very limited changes to occur, a substantial women's movement was essential. Its beginnings go back a century and more, and those who constituted the movement (as with their counterparts in anti-racist movements) were treated with scorn, contempt, punishment, and even imprisonment. Nor should it be overlooked that even now the lives of almost all girls and women in both rich and poor countries remain more like those of the deep past than of the emerging present; at home, at work, in school, on dates... wherever. Moreover, as also with anti-racist reforms, it is doubtful if a majority of men have agreed with or acquiesced in the beneficial changes that have occurred;

for most men, the progress has been accompanied by disbelief, resignation, stupid jokes, scorn, rage. Here are some examples (mostly from the US, but...) to make the point.

Get 'em while they're young

Boys and girls at home, in school, at play, in dress and in speech, attitudes and behavior are learning to be a "boy" or a "girl" in numberless ways, in lessons very difficult to "unlearn" and with *very* different consequences for boys and girls. In the US, for example, little Sally wears pink, and Billy wears blue even though both would look good in blue *or* pink (or green). Usually without parental deliberation, "Sally" will be treated as a girl en route to becoming a young woman, and then a mother; "Billy" as a boy en route to manhood and becoming "the man of the house." The lessons will be provided by their parents (who learned them from *their* parents), by their teachers, by their peers, from story books, from films, from TV...

Then, at school they will be self-segregating in terms of those with whom they chat or play, which games they play, with whom they become friends, and so on, year by year. All this is done in a set of processes as natural as breathing in and out; unspoken, unconscious, and unexamined: "normal." To be sure, much of that has changed and may (or may not) change even more, most visibly in sports where girls/women are now learning/being allowed to play. That can have a meaning going well beyond what is done and seen; could become significant in and of itself. There has been a similarity in sports also for blacks, except that even those whites who see Willie Mays or Tiger Woods as heroic continue to see blacks as a "group" in unchanged ways: "wouldn't want their sister to marry one," as the saying goes in the US. That a black man has now become President of the US means "the times they are a-changing." How much and for whom they have and have not changed will be discussed later.

Get 'em while they're watching

What children (and adults) see on TV and film screens is a dreadful combination of violence, sexism, aggression, and other values of

Macho US. They are "virtual realities" skillfully done, allowing watchers to become accustomed to violence (etc.) in such a way as to lose any sense of what such behavior might mean in actual reality. It is not hard to believe that today's increasing violence among children is thus stimulated; that children who become adults have "learned" *not* to see violence and other horrible practices for what they are (Postman, 1985).

By the time they are in high school, girls have learned that to be popular with their male counterparts is to be "good sports" about sex; so, for example, if there is an unwanted pregnancy it is generally not the man's to resolve. Boys learn that a real guy is one with physical prowess, at sports and with "chicks"; up to and including common rapes at fraternity parties.

In short, girls and young women are "taught" to take for granted, to admire, and to seek to become like the very stereotypes the women's movement has sought for so long to banish; as, meanwhile, boys learn to be fools, brutes, and sexual cowboys; or be ostracized.

Hey guys! Now you're a man: When walking down the street and a young woman is coming the other way, have you ever wondered why they almost always look down or away from any eye contact with you?

And the rest will follow
"The rest" includes jobs and education, among other important matters. Ponder this, for example: As will be seen in Chapter 9, a "living wage" sensibly defined for the US would pay at least $10 an hour for 40 hours a week. Only 20 percent of US workers receive that wage or higher; that is, the other 80 percent must try to live on *less* than a living wage. Thus it is that at least two-thirds of all wives/mothers also need to find survival jobs. With those uninteresting and poorly-paid jobs, most husbands and wives get home from work tired and bored; the wife somewhat more so, for she had probably taken care of the kids and breakfast and even some cleaning up before leaving for the "real" job. Neither those women nor their husbands are in the mood to have to put

up with the kids after a long day; but it's usually Mom's job to do so, and she *does* so, before, during, and after the dinner she has cooked; while Dad is having a beer or a shot or two in front of the TV.

Then to bed

The first few years of even what will become a bad marriage are usually sexually lively and pleasant; then, after the marriage settles, the jobs go on, and as the kids and the bills and the mountains of debt demand attention and worry, sex can become a routine; something the husband usually feels is his due, even if his wife feels only exhaustion. Not that there aren't wives who are just as sexually lively as men (or more so); it's just that after a couple of kids, not enough money, plus a bored/boring husband, at the end of the day, the wife is more likely to want to rest than to have a workout in bed. If she does want sex, fine; if she doesn't, hubby will all too often see it as "her duty."

There is much more that is unpleasant to dwell upon; suffice it to say that in a non-sexist world, the normal passions of males and females could, if left to themselves, produce both a physical and non-physical life for men and women considerably more satisfying than the distortions now marking the lives of almost all. In sum: much has been lost, also for "the masters of all they survey."

Jobs

Most jobs are neither clearly useful nor interesting for men *or* women; but for women more often than men, jobs are another area of oppression and injustice. For people in the poorer countries, conditions are of course considerably worse than in the rich countries; not only in terms of how very wearying and life-shortening their work is, but how little control women have over their lives, including their education, their sex lives, and their health. A main element of job inadequacies for women is the formal or informal distortion of education between them and males, and thus which "tracks" they can or are forced to take. Such treatment is also meted out to males, where the "push" is determined by class and "race," not sex; for young women, it is all of the above. Heaven help the young woman who is also not "white": she is destined to work in a Wal-Mart or a hospital hallway or, if a bit luckier, in an office or as a nurse, etc. Then, if and when she becomes a nurse, valuable though she is to the hospitalized patient, she will work more hours, be paid much less, be treated as a servant. Countless women with talents equal or superior to men have been tracked into stupid and low-paying jobs; countless are the women who, with equal education and opportunity, could have made a considerably greater contribution to their own lives and to society. Then there is what happens to a woman on an *identical* job: Often as not, she works more hours, is paid less, is treated shabbily to the point of *mis*treatment (including sexual abuse), and is less likely to have a union to assist her toward better conditions, pay, and benefits. In short, she is abused and exploited.

But surely that affects only a small minority of wives with children? Wrong; not least in the US. The socio-economic changes that began to emerge in the 1970s and that went through the roof from the 1980s on did so as the US had the world's highest ratio of two-income households, with its hidden, *de facto* tax on time and families. Whereas back in 1960 only 19 percent of married women with children under six had worked, by 1995 fully 64 percent did, exceeding all other industrial nations. By 1999, the Bureau of Labor Statistics reported that the typical American worked 350 hours more per year than the typical European (that's *nine* work weeks) (Phillips, 2002).

That's for the US; given all the woes concerning women and children and jobs noted earlier, it is revealing to compare what happens in, say, Italy, Germany, Austria, Sweden. In those and other Western European countries, when a married working woman has a child, she is entitled by law to one *year* off *with* pay. (As will be discussed further in Chapter 12, there are additional assistances.)

The inadequacies and cruelties referred to above are concentrated mostly on the rich US. Such treatment in the poor countries *might* conceivably provide something of an admissible basis for an excuse; but not in the richest and self styled most democratic" nation in the world. To repeat what will also be noted under racism: what girls and women have lost through all this, everywhere, has in different degree and with partial responsibility also been lost to men; men who have never been able to have a full life for themselves, partly because they have participated in denying a full life to *all* the women they have known: mothers, wives, and daughters.

In sum
So OK, most in the US would say; we're still the best place in the world; OK, we're stupid in things like spiked heels and lousy jobs and distorted education and...; but hey! that's not as bad as bound feet, having to wear a burkha, being burned to death on a ceremonial fire because your husband has died, not being able even to *go* to school if you're a girl... At least here things are nowhere near as bad as that. Right? Sort of. Women in the US are not subjected to all rotten possibilities; however, as regards the treatment of women, neither in the US nor the other rich countries are we even close to being as good as we men like to think we are; nowhere near as good as we would be if we saw men and women – *all men and all women* – as having equal rights, equal needs, equal possibilities going way beyond what all have now. From childhood to old age, all of us have an equal craving for the dignity now denied to almost all; especially if we're women, and/or not "white." But at least we are closer to that today than we were a century ago? "Closer," but with a very long way to go: few if any men would trade places with almost any woman. We are as far away from that goal as we are from what where we could and should be for ending poverty and racism and militarism. What fools we mortals be! (Especially us guys.)

Racial Inequality

What we call "racism" probably began soon after our species came into existence and had progressed enough so that "different" peoples would come into contact with one another. Then, understandably, they might well have viewed each other with attitudes of envy, or fear. In the primitive world of enduring scarcities and the mere beginnings of technology, such attitudes and associated behavior patterns would have been considerably less irrational than today or our species wouldn't have survived: consciously or not, they ultimately must have understood that the differences among and between them were minor when set against their common needs.

Would that we could recognize that truth today; for we are all members of the same "race." Finally: why the quotation marks? Because there is *no* biological basis for distinguishing human groups along the lines of "race"; such socio-historical categories used to differentiate among human groups are either imprecise, completely arbitrary, or both (Winant, 2001).

We usually have skin *color* in mind when thinking of "racial" matters; in practice, however, color is only one of its many bases. Think only of the "racial theories" of the German Nazis, which focused more heavily upon Jews than any others; despite that (1) not all, but most Jews are "white," and (2) when Jews are victimized, it is usually seen as "anti-Semitism," although not all Jews are Semites and not all Semites are Jews. Note this definition in *Webster's International Dictionary* (1911): "*Semite*: A member of a Caucasian race now chiefly represented by the Jews and Arabs, but in ancient times including also the Babylonians, Assyrians, Aramaens, Phoenicians et al."

But what about "black and white and brown and yellow *genes*"? Or, for those whose religious and national prejudices edge over into racism, what about the "genes" of Jews, Catholics, Protestants, Muslims, and Buddhists…, and/or Germans, French, Italians, Turks, Greeks…? Moving from color to religion and nationality and the intense feelings involved in all of those and other hate-and-fear-raising differences would usually bring strong affirmative answers to that question from those who hate and fear in "racist" terms: "Wake up, jerk: it's the punk's *genes!*"

The differences among peoples *within* a given category – color, religion, etc. – are at least as great as those *between* those different categories, whether the measuring criteria are those of intelligence and strength or, to shorten the list, bravery and honesty and health (Balibar and Wallerstein, 1991; Steinberg, 1981).

The oft-cited data regarding crime, education, health, etc. seem to (or are meant to) confirm racist views. But, and merely as an instance of what will be discussed more fully below regarding various economic and social indices, consider the most "physical" of those data; namely, health. In the *New York Times* feature article "As Black Men Move Into Middle Age, Dangers Rise" (September 23, 2002) the data provided showed conclusively that the death rate from strokes and diabetes for men aged 55–64 years old in the year 2000 was three times higher for black than for white men; and 50 percent higher from cancer and heart disease.

So it *is* genes? Not quite. The *same* article quoted the Deputy Secretary of the US Health and Human Services Department as stating: "All those causes are preventable or treatable with great survivability...; the central task is improving access to health care... We should not be losing people because we have not provided access to care, treatment, information and education in a timely manner." Moreover, although the economic element of the problem is greatest for low income blacks, income alone is not the reason. The Institute of Medicine, on the basis of 100 studies, reports that "...even when African-Americans and other minorities have the same incomes, insurance coverage, and medical conditions as whites, they receive notably poorer care. Biases, prejudices and negative racial stereotypes...may be poisoning the reaction of doctors and other health providers" (*NYT*, ibid.).

And, of course, the same goes for the reactions of police, teachers, employers, et al. Here the focus will be mostly on racism in the US. The dominating sets of institutions in US history have been nationalism, capitalism, imperialism, militarism, *and* racism. As noted earlier, racism very probably existed millennia before all other "isms." However, racism in the US has been much intensified by its interaction with the other four social processes, and the interaction itself greatly contributes to the strength and power of those same processes. How and why?

It should be unnecessary to make that argument at any length regarding nationalism, imperialism and militarism: *greed, envy, hatred, fear*, and attitudes of *superiority* are the heartbeats of all three. Their success has always utilized and required force and violence, the recruiting for which is facilitated when those against whom it will be used are deemed "inferior" and/or evil. Less obviously but just as surely – keeping slavery and immigrants in mind – this has been so for the relationships between racism and *capitalism*. Nowadays in the US, the term "class" refers to one's income group: high, middle, or low. In this age of "consumerism" people are generally identified by others and by themselves in terms of their purchasing power, not (as Smith, Ricardo, and Marx did) by the *source* of their incomes. Before World War II, however, one's "class" was usually identified by whether one was a worker or someone who hired workers: working class or capitalist class. The working and capitalist classes were often in conflict, but that conflict was and is reduced when workers' solidarity is weakened by the racism that pits worker vs. worker. Here is Marx's comment (quoted in Delany, 2001):

> All English industrial and commercial centers now possess a working class *split* into two *hostile* camps: The ordinary English worker hates the Irish worker because he sees in him a competitor who lowers his standard of life... He cherishes religious [i.e., anti-Catholic], social and national prejudices against the Irish worker. His attitude is much the same as that of the "poor whites" towards the "niggers" in the former slave states of the American Union. The Irishman pays him back with interest in his own money. He sees the English worker as both the accomplice and the stupid tool of *English rule in Ireland*. [Marx's emphasis]

The same processes were already common in the urban US North in the early nineteenth century; they are the main concern of the meticulous study of *The Wages of Whiteness* (Roediger, 1991). Working class formation and the systematic development of a sense of whiteness went hand in hand for the US white working class; race has at all times been a critical factory in the history of US class formation. Roediger was concerned mostly with the two decades before the Civil War. He delineates how the Irish in Boston, for example, had difficulty finding even poor jobs, and were treated shamefully both at work and also at pubs: "Micks and Dogs Not Allowed." At the same time, the Irish workers "learned" to see the pre-Civil War free blacks as competitors for jobs – in terms reflecting the ways in which they themselves were seen:

> The crude, violent "Know Nothing" persecutions of Irish Catholics in the 1850's had been supplanted (especially but not only in the South) by social and class arrangements which achieved the same ends – "white, Anglo-Saxon, Protestant" (WASP) advantages in jobs, money, power, esteem – by more subtle, systematic discrimination. This was the post-Civil War period after the failure of "reconstruction" of southern slavery when WASP Americans improvised a caste-like social system incorporating racist prejudices, discriminations, segregations and denial of civil rights against blacks and the Irish Catholics – a system which subsequently has been used against every people to immigrate to the US (Delany, 2001)

Ubiquitous over time and space, racism has of course taken on diverse as well as similar ways and means over the globe. The US, however, stands alone as regards its racist history; much more easily than any others we *could* have risen above that blight. How and why?

First

More than any other society the US has drawn peoples of every nationality, ethnicity, color, and religion to its shores. That *could* have served as a multicultural spring of social vitality; instead, the US ideal for immigrants was for them to become part of the "melting pot." Sounds OK, but in practice what was "melted" away were the immigrants' culture, language, and identity – leaving them to be discriminated against until they had done so completely; or, if they were not "white," for life. The "melting pot" is generally seen as a benign notion in a model nation; in fact it has served as an imperative: You will be accepted – *despite* your origins – "so long as you become like us." The "us," consciously or not, came to mean the "WASPS." Of course variety has persisted, and of course some significant percentage of immigrant families has risen to levels of comfort and dignity. But, each new group was pitted against its relatively more assimilated predecessors: the once despised "Micks" against the newly-arrived "Squareheads" (Germans) or "Yids" (German Jews) or "Frogs" (French) or "Wops" (Italians) or "Polacks" (Polish) or "Gooks" (S.E. Asians) or...; with *all* former Europeans vs. the "Niggers," the "Japs," the "Chinks," and the "Greasers" (Latinos).

That social crime was preceded by a worse rottenness: what was done to the native tribes whose lands we stole and whom we have since called "redskins" or "Indians," and the millions of men, women, and children stolen from Africa and enslaved. Consider that in the fifteenth century there were 100 million native people north and south of where Columbus landed; their descendants are now down to 10 million (Wright, 1992; and see below).

Second
Just as the richness of the US demographic mix *could* have led the US to become the least racist of all societies, the richness of its natural resources *could* have led to a minimal fear of "the other." All other societies have emerged in a world of dire scarcities; the US stands out as uniquely opposite without any *material* basis for racism, its abundance unmatched in past or present and with always plenty "to go around." Also, and importantly, until 1941 the US lived safely within surrounding oceans; which should have removed a basis for a militaristic population.

Also, and although the hemisphere's original inhabitants were friendly and cooperative with the invaders, an accelerating violence against them took hold. The consequences for the native peoples were genocidal in nature, matching the virtual extermination of the North American buffalo. It needs adding that the earlier millions of "primitive" people, whatever the dangers and hardships of their existence, were very probably better fed, clothed, and housed – and with more dignity – than their descendants have been for the past few centuries (Mander, 1992).

If there were any excuse at all for the *pre*-1776 murderous behavior of what became "the Americans," it would be the weak argument that they were merely part of the ferocious campaigns of the Spanish, the French, and the British. However, ferocity even worsened as the colonists took on their "American" identity and became dependent upon the simultaneous mistreatment of chattel slaves and the peoples native to the hemisphere; and their lands.

The hard core of US racist history is found in its centuries of subjugation, displacement, exploitation, and/or slaughter of "Indians" and black slaves. Racism served as a rationale for otherwise unspeakable behavior in those histories; and it set the stage for today's continuing variations.

Now some details of three realms of that socialized and accepted behavior in the US.

1. *Life and death*

The place to begin is the slave trade. The accepted estimates are that 20 million Africans were kidnapped from their homelands and that only about a fifth survived the months' long voyage. The many years of that "trade" were equal to or more horrifying, inhuman, and murderous than the Nazi's Holocaust (Nordholdt, 1970; E. Williams, 1944; Haley, 1977).

Add the poor health and life expectancies of slaves on the plantations. Slaves were productive "assets," so there was ample reason for the merchants and slave owners to treat them with care; as some did. Some, but not most; so deep was the racism of slave owners that they often maimed, raped, and killed their "assets." Then, after the Civil War, the physical mistreatment of freed blacks in the South plunged to even greater depths. (See below.) Add the decimation of those called "Indians" from the seventeenth century on. Literal "decimation" would mean a 10 percent reduction of the tribal population from 1500 to modern times; as noted earlier, the actual reduction was closer to 90 percent.

New victims from Asia arrived from the 1860s on: the Chinese, Japanese, and Filipinos; the Chinese in vast quantities to build the railroads of the West. They worked and sweated and died prematurely for decades, indistinguishable from slaves until the 200,000 miles of railroad construction were completed. As they mostly settled into towns and cities along the Pacific Coast, the Chinese underwent persistent "racial" persecution and discrimination, up to and including the hundreds of lynchings in San Francisco, then the largest city on the West Coast and, also, the city with the greatest number of Chinese and the most-organized (white) working class in the United States. Then as still, "white" workers allowed racism to direct their fears against the wrong target (Chang, 2003).

In the late nineteenth and early twentieth centuries, the Japanese arrived; by the end of the 1930s they numbered well over 100,000 (almost all on or near the Pacific Coast). After working hard on others' farms, they became able to be independent farmers: until Pearl Harbor. Soon after the attack, at least 150,000 Japanese men, women, and children were rounded up, placed in concentration camps and, without access to lawyers or visitors, left there until war's end. These camps were the precedent for post-9/11 Camp X-Ray, Guantanamo Bay, Cuba. No charges were made, nor was there public opposition to their imprisonment. Almost all lost their farms, etc., "guilty" of being Japanese (Winant, 2001).

2. Socio-economic conditions

The malevolent treatments of the peoples of diverse national, ethnic, and religious origins in the US have varied considerably in both degree and kind. Among European immigrants, those from its east were treated worse than those from its west; from the south worse than those from the north, with none receiving the harsh treatment dealt out to Latin Americans, Asians, or worst, "Indians" and African Americans.

In all these respects, conditions throughout the US before World War II were usually more severe than today. Since then, however, and despite numerous reforms, the incidence and seriousness of racial discrimination is still great. The results, among other miseries, include inescapable poverty and desperate lives for at least a fifth of the nation (measured conservatively), even in the "prosperous" 1990s (Mishel, 2002–03). Among the abiding accompaniments of the stunted lives of discrimination's victims are the explanations offered by the comfortable rationalization that "women and people of color are lazy, ignorant, immoral, inferior…etc." "Blaming the victim" soothes those who support racism while, at the same time, adding to the several vicious circles maintaining an ugly status quo; most clearly in the wholesale denial of equal access to education. That is an especially "vicious circle," meaning poor jobs, low wages, terrible housing in dangerous neighborhoods with terrible schools, where both students and teachers are demoralized. "Round and round it goes." (See Chapter 10.)

The vicious circles for poor people of all "colors" have become a noose. Those who defend past and present status quos in these respects and who see the plight of the poor people of color as "their own fault" point to the existence of blacks in the past who "made it": A black doctor or judge – or, now, a president – *proves* that opportunities exist for those who have sufficient strength, talent, and intelligence and who are willing to make the needed effort. Implicit in such arguments is that those who *are* well off *do* have the strength, and *did* make the effort. When such arguments refer to poor blacks, they neglect how very much was required of black individuals in the "pre-civil rights" past and forget that the achievements made by some since were much assisted by the very social reforms so strongly opposed by those same racists (including, most disgustingly, Supreme Court Justice Clarence Thomas who vigorously opposes the very policies that put him where he is; most clearly, but not only, his legislated ability to gain a university education). Before the 1960s, such individual achievement required amounts and kinds of effort rarely found in *anyone*, "regardless of race, creed, or color": Paul Robeson or Marian Anderson as singers, Zora Neale Hurston or James Baldwin as writers, Thurgood Marshall as a Supreme Court Justice, W.E.B. Du Bois as an intellectual prodigy – or, on a humbler level, Claude Brown, born in the slums, a captive of poverty and imprisoned for petty crime, who, befriended by a prison counselor, struggled to get an education and wrote a stunning book on his saga (Brown, 1965).

Little indeed can those who have not been directly afflicted by racism even begin to imagine the struggles and pains of such an effort. Reforms since the 1960s have helped; but only somewhat. It may be hoped that the needed substantial reforms will be forthcoming in the near future; if and when they take hold, it is important to remember that up to now, those mostly assisted have seldom been the most needy when they received it (Feagin and Sykes, 1994; Litwack, 1980; Omi and Winant, 1994).

3. The law and the police

To all of the foregoing it is necessary to add the systematic mistreatment of racism's victims by the police and the US legal system. As noted, and as all know, the US Declaration of Independence stated that "All men are created equal," that "all stand equally before the law." The reality blatantly violates that ideal, to the advantage of the rich and "white" and, regularly, to the harm of the poor and "non-white." In consequence, the disadvantaged are arrested more frequently and on occasions when others would not be, for using or selling drugs, for "driving while black" (or in the Southwest, "brown") and for other assumed crimes, now including suspected terrorism. Once arrested, they are frequently represented badly (or not all) by lawyers, receive longer prison sentences for a given crime, and are subjected disproportionately to the death penalty.

More generally, if and when those higher up on the socioeconomic pyramid are arrested for "white collar crimes," they are well-represented, and, if convicted, typically serve little or no time. Meanwhile, as the number of prisoners has burgeoned in recent decades, that has also provided "good arguments" for the rapidly growing prison-industrial complex. *Fact:* the State of California spends more on prisons than on education.

Such ill-treatment of human beings is by no means confined to the US; but we quantitatively outdo all other democratic societies with imprisonment: the US has over 2.5 million behind bars, most of whom are poor and black.

Such are only some of the consequences of racism for those singled out as "inferior," or dangerous, or...something. But there have also been grave consequences for the racists and their societies, not least for the US. (For further details see Chapters 9–10.) Now a summary of only some of the price paid by society as a whole.

Unintended Consequences

Whether it is "whites" mistreating people of color, or men mistreating women, dehumanizing consequences are suffered by both victims and by the perpetrators. Like it or not, we are all in the same boat. When born, we are like soft clay; our lives at home and school and in the larger society shape us to become who and what we are and are *not*. Although the Obama presidency may bring desired changes, they are most likely to fit into the status quo. More significant changes for better will depend upon strong pressures from a significant percentage of the people; and/or for worse, from continuing wars, economic worsening. Much of it is up to us, one way or the other.

Almost all of us have grown up in a pervasively racist and sexist society, so our "normal" feelings, thoughts, and behavior will be racist/sexist in one degree or another, depending upon time and place. That includes even those who have joined the struggles against racism/sexism: we too have been "taught to hate" (as the song in *South Pacific* put it); but our lives have been lucky enough to at least give us second thoughts.

It is generally accepted that "human nature" has both a constructive and destructive side to it. Thorstein Veblen, writing on the eve of World War I, agreed, but in seeing the "parental bent of the instinct of workmanship" as being in constant struggle for dominance with the "predatory bent of the instinct of sportsmanship," he also saw our destructive side as usually winning because of the driving forces of capitalism and imperialism. He called those forces our "imbecile institutions":

History records more frequent and more spectacular instances of the triumph of imbecile institutions over life and culture than of peoples who have by force of instinctive insight saved themselves alive out of a desperately precarious institutional situation, such, for instance, as now faces the people of Christendom. (Veblen, 1914)

Not just capitalism, imperialism, and militarism, but racism and sexism are among those "imbecile institutions." They function in a mutually strengthening set of processes that damage all people, all social wellbeing, and all of nature: workers divided by racism and sexism; citizens "bewitched, bothered, and bewildered" by consumerism and hyped-up nationalism; big business allowed to have its way in ravaging the environment; militarism running wild.

No species has ever survived except by mutual support, the modern term for which is "solidarity." That term need not connote affection or anything like it; it does connote recognition of life-serving mutual interests. The US is the global leader today for trampling those mutual interests. Will we wake up, grow up, and wise up, or will we continue to allow this cruel and insane system do us in?

4

BIG BUSINESS AND INEQUALITY

The inherent class of inequality capitalism noted by Smith, Ricardo, and Marx from 1776 to 1848 was in reference to the small companies of birthing industrialization, owned and controlled by individuals or their partners. In sharp contrast, the technological progress after the 1850s created the need for large companies and, for their financing, the modern corporation. The economic and political dynamics of that process have continually accelerated ever since, much provoked and stimulated by the two world wars and the globalization of today. Thus, what in the early twentieth century were seen as big companies (e.g. Standard Oil and US Steel) have since become *giant* corporations.

Item: In 1955 *Fortune Magazine* began its annual listings of "the 500 largest industrials." As the twenty-first century opened, *Fortune* noted that "the 500" by themselves had revenues equal to about two-thirds of the production of the entire US economy and which exceeded that of the economies of Japan and Germany, the next two largest *nations*. Now, that's *really* big business.

Today's giants have become "TNCs" – transnational corporations – whose production is "outsourced" to cheap labor and unregulated countries, and neither the markets nor the production of the TNCs are centered on their own nations, whether as regards products or services. Thus: accelerating over time, well *before* the current economic crisis, those who earlier had good jobs in the US and Europe had lost them and have since been unemployed or working at lower level jobs. In addition, the always greater concentration of business power has of course meant an always greater concentration of both political and social power; *and*, therefore, intensification of inequality, as the business world's ability to reduce the power of all others increases.

Whatever power may have been possessed by workers, educators, doctors, scientists, governors, or senators has been bought or stolen in the US and elsewhere by a few dozen of the "500." (See below.) Despite that always greater concentration of power in the hands of those few companies, the ideology of capitalism continues to be that of Adam Smith's *Wealth of Nations*, written when the size of the largest businesses was measured in hundreds of workers in local factories.

From Small Factories to the Fortune 500

When Adam Smith wrote, he trusted "neither the means nor the ends of businessmen, an order of men," he said, "whose interest is never exactly the same with that of the public, who have generally had an interest to deceive and even to oppress the public, and who accordingly have, upon many occasions, both deceived and oppressed it" (Smith, 1776). *Wealth of Nations* was an appeal for an economy whose hustling competition would *frustrate* business attempts to achieve the unlimited profits and power they seek. Smith's main aim was to get rid of long-standing "mercantilist" economic controls and legalized monopolies. Smith's ideal was an economy of competing small firms.

It was not a crazy idea in his time. The industrial revolution (usually dated as 1780–1850) was gestating and nobody could foresee the massive machinery that would come later: not even the first, and tiny, industrial factory with machines was born until 1815. For some decades after that, one company's percentage of a given industry's output was so insignificant that none could even imagine any control over supply (Mantoux, 1906).

Thus, in his time Smith's dream of an economy in which all firms would be restrained by an "invisible hand of competition" that would transform individual self-seeking into the wellbeing of all was plausible (setting aside, for the moment, worker exploitation). But the "industrial revolution" inexorably transformed small into large, larger, and then giant companies. That continuously exploding process went on in ways and degrees such that today, a company like General Electric not only produces your toaster, but airplane engines, and ships; is a media company, a finance company and...so on; with innumerable other companies knowing that they had better become big, bigger, biggest or be swallowed up by those that have.

However, even when and where Smith's dreams of an "invisible hand" of competition had become real, it was accompanied by ugly realities. Thus, for example, in the US the competition Smith depended upon *did* prevail here and there into the twentieth century: in staple agriculture, coal mining, and cotton textiles. But it was devastating for most farmers, *workers* and for many owners, in one way or another. So it was that (a) farmers began in the 1920s to demand and to get some governmental control over their output and pricing; (b) free competition in coal mining produced ruined lives for the miners and bankruptcies for their small owners; and (c) the perfectly competitive cotton manufacturing industry could not survive even with its brutal exploitation of workers. In consequence, (a), (b), and (c) asked for and received either governmental market intervention and/or were taken over by big business (Du Boff, 1989). Furthermore, Smith's ideal economy took as given that if profits were to be made workers *must* be exploited. Because they were property-less, they could survive *only* by working on the terms of those who owned and controlled the means of production; that is, the means of life. Nonetheless, Smith, gloomy Scot that he was, saw that future as "the best of all possible worlds." A few decades later, David Ricardo, his most important follower, argued that there should be "external" freedom"; that is, *no* barriers to foreign trade, even if it meant imperialism (Ricardo, 1817).

Neither Smith nor Ricardo foresaw that their ideal "*free* markets" would be snapped up by giant and politically powerful companies which would use those very arguments to disguise *their* market controlling policies; the problem was "reality." It was and is in the very nature of the industrialization process to obliterate the tiny firms required if the "invisible hand" were to function.

Half a century or so after the first small factory, the galloping technological advances unleashed by industrialization and mass production had begun to make it both possible and, if they were to survive, *necessary* for business firms to enlarge, and to move toward becoming gigantic if only in order to defend themselves from their enlarging competitors and "destructive competition"; *and* possible to increase their profits by their ability to control their markets. "The best defense is a strong offense" applies as much in business as in boxing.

As the nineteenth century drew to its end US companies took the lead, facilitated and stimulated by rich resources, vast spaces, large population, and broad national markets. In the decades after 1860, when the mergers of formerly competing companies sped up in railroads, then in metals, then oil, then in..., they created "the combination movement." By the first years of the twentieth century, the "invisible hand" had becoming a "visible fist": what had been 5,300 US industrial firms in 1897 became only 318 corporations in less than a decade. Most spectacular were the mergers in iron and steel which in 1901 created US Steel – the first billion-dollar company: one company replacing what had been 750 different companies (Josephson, 1934).

Before the 1920s, mergers had always been of many small companies into one, all in the same industry. But the interacting economic demands and technological/scientific jumps during and after World War I created a set of strong stimuli for mergers of three kinds:

- "horizontal" (within an industry; e.g. steel)
- "vertical" (between industries; e.g. steel companies buying up bridge building companies)
- "conglomerate" (among and between companies in different sectors, as by General Electric, noted above)

All records were broken during the 1920s (for a while), not only in terms of mergers' numbers and values. It was then that today's merger processes of very big companies buying up other very big companies took hold. Thus, by 1929 the assets of the largest 200 non-banking corporations had doubled, rising at an annual rate of over 5 percent, while others' assets enlarged by only 2 percent (Berle and Means, 1932). By 1955, as noted above, *Fortune Magazine* (self-styled "Magazine of Big Business") began its annual "Fortune 500 Largest Industrials." Since then it has added special issues for the "50 Largest Financial, Utility, etc." and, in the 1990s, the "500 Largest *Global* Firms." Since then? See below.

As was briefly noted in Chapter 2 and will be detailed below, what was in the 1920s inaccurately called "competitive capitalism" in the US had by the 1960s matured into "monopoly capitalism" (Baran and Sweezy, 1966). The developments from the 1970s on require that we distinguish between two stages of monopoly capitalism: "I" for the 1950s–60s, and "II" for the years after the 1970s. II is the latest stage of capitalism, birthing ever more gigantic "globalized" companies. That in turn was dependent upon consumerism and reckless debt at all levels, and stimulated what will later be termed "Las Vegas, Inc." All of that held hands with the giant media. (See below and Chapters 5 and 7.)

The giantism of US monopoly capitalism was a product of the combination movement's post-World War II transformation into "mergers and acquisitions" (M&As). Commencing in the early 1950s, merger activity registered progressive increases and reached a frenzied pace in 1967–70, when more than one of every five manufacturing and mining corporations with assets exceeding $10 million was acquired. (See Adams and Brock, 1986.) The best – or worst – was yet to come. As capitalism developed over time, it produced what it must: more and more change in always more areas of social existence, faster and faster; as private gain and social harm both increased, and as we moved into what the twentieth-century capitalism would become.

Monopoly Capitalism

Monopolistic arrangements go far back in time: in ancient, medieval, and early modern societies. However, with industrialism they became both more essential for "good business" and easier to arrange. In one variation or another they were common in all industrial capitalist nations by the late nineteenth century. By the 1930s they had become more essential, more pervasive, *and* more dangerous: of the six major capitalist powers between 1920 and World War II, only two (the US and Britain) did *not* become fascist (R. Brady, 1943).

After World War II there were repeated waves of M&As, varying in degree and kind from country to country but with one characteristic in common: an always greater concentration of economic and political power. As the century ended, M&As within and between industries, sectors, and nations had become the rule, and dangerous in ways going well beyond costs, prices, and profits (Cypher, 1987, 1991, 2001, 2002a, 2002b).

Capitalism has always been a *social* not just an economic system; has always meant more than the existence of privately-controlled markets for goods or services. Monopoly capitalism is the "mature" form that capitalism took in the late twentieth century. It has meant an always deeper subservience of the entire society to the aims, ways, and means of a big business-dominated socio-economy, a domination expressed usefully through the six interdependent and interacting clusters of US "monopoly capitalism, to which we now turn:

- giant corporations
- a giant State
- consumerism
- globalization/financialization
- the military-industrial complex
- the media.

All will be examined in detail in the pages that follow. ("State" is capitalized here to distinguish it from the individual "states" of the US, e.g. New York.)

Each "cluster" is complicated in itself, but all depend to a critical degree upon their dynamic relationships with the others in an always more integrated *global* economy. Separately or taken together the "big six" required technological and organizational developments that neither did nor could exist until the mid twentieth century. In consequence the joint powers of business and the State have been recast such that the economy is able to function to the satisfaction of giant business *only* insofar as *all* of social existence is increasingly shaped to satisfy the felt needs and desires of capital – everywhere.

As we now examine that reality, most of the analysis and data will center on the US. Were this study to have been written a century ago, the emphasis would have been on Great Britain, then the "hegemonic" power of "competitive capitalism." But at least since World War II, the US has dominated not only with its economic and military power but with its politics, its culture, and its ways of thinking; all in considerably greater degree than Great Britain did or could have. (Chapters 6, 7, and 10 will argue that the era of US "hegemony," as earlier with the British, is dwindling, if for mostly different reasons.)

Capitalism Unleashed

Unevenly, and rapidly or slowly, the main elements of monopoly capitalism took shape as the late 1940s moved toward and through the 1950s and 1960s. As its six elements grew in strength, each depended upon, fed, and was fed by the strengthening of the others. Thus:

(1) The vast increase in both the absolute and the relative power of *super corporations* required and facilitated (2) an equally striking increase in both the quantitative and qualitative roles of the State in all functional and geographic areas, and at all levels. Given that both of those developments constituted a marked departure from traditional US notions of what was "proper," it was essential for the maintenance of socio-economic stability that there be vigorous economic *expansion*. Up into and through the 1970s, what was needed was made possible by (3) the strengthening and spread of *consumerism* (see Chapter 5) in the United States and its increasing replication in all of the leading, and some of the lesser, economies in the world. That in turn required and

facilitated (4) the re-creation, transformation, and deepening of an expanding world economy through "globalization" and "financialization" (see Chapters 6–7). That was led and, until recently, easily dominated by the US. It was enabled to do so by (5) the economic stimuli of the US *military-industrial complex* and the "Cold War" that rationalized it until the Berlin Wall fell in 1989. The ensuing vacuum was filled by the "war on terrorism." (See Chapter 8.) But none of the foregoing developments – economic, social, political, military, national, or international – could have reached the levels or taken the form achieved by the 1960s had they not been created, lubricated, and sustained by (6) the extension and refinement of the techniques of mass communication for selling products, politics, and ideology (see Chapter 5).

Such were and are the indispensable lubricants of monopoly capitalism's ways and means. Critical among those "lubricants" have been past and present huge military expenditures by the US: well over $12 *trillion* since 1950, with its current expenditures set to exceed both those of World War II and the Cold War years (after accounting for price changes). By whatever name, those expenses seem destined never to end, unless, along with all else, with World War III. If there is such a war, then, as a song in the 1960s went, "We'll all go together when we go." The economist James Cypher, referenced above, has become the authority on our massive military expenditures. (See Chapter 8.)

As all of the "big six" strengthened from the 1970s on, already existing inequalities were worsened:

- giant business has meant dwarfed workers' power
- the State in monopoly capitalism is effectively "bought and paid for" by the rich and powerful
- consumerism deflects attention from public needs into individuals' buying and borrowing
- globalization has meant both the economic and the political weakening of workers and their unions in all the rich nations and, with financialization, increased fragility

- as militarism deflects attention from social needs toward war, it also raises already high barriers against decent domestic policies and expenditures
- and the media, themselves part of big business, facilitate all the foregoing in favor of their fellow "monopoly capitalists."

Thus:

- what was already harmful for a majority of the world's people has become worse, as existing inequalities have deepened and magnified, as noted in today's news. (A fuller discussion will follow in subsequent chapters.)

The "normal" functioning of the first decades of monopoly capitalism brought troubles to itself, so much so that by the 1970s (see below), it seemed as though the traditional capitalist system had done itself in; that if capitalism were to survive, let alone to prosper, it had to cease parading itself as "competitive capitalism" and move beyond "Monopoly Capitalism I" toward a newly-invigorated but even more dangerous "Monopoly Capitalism II." That's where the US is now, but in always more serious troubles: economic, political, and military troubles. As Obama occupies the White House, the daily question is "What's next?" (See ensuing chapters and the Epilogue.)

Neither the corporations nor their spokespeople call themselves "monopoly capitalists," nor have they ceased to use the term "competitive"; nor have the spokesmen of capitalism ever seen its realities as "exploitative, imperialist, or plutocratic"; of course not. Those defining characteristics of "Monopoly Capitalism II" will be examined soon; but first, what went wrong with "Monopoly Capitalism I"?

The answer is partially provided by a term first used in the 1970s: "stagflation" (Sherman, 1977). The term refers to the uniqueness of the economy's behavior in those years: the unprecedented combination of a *stagnant* economy's high unemployment *and* rapidly rising prices. Before those two problems joined hands, it was seen as impossible by economists. Stagflation seemed to be on its way again in 2007 here and there; whether or not it will take hold cannot be known yet. In Monopoly Capital II's early period the financial *boom* was strong. That boom began to bust in 2007. As I write this in early 2009 a full financial collapse has carried with it already serious unemployment and a recession lurching toward depression. (See Chapters 7 and 11.)

Here we look only at the past; in later chapters we examine the present. Du Boff (1989) saw the cause(s) as being due to the combination of the triumphs *and* troubles Monopoly Capitalism I had provided:

> The impasse of American capitalism in the 1970s was defined by the tightening [of the] constraints [of] accelerating inflation led by energy and food prices, expectations of annual wage and benefit increases in the face of pressure on corporate profitability, more frequent intervention by government in ways that threatened freedom of action by business, an emerging import penetration of consumer goods markets [with domestic job losses], and the seemingly sudden loss of international hegemony symbolized by military defeat in Vietnam in 1975 in the longest, costliest, and least successful of a series of postwar interventions against the socialist and communist left all over the world. (Also see Sherman, 1977)

In that long quote of Du Boff, note the phrases: "expectations of annual wage and benefit increases...; more frequent intervention by government in ways that threatened..." That is, from the point of view of business, something had gone awry: others were having a voice about matters that were "none of their business."

Why? The answer to that question is found in what the depression of the 1930s meant to US politics, and what World War II meant to the "political economy" of capitalism; an "answer" that centers upon the meaning of World War II to the US, as compared with other nations. The war (and what preceded it) was a total disaster to Europe and Japan for both "winners" and losers. However, and setting aside US dead and wounded soldiers and sailors (and I say that as one who was with them in combat for over three years) the US economy and its people "never had it so good." Nor did the "good" start only when the US entered the war or vanish with its end. Rather, it began its long lift out of the depression as the 1930s went on because of the socio-economic policies of the "New Deal" and increased exports of critical materials to friends such as the UK (and, until Pearl Harbor, also to Italy, Germany, and Japan). After the war, such exports rose even higher, to almost all of Europe and elsewhere, including Japan. That was economically significant; even more so was what happened to the US economy after 1941. The US economy by then was beginning to run well, greatly sped up by what would become 16 million in the armed forces, and the associated highest demands ever for iron and steel, coal and timber, machinery, tanks, guns, aircraft, ships, trucks, and clothing – not least for those 16 million soldiers. (See Cypher, 2002a, 2002b.)

Put all that together and it meant *really* full employment. A moment's reflection tells us also that it meant some years of a significant *decline* in inequality. Because others than those 16 million at war had to make all that stuff:

- discrimination *had* to be reduced against blacks and women
- unions inexorably gained in strength and influence in their jobs and in politics
- average buying power rose greatly in the US both during the war and, much more, after its end
- but because of improved wellbeing for millions of families, there was also better education, housing, and health care; not least for the military who survived, and who were eligible for the "GI" Bill, which paid for tuition, board and room, books and supplies, etc.

Putting all of that together goes a long way toward explaining why so many people of the US came to see war as "not so bad." Du Boff (1989) summed it up this way:

The true "American century" arrived between 1947 and 1972, the golden years of the postwar expansion. During this run, real GNP grew at a rate of 3.7 percent per year and real disposable income per person at 2.3 percent per year; civilian unemployment was at the lowest quarter century average since 1890, and corporate profitability rose over most of the period, peaking in the mid-60s.

Sounds great; but some of it didn't to most of the business world, especially when one considers that the "good times" for the average US citizen began (slowly) from 1935 on; that is, from the beginnings of the New Deal and the many and sustained beneficial reforms put in place from then until the very early 1970s. Among these reforms were those meant to benefit middle- and lower-income workers: minimum wages, maximum hours, no child labor, safe and healthful working conditions, the right to organize and to form (honest) unions, housing and educational projects, and so on.

Those were also the years when badly-needed governmental regulation was created and took hold, not only of working conditions, but of business behavior, especially in the financial world whose wild speculations had ended in the Crash of 1929, the repeat (or worse) of which is now raging. Why? Because those same regulations were entirely cancelled from the early 1980s on, with the easy cooperation of Congress and the White House, from Reagan, the first Bush, Clinton, and Bush II. (See Chapters 6 and 7.)

So what has gone wrong, whether in the US or elsewhere? Why have inequalities been both spreading and deepening? Why is the financial system in such scary troubles? Why, especially in the US, are health costs rising as, at the same time, health care is deteriorating from its already inadequate level? Those questions will be confronted in ensuing chapters (especially in 9–11).

At the heart of all those whys and wherefores are answers which point to today's unparalleled concentration of economic, political, and social power; how it is used and, importantly, has been accepted by an almost mute, more envious than critical public. There is grumbling, of course, but grumbling at imagined enemies while concentrating more on the next shopping excursion, the next debt payment, the next sporting event, the next movie or...something we have "learned" to see as the good life. Today's ongoing shocks may – or may not – change that. (See Krugman, 2007; Bromwich, 2008.)

While we were being conditioned to live out our lives in those ways, the business world was learning how to increase and to use its economic, political, and social power. Especially in the US, and with the help of their well-financed "research organizations," business has worked very successfully at its goals "off-stage" in four tightly-related realms: corruption, lobbying, campaign financing, and their media (TV, radio, film, and the press) and, of course, advertising. (See Chapter 5.) That takes us to the present.

Monopoly Capitalism II

Today's dangerous world of monopoly capitalism is blood brother to what emerged in the 1960s, but with importantly worrisome differences. We go by the numbers 1–6 again (if not in the same order):

1. The giant corporations of today – most clearly the transnational corporations (TNCs) make even the giants of the 1950s–70s seem relatively small.
2. The State is still "super," but it functions always more at the beck and call of giant TNCs, Wall Street, well-organized gun-lovers and religious groups and much less or not at all, indeed against, social wellbeing.
3. The global economy is considerably more integrated *and* considerably more disruptive and dominated by speculative finance than earlier.
4. Although the Cold War ended along with the 1980s, the "war on terrorism" is giving us high and always rising military expenditures. (See Chapter 8, and Cypher, 2002a, 2002b.)
5. Consumerism (see next chapter) has spread and deepened all over the globe *and* (like much else) become tightly intertwined with clearly precarious debt accumulation exploding in 2007, and spreading to all realms of global finance. (See Krugman, 2007, and Chapter 7.)

6. The world of the media, earlier noted as one of the "lubricants" of monopoly capitalism, has taken on forms and power that make even its great strengths in the 1960s seem paltry. (See next chapter.)

But that's not all:

"There's a sucker born every minute"
That warning is attributed to the US circus genius Barnum, long ago, as he explained some of the illusory tricks he was using on customers. In today's world, consumers and voters are the "suckers." In allowing ourselves to be spellbound by consumerism, many ceased to be even the casually involved voters of the past, especially damaging for workers and their unions who were significant for national politics. Now, except for a union here or there, that political significance has melted away; from the 1970s on, worker solidarity has weakened, and as their political power has faded that of business has inevitably strengthened. The ongoing economic crisis and a different White House may change that.

All of the foregoing was much assisted by the multiplication of mergers and acquisitions and greater associated concentration of power. In the US, for example, the "Fortune 500" companies took over legislators and the White House, beginning with the Nixon administration of 1969–74. Exploding in the Reagan years, that continued with only some illusory interruptions in the Carter and Clinton years, and paradise unbound in the Bush II years. (See Bacevich, 2008.) Whether or not those processes will be reversed in the Obama presidency will depend on "us the people."

The conservative-reactionary process was created; it did not "just happen." It was much assisted by "off-stage" developments examined in chapters to follow. In the US that assistance is found in four tightly-related categories: corruption, lobbying, campaign finance, and the always more guileful "spin" skills of the media (itself among the giants). We take them up in that order and give close attention to the media in Chapter 5.

Corruption

The word signifies betrayal of function, whether of one's self as a person, of a public or private office, of a process, of an institution. It is another name for succumbing to temptation for sexual, monetary, political, or other forms of anticipated advantage; for "selling out." Doubtless it has existed in all societies. However, to say that corruption has been timeless, ubiquitous, and multi-dimensional does not mean we can shrug it off. As with our increasingly polluted air, unless we clean up our society we will be done in by the individuals, institutions, or nations that portray themselves as exemplars of all that is good; ourselves included. (The several books of Phillips in the Bibliography serve well as an intensive survey.)

Although corruption has always and everywhere been with us, in what follows I will deal mostly with the US; adding that, living and working more than 20 years in Italy I have learned that Italy easily outdoes the US in ways that make it seem corruption was invented there, most vividly in its southern parts, and presently at its hottest in Naples and its "Camorra." Worth noting is a recent book, *Gomorrah* (2006), showing how corruption functions, its dangers to all of Italy and indeed to the world, as regards the environmental damages the Camorra has caused by making the region surrounding Naples into a lethal garbage dump for the rest of Italy and, increasingly, the rest of Europe. (The book's author, Roberto Saviano, is under police protection.)

Now, running a close second to Italy for the corruption prize, is, the US. This home of "rugged individualism" and the richest ever of all nations offers great opportunities and rewards along with the mildest of punishments in the practice of corruption. Already in 1904, Veblen summed it up in his usual ironic manner:

> It seldom happens, if at all, that the government of a civilized nation will persist in a course of action detrimental to or not ostensibly subservient to the interests of the more conspicuous body of the community's businessmen... There is a naive, unquestioning persuasion abroad among the body of the people to the effect that, in some occult way, the material

interests of the populace coincide with the pecuniary interests of those businessmen who live within the scope of the same set of governmental contrivances; that, in the nature of the case, the owner alone has, ordinarily, any standing in court. All of which argues that there are probably very few courts that are in any degree corrupt or biased... Efforts to corrupt them would be a work of supererogation, besides being immoral.

Before the modern era, few indeed were those who had an opportunity to be corrupted; such openings were confined largely to the very small percentage of those who sat at or near the apex of power: top political (usually military) and religious functionaries. On the other hand, whatever the rewards for becoming corrupt in that era, the punishments were severe, including a usually freer and terrifying use of executions (by fire, being torn asunder, beheaded...).

Jumping to the present shows that the opportunities are now "mass-produced" and "democratized"; no longer confined to the powerful. Individuals of merely comfortable incomes can corrupt themselves: for example, university professors (in refraining from writing or teaching in ways that might hold back their careers); doctors (in attaching more importance to their incomes than their patients' health); businessmen in cutting corners qualitatively, engaging in "planned obsolescence" (as with cars and computers) as a means of enhancing profits; CEOs lying about their companies' earnings; professional athletes and drugs; and so on.

This points to two of the dominating characteristics of today's capitalism: commodification and competition. When almost every*thing* has a price, almost every*one* will have a price. After all, as we have learned to believe that competition is an acceptable and ongoing basis of social existence and that "It's each for himself and God for all," it becomes more likely to see others as opponents rather than as fellow men and women; whether in the office, the classroom, in sports, business, politics, wherever.

That points to another set of tightly interacting processes: those that center upon *decadence*. What has decayed in a decadent society are its functioning ideals and principles and the traditional constraints within which they exist; for example, when commodification puts a price on goods and services that should be provided on the basis of human need rather than income and when competition sets us against one another and cooperation withers and dies. But the most dangerous decay is when we acquiesce in the commodification of our politics through lobbyists and of our culture through advertising and the media.

What is common to all of the foregoing is an individualism that emphasizes personal gain or status, and lets *social* wellbeing take care of itself. We have allowed competition and commodification to contaminate and erode our humanity and the traditions that support it. Our focus is mainly upon inequality of the US. Its kinds and degrees stand in sharp contrast with the "rock of idealism" upon which its people like to think their nation was founded and stands; a nation which, in a debauched world, sees itself is a paragon of virtue. As such, the US should stand in horror at the degrees and kinds of corruption that have marked it from its beginnings and that have intensified in our own day. Here are a few more sad examples:

Those who first settled and developed the original colonies were Christians, the Puritans among them devoutly so: their treatment of the native tribes was from the first a murderous corruption of anything to be found in "The Gospel of Christ" (Wright, 1992). Nor can anything better be said for the almost immediate adoption of slavery as a crucial basis for the colonial and national economies. How marvelous the inspiration of the words of the famed "Declaration of Independence" of the US: "We find these truths to be self-evident, that all men are created equal, that they are endowed by their Creator with certain unalienable Rights, that among these are Life, Liberty, and the pursuit of Happiness..." They were inspiring then and are now. But neither then nor now can we reconcile those words with the fact that so many of the Constitution's signers, Jefferson and Washington among them, held slaves. The colonists and those who practiced or abided in slavery up into the Civil War were at least as aware of what slavery meant to those enslaved as were the "Good Germans" who watched the departing trains of the

Holocaust in the 1930s. Nor have the many-headed practices of racism in the US been either unknown or, except for a minority, unwelcome (Genovese, 1966).

That is merely suggestive of the innumerable dimensions of corruption in the US, past and present. Already in the late nineteenth century, Mark Twain famously saw those years as "The Gilded Age"; the historian Vernon Parrington called them "The Great Barbecue." What was golden and being barbecued were the resources and economic possibilities of the new nation. In those same years, the US Senate was accurately called "a rich man's club," as senators were openly bought and paid for. Now (see below) almost *all* political offices and most policies are bought and paid for through campaign finance and lobbyists; now it has become virtually impossible to find a candidate for any office, or any proposed policy, not "up for sale"; all of it enhanced and worsened by the always more powerful and tightly-controlled media. (See Phillips, 2002; Kuttner, 1996; McGinnis, 1969; Frank, 2008.) Consider this warning from the *International Herald Tribune* ("The Selling of America's Presidential Candidates," December 14, 2007) concerning the then oncoming 2008 US elections:

> The sticker price for US presidential candidates and congressional elections is rocketing toward $5 *billion*, shocking even political professionals who figure the ante in the opening Iowa round may cost at $500 *per voter*. The campaign is harvesting record amounts of money, watered by the willingness of candidates and party machines to ignore the spirit of the law and fertilized by the bottom lines of TV companies. By next Election Day the two presidential candidates will be at the $1 billion mark in combined spending – a 50 percent rise over the outrageously high price of the 2004 campaign.
> [Postscript: Although a good deal of Obama's financing was small amounts from "plain citizens," he too had big money from several of "the usual suspects."]

Corruption is not limited to politicians and policies; it is not limited at all. In the US, for example, it exists in the attitudes as when "voters" acquiesced in the deaths of 3 million or more Vietnamese, Laotians, and Cambodians in a war for their presumed freedom; when we today ignore and literally "don't count" the deaths of hundreds of thousands of children in Iraq as a direct result of our earlier embargo and present war. If (and when) others behave like us in these and other respects, we accuse them of employing a double standard, which they and we are. In addition, corruption of course extends well beyond the political sphere, most famously in the scandals concerning US CEOs and their companies (such as Enron, Tyco, Citigroup, MCI/WorldCom), in our health care system, and in our universities; etc. (See Chapters 6, 9 and 10.)

Long, long ago, it was said that "crime doesn't pay." For many corruption in sports is the most heart-breaking crime of all: "Can't we trust *anyone*?" Maybe not. Here's a quote from an aptly-titled article, "Something Is Very Rotten in US College Sports" (George Vecsey, *NYT*, October 19, 2002):

Free sex to entice athletes at many universities, uniforms with ads on them, dependence upon TV revenue to finance sports teams, binge-drinking associated with college sports fans... In the United States, people know all about the corruption, the phony admissions standards, the payoffs, the boosters that permeate college sports. School administrators know. Fans know. We all go along.

That was in 2002. Today? Everyone's doing it. Among the most disgusting and frightening of the members of that "everyone" – and closest to home – are our doctors, especially in the US. (See Chapter 9.) Farther from home are those who have successfully bought our politicians:

Lobbyists

In US politics, lobbyism and contemporary campaign financing have been significant for only about a century. Lobbying is called that because in the bad old days those who sought to create, eliminate, or modify governmental policies hung out in the "lobbies" of Congress and state legislatures, waiting to buttonhole those with open pockets in order to induce them to vote yes, no, or maybe. Election campaigns in that youthful past were not significantly dependent upon the media. Except for the downright and common buying of votes, campaigns were effectively costless. It's always been a game of "them what has, gets"; but today "them what already have more can get *much* more."

There is a difference between lobbying and campaign financing in the US, but this has steadily vanished for elections as they have become tightly interdependent for influencing or controlling legislation, most especially for those businesses who know just what they want and how to get it, such as "Big Oil."

Item: In the election of 2004, oil and gas companies spent $17 million on Congressional campaigns, 80 percent for Republicans; in 2006, that went up to $20 million. But for *lobbying* they spent about *six times* as much. (See "The Political Economy of Oil," *Multinational Monitor*, September/October, 2007. For the full story of lobbyists see Kaiser, 2008.)

Literally sitting in the "lobby" is now quaint in the US, except for those who wait around in doctor's offices. The lobbying business – and it's a *big* business – is more efficient now; no need to waste time hanging around; instead, just "press a button" (Kuttner, 1996). Given that life and death are fundamental in health care, perhaps the most shameless games are those played by doctors and pharmacists. In the US they (my own pharmacist told me this) are annually invited to *all*-expenses-paid-for conventions at a summer or winter resort (usually in distant places) for presentations; and the beach or ski slope is "the lobby." That is only one of a very long list of political corruptions which we end up paying for: with higher prices for our medicines, yielding higher profits for "Big Pharma." (See Chapter 9.)

Lobbyists' successes often go well beyond such matters in other important areas. Some examples: for the oil companies, so they can drill into forbidden or sensitive areas; for matters that have or will lead to wars. It's a long list: oil, autos, steel, trees, fish, chemicals, HMOs, taxes, military expenditures, media, guns, credit cards, subsidies, etc. Wherever there's an industry or a law or anything where there's lots of money to be gained or lost... *voila!* you will find the lobbyists. Their annual incomes averaged $250,000 in the 1990s. And today? Who's counting? They are. Who's paying? We are. Who cares? They do. (See Chapter 9; read it and weep.)

There are tens of thousands of lobbyists. In his penetrating study of political corruption, Kevin Phillips (1994) pointed out that in Washington DC in 1991 there were already over *90,000* lobbyists at work (many of them ex-legislators), with an additional 50,000 putting the pressure on at the local and state levels. That was more than a decade ago, so add at least 20 percent. Then take a look at the next dirty realm:

Campaign Finance

This has to do with the money *admitted* to have been directly raised by candidates on all geographic levels for all offices (including, mind you, *judges*). In the US there are legal upper limits for contributions from any one person for any one candidate, as there perhaps will be for the critical "soft money" raised by a political party when it is used to support a particular candidate "indirectly." Are those laws strictly enforced? Hmmm. Although it *is* illegal, the common practice in many businesses is to "ask" their employees to contribute to a particular campaign. It works, of course: one doesn't have to have a great imagination to assume that a very high percentage of employees would find it wise to make such contributions in their individual names, with most, surely, being given the money to do so by guess whom?

Campaign finance as generally understood in the US has two legs to stand on, one called "hard" and one "soft." The hard money is given directly and "legally" and the soft money indirectly and illegally. The amounts are substantial: individuals, organizations, and companies gave a total of nearly $3 *billion* to national campaigns already in 1999 and 2000. "[However], organizations spend 10 times as much on lobbying as on direct campaign contributions, *and* they spend undisclosed millions more to establish special-interest research institutes, or so-called think tanks, which do not legally count as lobbying activities but are intended to manipulate public opinion and public policy" (Alan B. Krueger, "Lobbying by Businesses Overwhelms Their Campaign Contributions," *NYT*, September 19, 2002). For 2008, add some zeroes. (It is estimated that Obama raised and spent $600 million; fortunately.) But what's to worry? We live in a democracy and Congress knows about all this, passed laws against it, and since then it's been clean hands all around, no? Not quite. Look back a few pages at the quote from the *IHT*, "The Selling of America's Presidential Candidates."

Setting aside further ugly details, wasn't it always thus? Sort of. In the past as now, "democracy" was more "plutocratic" than "democratic"; however, that past was considerably more fluid than this present. Today in the US we are confronted with the cooperative club of a few *dozen* giant companies, their media buddies, two political parties whose differences are more of degree than kind, and a population bewitched, bothered, and bewildered by consumerism.

Whatever the limitations of US democracy a century or so ago, there were at least some democratic intervals on the local, state, or even on regional levels, such as the "Populist" movement of the late nineteenth century. The limitations of those trouble-makers were substantial, so lobbyists and organized campaign financing were irrelevant and unnecessary. (See Faulkner, 1947.)

Both lobbyists and campaign finance came to be in the twentieth century for at least two overlapping reasons: (1) the emergence of the federal government as an always more essential agency to influence the overall direction and health of the economy, at home and abroad; (2) the growth and emerging dominance of big business and *very* high finance. Already by 1910 the quantum leap between then and now had begun, a "leap" overarching all sectors of the economy and intersecting with both domestic and international politics. The US was "growing up," as were all other capitalist powers; dangerously so, as subsequent developments revealed. (See R. Brady's *Business as a System of Power*, 1943.)

By the early twentieth century a strong national state became imperative if continually precarious situations were not to become worse. In the US, Woodrow Wilson won the election of 1912 after a campaign in which he proclaimed that "When government becomes important, it becomes important to control the government." He didn't have to tell that to the business world; they told him. The first years of the twentieth century gave the appearance of promising that Wilson's "control" could be, even might be, by and for an informed electorate: education had taken a big leap, so that a high school education became not just common but a necessity. And, with literacy becoming widespread, so too would information and understanding, no? No. For just those reasons, that period produced the modern media, advertising, public relations, and "spin," all of which were from their beginnings more inclined to sell and manipulate than to "inform." However, the inclination to control in the pre-World War II era was paltry by comparison with what has occurred since then in the US. (For the 1920s see Soule, 1947; for the 1930s see Mitchell, 1947.)

The late twentieth century was made to order for rule by big money, much facilitated by enhanced techniques of "mind management" and "infotainment," and the armies of well-paid lobbyists and heavily-financed candidates at all levels. A major similarity between the distant past and today is that nowadays it is becoming increasingly common for *very* rich men to use some of their many millions to buy an office: for themselves, as a governor, Congress, or president, with some help from their brothers in wealth.

So, there's something rotten in the US. But what about Western Europe? Isn't it like that all over the world? The answer is both yes and no. Even though things are far from ideal in the EU, at least their *elections* aren't bought and sold as easily and disgustingly as in the US. Nor, relevantly, are their inequalities as deep or as painful as ours; although in recent years they have been trying to catch up. (See Chapter 12.)

But what about workers' unions in the US, and the Greens, and the teachers...? Aren't they and other groups also "buying" votes? Good question; here's an answer in excerpts from a well-documented study in the bimonthly *Dollars & Sense* ("How Money in Politics Hurts You," July/August 2000):

> Most of the money flows to the politicians serving on the congressional committees that oversee each industry. For example, most banking-industry money goes to members of the finance committees, regardless of party…[etc.] Business interests "out-gave" labor interests by a factor of 11-to-one in the 1997–98 election cycle… Dirty industries – oil and gas, mining electric utilities, automobiles – outspent the Greens, spending more than 40 times than environmental groups. Only one-quarter of one percent of the population makes contributions in excess of $200; only 170,000 people contribute $1,000 or more; 80 percent of all donors make more than $100,000 a year.

Money talks; big money SCREAMS. If we are ever to have a truly democratic society, we must get together and SHOUT.

5

TODAY'S INEQUALITY AS WORSENED BY CONSUMERISM AND THE MEDIA

"Nowadays people know the price of everything and the value of nothing," Oscar Wilde had one of his characters say. Wilde's setting was late nineteenth-century England. Today, with consumerism at the center of our existence, what would Oscar say? In Chapter 4, consumerism's emergence, and its economic, political and social meanings were discussed briefly; now, because of its key role in monopoly capitalism's deepening of inequality, it will be discussed at some length.

Consumerism as a Social Disease

The production *capacities* for high levels of consumption existed in the years preceding World War I for all of the industrial nations: Britain, France, Germany, Italy, Japan, and the US. But consumerism requires that two other imperatives must be met: mass purchasing power and a supportive culture. The US was the first to meet both of those imperatives.

To be able to so, it was much assisted by two world wars. Except for the US, both of those wars had much more negative than positive socio-economic consequences for all nations. The enrichment of the US economy by World War I was the basis for what came to be called "the prosperity decade" of the 1920s. That "prosperity" was real for less than 25 percent of its people (H. Miller, 1971; Soule, 1947). It was not until World War II ended that there would be sufficiently widespread purchasing power for consumerism to take full hold in the US; and not until a decade or so later for Europe. Nor was it until the 1960s that the broad and deep US household *indebtedness* central to consumerism began to take its grip.

Wilde's witty comment now applies to much of the world's people; but he would have to add that we know neither the *value* of anything nor its *costs*. The plural of "cost" refers both to the unit costs of getting a product to market and sold, *plus* the even higher costs of advertising and packaging, *plus* the costs of borrowing for the bedazzled public, *plus* the environmental costs of today's wasteful production.

Item: Under investigation by the US Federal Trade Commission in 1939, General Motors admitted that a Chevy priced at $950 had *production* costs of only $150; the other $800 went for advertising, distribution, and profits; but a good third of the costs of production were for the annual change in the "looks" we have been taught to desire (FTC, 1939).

It would be fun to know how Wilde would characterize today's insanities. The wastes of automobile production are but one item of a very long list that neither begins nor ends with cars. The grip of consumerism continually tightens for *all* products and services; so much so that today's wasteful production and consumption have brought us to the brink of environmental disaster. That such would be the result was perceived soon after World War II by a respected economist (Kapp, 1950). He was ignored.

Toward Self-Destruction

Consumerism first took hold with cars and cigarettes, dangerous to the health of both us and Mother Nature. They were the first steps toward building ourselves the madhouse in which we would do ourselves in. By World War I, all of the industrial nations had the technologies for mass *production* but not the socio-economic conditions for the mass *consumption* of what *could* have been produced. Except for textiles and some food stuffs, industries were largely those of producers' ("capital") goods:

most importantly in metallurgy, machinery, heavy chemicals, and transportation equipment.

Those facilities largely duplicated each other in several nations and were rapidly heading toward excess capacity; thus the need was to find mass consumer markets for such capabilities. There were only two possibilities: mass consumer durable goods markets, or military markets. The world was finding many reasons to go to war in those same years, and did so; but there was little or no serious attention paid to the possibilities of mass markets for consumer *durable* goods. But what about Ford's "Model T," produced from 1908 on? It was first produced as a capital good for farmers, and it was the war and its sustained incomes and savings that allowed what had been a small "truck" to be transformed into being among the first giant symbols of consumerism (Sward, 1948).

When World War I ended, only the US was in both the social and the economic position to move toward what soon became "consumerism." The other nations were either flattened by the war and/or entangled in what became deadly political struggles. (Japan, not a part of World War I, was an exception for its own reasons.) The US was unique. Except for the dead and wounded and their families, the war was "manna from heaven"; as would be World War II, only considerably more so.

Although the 1920s came to be seen as "the Jazz Age" and "the Prosperity Decade," those same years meant poverty for the 50 percent who were unemployed, the many disabled and displaced veterans of the war, and those just plain poor because of racism, sexism, ill health, and/or old age. It was also the 1920s that birthed consumerism and early "financialization" and the "Crash of 1929." (See Chapter 7 and J.K. Galbraith, 1955.)

Until the 1920s, the durable goods now bought by all were either "rich men's toys" and/or just beginning to be produced: cars, radios, telephones, refrigerators, washing machines, vacuum cleaners, etc., previously beyond reach for almost all.

Item: There were hundreds of automobile companies in the United States from the 1890s into the 1920s. As mass production began (much stimulated by the war), their numbers swiftly shrank, so that by the early 1930s, there were just 30. Then, by the early 1940s only three were "healthy": GM, Ford, Chrysler (Soule, 1947). Now even they are hospitalized.

The movement toward mass production and mass markets for the durables noted above was also toward the elimination of many small firms, whether by failure or takeover by the always fewer always bigger ones. The producers of durable consumer goods became "household names": Standard Oil, Texaco and Shell; GE, Westinghouse, and Maytag; RCA, Philco and, of course, the Big Three of cars and the other giants which, taken together, later became the "Fortune 500," functioning in a political economy dominated not just by business, as earlier, but by *big* business.

Only giant firms had the capabilities for the effective marketing, product variation, and advertising of consumer durable goods; to which we now turn.

Advertising as Narcotic

The first breakthroughs in modern advertising came in the cigarette industry in the 1920s: "Reach for a Lucky instead of a Sweet." But the techniques of creating markets were carried to the threshold of insane consumerism by General Motors, the first completely modern corporation in its combination of organization, productive techniques, and marketing.

In 1923–24 GM realized that the sales of *new* cars was approaching its ceiling. In order to keep that ceiling rising, GM undertook a multi-faceted campaign: (1) to create always more new sales by annual model changes and what they called "deliberate obsolescence"; (2) to create massive advertising campaigns; (3) to establish a used-car market; and (4) to become a big lender, with GMAC, the General Motors Acceptance Corporation (Soule, 1947).

In one variation or another, all of those techniques were adopted for the whole range of consumer durables from the 1920s on. Now these techniques are applied to almost everything – including the realm of "subprime lending," the first big step toward today's *global* financial crisis. (See Chapter 7.)

In 1948 George Orwell wrote what became his most famous book: *Nineteen Eighty-Four*. In it he sought to show the dangers of a "Big Brother" presiding over a totalitarian society. There were all too many examples of such societies both before and after 1948, in nations both rich and poor, capitalist and non-capitalist (including Germany, Italy, France, Japan, Spain, Portugal, Hungary, Greece, Chile, Argentina, and the Soviet Union). Their rulers combined force and violence with tough or clever persuasion to gain and to hold power.

In our time, such powers do not usually require force and violence, nor *need* an Orwellian "Big Brother." (See Epilogue.) Orwell's book was very popular, but few remembered that 20 years earlier Aldous Huxley had also raised a strong warning of what was on its way. Accordingly and usefully, a warning that fits our consumeristic era was issued already in the 1980s, by Neil Postman, as he adjusted Huxley's warning to the present:

> In Huxley's vision, no Big Brother is required to deprive people of their autonomy, maturity, and history. As he saw it, people will come to love their oppression, to adore the technologies that undo their capacity to think. What afflicted people in *Brave New World* was not that they were laughing instead of thinking, but they did not know what they were laughing about and why they had stopped thinking. (Postman, 1985)

Orwell, Huxley, and Postman were all pointing to how demented our political minds could, and have, become in the "age of consumerism." Most of us have learned to believe that consumerism keeps the economy going, and going, and going. A few years ago, consumption accounted for "only" 66 percent of gross domestic product (GDP); before its present contraction, it was up to 72 percent. However: until the present financial collapse, that sounded pretty good, even though, led by the US, it required massive borrowing by almost all households. Monthly payments on household debt in the US have long exceeded monthly incomes by at least 25% and must *continue* to do so always more.

As I write this, in early 2009, the essential rise in borrowing and buying has hit a large bump in the road. (See the extended discussions of "financialization and speculation" and recession in Chapter 7.) Here a sample of what's now underway and why, as seen already in 2007 by Stephen Roach, head of Morgan Stanley Asia:

> The buying bulge has been increasingly supported by housing and lending bubbles. Yet home prices are now heading lower, probably for years, and the fallout from the subprime crisis has seriously crippled home mortgage refinancing. With weaker employment growth also putting pressure on income, the days of open-ended American consumption are likely finally to come to an end. That will make it harder to avoid a recession. (*NYT*, September 26, 2007)

In 2006 the US imported $2.2 *trillion* of goods and services; and in 2007 it approached an annual *trillion* dollar trade *deficit*. When the dollar drops because of that enormous trade deficit, imports cost more. Although that means others *might* buy more from us as the dollar falls, that holds only so long as they and we don't get busted by the "subprime" crisis (now only in its early stages).

The whole financial world is tied into the US crisis and its consumers' borrowing and buying. As I write this, in Italy, the crisis has spread as far north and east as Norway and Denmark and Iceland, and as far south and west as Argentina and Australia and Asia. In Iceland, the banks have already closed the credit card machines. Tomorrow the world?

It sounds like "The Roaring Twenties" all over again, except that it's much worse. Globalization and its financial gambling casinos have very much tightened economic connections among all countries. In this consumeristic age, neither the gamblers nor the consumers they depend upon have paid due attention to what they "should have known." Contemporary US consumer spending could not continue without the always greater indebtedness of almost all households *and* the always rising US trade deficits upon which others' economies depend. A reminder and warning from the past: the 1929 stock market crash was in October; from then until March 1933, it had its largest ever percentage *gain*; but, as noted above, the US economy stayed in *depression* until World War II, with 10 percent unemployed into 1942. (See Chapters 7 and 11.)

Today's perilous state of affairs did not "just happen"; nor was it "intentional." It was brought about by a set of "unintended consequences," increasingly strengthened by the interactions of consumerism, capitalist ideology and politics, *and* today's powerful and ubiquitous media complex.

The Media Plague

When, in 1948, Orwell wrote *Nineteen Eighty-Four* his focus was upon the social shaping and pollution of what has come to be called "hearts and minds." A main focus of his book was what he called "doublethink." Reviewers tended to see the book as a critical satire whose target was the USSR. Doubtless Orwell had the USSR in mind, but much more than that: Orwell was a passionate believer in freedom and full-fledged democracy, and he backed those beliefs both by his writing and by fighting against and being wounded by the fascists in Spain (see his *Homage to Catalonia*, 1938).

Orwell's political books were prompted by Europe's interwar totalitarian states, but he was at least as much concerned with ongoing developments in the democracies, including his Britain. He never showed explicit concern with the US; but the Cold War and its bedmate McCarthyism (which began to flourish just as Orwell died) fitted his concerns all too well. So, what is "doublethink"? Early on we come to know *Nineteen Eighty-Four*'s "hero" Winston Smith:

His mind slid away into the labyrinthine world of doublethink. To know and not to know, to be conscious of complete truthfulness while telling carefully constructed lies, simultaneously to hold two opinions which cancelled out, knowing them to be contradictory and believing in both of them, to use logic against logic, to repudiate morality while laying claim to it, to believe that democracy was impossible and that the Party was the guardian of democracy, to forget, whatever it was necessary to forget, then to draw it back into memory again at the moment when it was needed, and then promptly to forget it again, and above all, to apply the same process to the process itself. That was the ultimate subtlety: consciously to induce unconsciousness, and then, once again, to become unconscious of the act of hypnosis you had just performed. Even to understand the word "doublethink" involved the use of doublethink.

In its setting of "Oceania" "doublethink" is partially represented by its "Ministries of Peace, of Truth, and of Love," whose functions are diametrically opposite to their names.

Item: From 1800 until 1947, US military affairs were in the hands of the Department of War; since 1947, its name has been the Department of Defense. What's in a word?

"Doublethink" and "non-think" have blended, spread, and deepened over the past century; and not only in the media. "Education" in those arts begins at home, at our parents' knees. The many-headed media (newspapers, magazines, radio, film, TV, and now the Internet) have become our basic socialization process; and, as Orwell argued, instead of jackboots or whips we are led by dazzle and the semi-hypnotic tricks learned in media schools and sharpened in advertising agencies. A ruthless "Party" was the root source of Orwell's totalitarian society; such a "Party" and its accompanying means of punishment, are now less necessary and less used. Doublethink is the polluted air we breathe daily and "freely," taking us toward a *de facto* totalitarian society with chatters of disagreement.

It may be hoped that the 2008 election in the US pointed to a better future. But it must not be forgotten that in the US – as we moved from Lyndon B. Johnson's "Great Society" to Reagan's "Supply-Side Economics," to Clinton's "It's the bond market, stupid!", to Bush II's "compassionate conservatism" – we looked the other way and, most of us, continued to compliment ourselves as being the most democratic society of all time. We barely grunted as an anti-democratic, plutocratic government lowered the taxes of the very rich, cut already inadequate social programs for education, housing, and health care and, among all too many other matters, created ruthlessly disastrous wars in Iraq and Afghanistan. We too have learned to "doublethink." (See Chapters 7–8.)

The media were not the only source of that self-delusion, but it couldn't have occurred without them. In their various forms, the media perform three overlapping social functions: entertainment, information, and advertising. The content and intentions of what we see and hear serve the needs and desires of the media's business and political clients; their *means* are devised by the experienced "mind managers" of the overlapping advertising and public relations worlds. In doing so, the media intermingle and interact business with politics, profits with power, and talking peace with making war. They have provided a new word to our vocabulary, "infotainment"; amusing as a word, but dangerous in its doing. (See Hersh, 2007; Schiller, 1973; Herman and Wuerker, 2002; Chomsky and Herman, 1988.)

To comprehend the media's ends and means, what follows will examine: how the media came to be what they are; what they have helped to bring about; and their structures of ownership and control. (See authors just noted, as well as what follows.) Keep in mind that each of the foci discussed below is in itself a bundle of complexities.

They began to become a noticeable problem in the US about a century ago, leading to Upton Sinclair's scathing attack on newspaper corruption. Since then, there has been a substantial and badly-needed flow of critical books, very much stimulated by the years of the Cold War and subsequent dangerous developments. (See Barber, 1996; Sinclair, 1920; Stone, 1952; Liebling, 1961; Cirino, 1971; Aronson, 1970; Ensenzberger, 1974; Schiller, 1971; Bromwich, 2008.)

A Brief History of the Media

A century ago the word "media" as now understood was not used; had it been, it would have referred only to newspapers and magazines. Newspapers were influential in the political realm on the local and regional level, but considerably less so nationally; magazines were mostly influential in limited circles for matters of taste and culture. It was they, however, that gave birth to the beginnings of modern advertising.

The first significant jump in the US toward the modern media took place as World War I was edging over the horizon, aided by its technology and lifted incomes. In those same years cars became a consumer product (as distinct from a rich man's toy or a farmer's tool), and silent films opened the gate toward what would become Hollywood. In the 1920s, cars, cigarettes and soap became the major stimuli for modern advertising; that is, the advertising that "teaches people to want what they *don't* need, and not to want what they *do*" (Baran, 1969).

Radio was critical in those developments. As with so many other technological jumps, it was born as a military product; it became a consumer product in the early 1920s. By the end of that decade and through the 1930s, the impact of radio on public tastes and attitudes – whether frivolous or serious – became always more substantial; but compared with what TV has become, radio was a pygmy. More recently, the Internet has become a vehicle for the media, used as it now is for advertising, information, and entertainment. Thus, what only slightly influenced the average person's life in 1900 now dominates social existence; the media are no longer merely or mostly "products and services"; they are key shaping forces in society. That evolution was *not* intentional at their beginning: now it is.

What the Media Have Done To Us

As one who was a boy in the 1920s, I am struck by the sea-change in the role of the media since then. Even as late as the 1950s the media were merely a now and then "presence"; now they are "in our face." No matter what our age, and whether or not we are conscious of it (and mostly we are not), there are few indeed of our thoughts, our feelings, our inclinations, our behavior patterns, that are not shaped or directed in significant degree by the media.

Business knows that, politicians know it; most of *us* know it. Yet almost all who know it unconsciously "make believe" that what is true is *not*; that what is *not* true *is*: Doublethink.

Those processes are what Chomsky and Herman called "manufacturing consent" in their 1988 book of that title. It is not difficult to find instances of these phenomena; quite the opposite. Because what happened in the Bush II administration was and remains so dangerous, here we take our examples from its manipulative media tactics, beginning with three episodes early in the Iraq war: at Mount Rushmore, at the Statue of Liberty, and on the aircraft carrier *Abraham Lincoln*. All three were discussed in an excellent article by Elisabeth Bumiller (*NYT*, July 16, 2003), "Keepers of the Bush Image Lift Stagecraft to New Heights." I quote:

> The White House positioned the best platform for the TV crews off to one side, not head-on as other White Houses have done, so that the cameras caught Mr. Bush in profile, his face perfectly aligned with the four presidents carved in stone.

> The White House put together three barges with giant lights, the kind used for sports stadiums and rock concerts, sent them across New York Harbor to the water around the Statue of Liberty and then blasted them upward to illuminate all 305 feet of America's symbol of freedom. It was the ultimate patriotic backdrop for Mr. Bush, who spoke from Ellis Island.

> Mr. Bush's speech aboard the Abraham Lincoln announcing the end of major combat in Iraq [was] the most elaborate event...; including Bush's landing in a flight suit, with the members of the Lincoln crew arrayed in coordinated shirt colors over Mr. Bush's right shoulder and the "Mission Accomplished" banner placed to perfectly capture the president and the celebratory words in a single shot...

If ever there were instances of doublethink, those and what followed must be among them. There cannot be many who watched those TV appearances who did not know or sense that they were being deceived by elaborate staging accomplished by highly-paid experts from the ad agencies and Hollywood. All of that is important; but it is only a small part of the larger problem constituted by the pervasive and deep-seated corruption of the media. It has usually been like this in some degree, of course; after all, newspapers, radio, and TV depend for their profits upon satisfying their advertising clients, on whose toes one never steps. However, the differences between newspapers a century ago and themselves and the media as a whole today are not merely those of degree; nor has that qualitative shift been only a matter of money from advertisers; it is of vital relevance to note the shared interests between the big media and other big business.

Many of the media giants also own and control, or are owned and controlled by, what once were *non*-media giants: General Electric, a pioneer in using its economic strength to gain more than economic power, was also the first to take the giant step of media ownership by an industrial or financial company when, in 1986, the Reagan administration (pressured by GE, and others) made legal what had been illegal (Wills, 1988). Given the business roots of the media, it is not surprising that they are "cautious" in their presentation of controversial subjects that touch upon business interests; like most others, they tend "naturally" to be nationalists.

Since the inception of the Cold War and McCarthyism, that natural tendency has led the media to be more hesitant than ever about criticizing aggressive US policies abroad or repressive policies at home. Moreover, the more aggressive and repressive such policies become, the greater the hesitancy. Given the importance of the media in our private and social lives, it would seem important that there be at least some degree of supervision, of control, of regulation. So it seemed to Congress and the President and the Federal Communications Commission (FCC) when in 1939 it stated:

> To the extent that the ownership of and control of broadcast stations falls into fewer and fewer hands, the free dissemination of ideas and information upon which our democracy depends is threatened. (Bagdikian, 1983)

So, not to worry, right? Wrong. Note that those words and associated rules occurred in *1939*, when there was no TV, when Roosevelt was President, when the New Deal and deep support for it were in full swing. Forty years later, as the shift to the right was underway, Reagan was elected and re-elected as president for eight years. He was much loved despite being regarded by many as a full-blooded racist, militarist, and hater of the poor. It was he, more than any other individual, who re-opened the doors wide for the plutocracy that followed. The already weak rules regulating the media, finance, and much else were dumped; clearing the path for the mess we live with today. (See "Not Your Father's FCC," by Michael J. Copps, *The Nation*, April 7, 2008.)

Given all the above, it should also be noted that a good share of the critical information found in *this* work has of course come from the media, notably from the *New York Times* (which prides itself on "all the news that's fit to print"). However, as Herman points out, "the news" can wear many costumes, and the problem arises in who defines "fit."

> The New York Times, both as a media institution and the product that is delivered in its name on a daily basis, is built and thrives on structures of disinformation and selective information that constitute Big Lies. These structures do involve occasional direct lies, but far more important is their base in passing on the lies issued by official sources, lies by implication, and lies that are institutionalized by repetition and the refusal to admit contradictory evidence. It is possible to institutionalize a very big lie without actually telling a direct lie, although one can usually find them represented as well. (*Z Magazine*, May 19, 2003, "Commentary: Little Versus Big Lies and Structures of Lies")

There are so many instances of the foregoing that it is difficult to know where to begin. Not to be excluded are those "Big Lies" regarding Iraq and the lies of "weapons of mass destruction" that served as its *casus belli*. The list is very long; in his essay Herman selected the Cold War era shooting of the Pope which, the CIA told us over and over again was done by the Soviet KGB and the Bulgarians; even though, after the USSR dissolved, a CIA official testified to Congress that the CIA *knew* that was a not true.

Then note the thoroughly "institutionalized lies" about why we were in Vietnam and what was happening there ("light at the end of the tunnel"), and the compliance of the media in the US lies about the (false) "attack" of North Vietnam against our navy (Young, 1991; and see Chapter 8).

Given the dangerously deplorable state of most other newspapers and the rest of media, the *NYT* and a few other newspapers serve a vital function: "Beggars can't be choosers." Given the most recent media developments, we had better concentrate on how to *become* choosers. The reference is to what has come to be called "spin." It is a "four-letter word" with consequences going well beyond the other members of the media family. It is the presumably amusing way of describing a euphemism; that is, of speaking and writing that simultaneously confuses and softens what is being discussed. (See Bromwich, 2008.) In the 1940s George Orwell had already seen through the ways in which horrors are "spun" so as to leave the reader more in a mood to think "ho hum" than to scream. In his 1940s essay "Politics and the English Language" he could have had the news on Vietnam or Iraq in mind:

> Defenseless villages are bombarded from the air, the inhabitants driven out into the countryside, the cattle machine-gunned, the huts set on fire with incendiary bullets: this is called *pacification*. Millions of peasants are robbed of their farms and sent trudging along the roads with no more than they can carry: this is called *transfer of population* or *rectification of frontiers*. People are imprisoned without trial...: this is called *elimination of unreliable elements*. Such phraseology is needed in order to name things without calling up mental pictures of them. (1970)

Would that such doings were the end of the media's "bending on knee." The problems of our time, in and outside of the US, surely include US aggression abroad and repression at home, but they are only the most dramatic of many other problems, also at home and abroad, whether as regards health care or globalization, truth or falsities.

The information whose creature we have become is mostly that which meets the eye regularly on "the boob tube." The average adult in the US watches TV an average of four hours a day; for children the average is six hours. If or when the news is watched, it comes in sound bites or as "infotainment" rather than substantial and informative statements, with only rare exceptions.

(See Postman, 1985.) That leaves a momentous task for even the most searching and uninhibited of newspapers, books, and magazines to fulfill, if we are to depend upon them as our source for understanding what's going on; especially when it is recognized that those who own and control the media are as few in number as they are huge in power.

The Consciousness Industry

This was the title of the valuable book by Ensenzberger, back in 1974. The "industry" with which he was concerned, like all of modern industry, is mostly owned and virtually controlled by a few giants; not all newspapers, radio or TV stations, just yet; only the ones that count. By 1997, the media world was presided over by ten or so integrated media conglomerates, most of which were based in the United States. Along with thirty to forty supporting firms, the giants compete vigorously on a non-price basis. Their competition is softened not only by common interests, but also by a vast array of joint ventures, strategic alliances, cross-ownership, and their financial underpinnings in advertising and its thoroughgoing commercialism (Herman, 1999; Alterman, 2003). The five largest of these giants as the twenty-first century began were Time Warner, Disney, Bertelsmann, Viacom, and News Corporation. Among the others, control emanates from outside the media, as with Sony, Seagram, and General Electric.

The major actor in media mergers and acquisitions of the recent past has been and remains Rupert Murdoch and his News Corporation/Fox. Early on he tersely expressed what underlies the structures and processes of today's concentrated ownership (as quoted in *Business Week*, March 25, 1996): "We can join forces now, or we can kill each other and then join forces." They "joined forces":

All six major broadcast networks are owned mostly by giant media companies... GE bought NBC...right after Disney failed in a bid to do the same thing. Ten years later Disney got its network when it bought Capital Cities, which then owned ABC..., the same year Westinghouse bought CBS…, and that UPN was begun by United Television/Chris-Craft Industries and Paramount Television/Viacom. Four years later…after some other media mergers, Viacom bought CBS. That means Viacom owns CBS and UPN. As for the remaining networks, Fox, owned by Murdoch, was started in 1986 the product of a media conglomerate, and the WB is owned by Warner Bros. (McChesney, 1999)

The giants have continued to join forces and (with the FCC ruling noted below) will be able to do so always more voraciously. Advertising has always been dominant both to the birth and the strengthening of the media, and becomes always more so. As might be expected in the era of giant this and giant that, advertising is now dominated by the Fortune 500 global giants. Thus:

It is TNC advertising that has fueled the rise of commercial television across the world, accounting, for example, for over one-half the advertising on the ABN-CNBC Asia network, which is co-owned by Dow Jones and General Electric… In 1999, the United States still accounted for nearly one-half of the world's…advertising. Even in the developed markets of western Europe most nations still spend no more than one-half the US amount on advertising per capita and [its] 2.1 to 2.4 percent of GDP going toward advertising… [But] European commercial television is growing at a 10 percent annual rate, twice the US average… The top ten global advertisers [Nike, Procter & Gamble, GM, Philip Morris, et al.] alone accounted for 75 percent of the $36 billion spend by the one hundred largest global marketers in 1997. (McChesney, 1999)

Bigness had become characteristic of the media before World War II but, especially in the US, the NBCs and NYTs (et al.) of that era were tiny compared with what began to take hold after 1950. The decades from 1950 to the present must be divided into three phases: from 1950 up to the 1980s, from then until yesterday, and what is emerging as this is written in early 2009. As with other sectors of the economy long regulated by the state and federal authorities (e.g., utilities and finance) so it was with the realm of "infotainment." As noted in Chapter 4, in recent decades the boundaries both within and between industries, sectors, and nations have become muddied, and that has been true for the media as well. Once upon a time, however, and before the 1970s ended, there were rules whose aim was to prevent centralized control over the sources and dissemination of "infotainment."

Consider these numbers: from 1953 into the Reagan years ownership limits were fixed in the US by the 7-7-7 rule (7 AM, 7 FM and 7 TV stations per owner), and cross-ownership of newspapers and broadcasting stations within the same market was barred (although over a hundred exceptions were grandfathered). These limits were raised to 12-12-12 in 1985, with TV station owners allowed to reach up to 25 percent of the national population. The ownership limits for radio were raised to 24-24-24 in 1992 and owners were given the right to acquire multiple stations in each market. The 1996 Telecommunications Reform Act removed the national ceiling on radio station ownership and allowed as many as eight stations to be acquired by a single owner in the largest market. The ceiling on TV ownership was raised to allow a single owner to reach 35 percent of the national audience. (See Herman, 1999, and Alterman 2003.)

To some of us old-fashioned folks even "7-7-7" sounds like a lot, and "12-12-12" like a lot too much. But the greed for profits and power has neither bottom nor top, and the foregoing shows they know how to get what they want. When you read this, it may have gone to "36-36-36." Sound ominous? It does indeed; but as things go these days, before long it may well sound like widely-dispersed ownership and wide-open competition.

Already giant corporations are itching to become more so, and always more so since the 1950s, taking every available opportunity to pile up money both from creating and operating mergers. They have been much assisted by their thousands of lobbyists working to get rid of the few remaining constraints. The FCC ruling of June 2, 2003 gave them what they wanted (up to then). Since then, it has been anything goes, where the "any things" included the creation of media conglomerates such as Time Warner, News Corporation, and Disney, and their simultaneous ownership of book publishing, magazines, TV show production, stations, cable, and networks, movie production, and amusement parks. But no matter how big, it's never enough. Thus "their" FCC decision of June 2003, whose principle is *everything* goes:

Item: From "New Rules Give Big Media Chance to Get Even Bigger": as consumer advocates deplored yesterday's changes to media ownership rules as a blow to democracy, investors bought up shares of the biggest media companies. Both advocates and investors agree that the latest rule changes are likely to let media leviathans fortify their positions while increasing the odds against newcomers and small fry. (*NYT*, June 4, 2003)

So, the "solution" for the media is the same as that for the rest of those in power, whether as regards pharmaceuticals or military expenditures. In what has become a bought-and-paid-for democracy, political candidates have become almost entirely beholden to campaign financing; then, once in office, they are besieged, bothered and, if good little boys and girls, rewarded by lobbyists. That is exactly what happened with the FCC:

> The independent Center for Public Integrity examined the travel records of FCC employees and found that over the last eight years, commissioners and staff members have taken 2,500 trips costing $2.8 million that were "primarily" paid for by members of the telecommunications and broadcast industries... "The top destination was Las Vegas, with 330 trips..." [with many other trips to New York, New Orleans, San Francisco, Palm Springs, Buenos Aires...] ("Cozy With the FCC," *NYT* op-ed, June 5, 2003)

Lots of communications to worry about in Las Vegas... But that's only part of the story. The FCC presumably represents the People of the US. However: "The Center for Public Integrity reported that there were more than 70 closed-door meetings in recent months with FCC officials and representatives of the nation's top broadcasters [mostly with CEOs], to discuss the relaxation of media ownership restrictions. [But] the two major groups that represented the public...Consumers Union and the Media Access Project...met just five times with the FCC" (*NYT*, ibid.).

The *NYT* piece closes with this report: "...a survey of 500 thousand comments of the FCC web site showed that more than

97 percent 'were opposed to the new rules'." (See also Herman, 1999.) That's democracy for you: when it's 97 percent vs. 3 percent, the 3 percent gets what they want, *if* they have enough money; and they *do*.

There is much more to say on other matters concerning the media (and everything else). The troubled hero of Orwell's *Nineteen Eighty-Four* was Winston Smith; the villain was represented on posters stating "Big Brother is Watching You." That was crude stuff; nowadays *we* are watching Big Brother, day and night.

6

GLOBALIZATION: UNINTENDED CONSEQUENCES, INC.

Globalization is but the latest process by which powerful nations have met capitalism's imperative of geographic expansion and easy access to abundant natural and cheap human resources: it is today's version of colonialism/imperialism. There is, of course, a big difference: the countries exploited now have their own governments; or so they say.

The seeds of what would become industrial capitalism in the nineteenth century were planted in the medieval trading *cities* of Europe: Venice, Florence, Genoa, and Bologna in the south; Leipzig, the Hanseatic League, London, Bruges, and Paris in the north. The early modern period *was* modern by virtue of the economic and military strength of its emerging nations, but by the seventeenth century, the city-based medieval trading relationships between Europe, Asia, Africa, and the Middle East were giving way to colonialism and the regional monopolies controlled by *nations* and their great brute force.

Colonialism and Imperialism

Trading that had long existed in small quantities was transformed and expanded by improved navigation, larger ships, and greater firepower. Those processes were led first by the Portuguese and the Spanish through the sixteenth century. They were superseded by the Dutch in the seventeenth century. Later, the French and British would supersede them. (See Clark, 1947; Heckscher, 1935.) The nature and importance of that early set of national expansions were vividly described by Marx (1867):

The discovery of gold and silver in America, the extirpation, enslavement and entombment in mines of the aboriginal population, the beginnings of conquest and looting of the East Indies, the turning of Africa into a warren for the hunting of black-skins, signalized the rosy dawn of the era of capitalist production. Those idyllic proceedings are the chief momenta of primitive accumulation.

Just as colonialism had supplanted medieval trading routes, so did imperialism push colonialism aside; and just as pre-industrial capitalist colonialism was made possible and necessary by technological change and nationalistic rivalries, so too was industrial capitalist imperialism, but with quantum leaps and differences; as seen by Dobb (1937):

Imperialism required, as the colonial system of earlier centuries did not, a large measure of political control over the *internal* relations and structure of the colonial economy. This it requires, not merely to "protect property" and to ensure that the profit of the investment is not offset by political risks, but actually to create the essential conditions for the profitable investment of capital.

Among those conditions is the existence of a proletariat sufficient to provide a plentiful and cheap labor supply; and...suitable modifications of pre-existent social forms will need to be enforced (of which the reduction of tribal land-reserves and the introduction of differential taxation on the natives living in the tribal reserves of East and South Africa are examples); the political logic of imperialism graduates from "economic penetration" to "spheres of influence" to protectorates or indirect control, and from protectorates to military occupation to annexation.

Imperialism became central to the strengthening and spread of industrial capitalism from 1815 to World War I, a war made inevitable by that same imperialism. The ensuing decades, embracing global depression, revolution, counter-revolution, and World War II, left only the US standing as a strong nation: the Europeans and Japanese were flattened.

When the previously colonized areas sought to rid themselves of their foreign rulers in that new situation the US, pursuing its own long-term interests, sometimes assisted their struggles (as in India and Indonesia), other times assisted rulers seeking to hold on (as with the French in Vietnam), or remained aloof (as in South Africa).

The Modernization of Imperialism

As the 1940s became the 1950s, US aims and policies moved toward creating a new world economy and a new form of imperialism suited to the imperatives of the *very* different post-World War II era: as time went on, the evolving world economy and *its* imperialism were "spun" as "globalization."

The French like to say (in French, of course) that "the more things change, the more they stay the same." Is that so for the evolution from colonialism to imperialism to globalization? In some ways, yes; but for reasons to be discussed in detail below and in Chapter 7, both the intended and unintended consequences of globalization – despite its professed aims – seem all too likely to become even more destructive for both humans and natural resources than before the world wars. Imperialism wrought horrors upon those "imperialized" and made World War I inevitable; the combination of globalization and financialization has taken the entire world into economic collapse and the threat of the worst – and last – war ever. (See Chapters 7, 11, Epilogue and Preface.)

As globalization took over from imperialism, quantum jumps followed quantum jumps, with permanently deleterious effects in every realm of social and physical existence for all concerned. The soothing theme of today's globalization is that "a rising tide lifts all boats." But that pleasant thought requires a second look.

In the past the "boats" of the vast majority of the people of the poorer societies were the flora and fauna of their countries. In recent years those life and death resources have been commandeered by giant transnational corporations: agribusinesses such as Archer Daniels Midland, and by equally gigantic mineral and industrial companies. As it has affected *billions* of people "the tide" has combined a hurricane with a tidal wave, leaving all to suffer and die on a barren shore. (For an early grasp of the harrowing details concerning only the Congo, see Hochschild, 1999.) The larger discussion will see five different sets of consequences:

- economic
- political
- cultural and social
- environmental
- military

Remember that earlier inequalities are deepened by the constant interaction within and between themselves and the strong and the weak societies.

Economic Consequences

The delineation of globalization's consequences for all concerned will focus mostly upon the US as their "master," with the implicit understanding that a review of all others would have only a mild lessening effect on the analysis. (And note that the "financialization" discussed in the next chapter intensifies the harms of "globalization.")

The "economics" of globalization have been positive for a few but damaging for most in both the rich and poor societies. We begin with the strong economies. In 1997, Greider wrote an illuminating and readable analysis: *One World, Ready or Not.* The world was not "ready" but the giant TNCs were: globalization could not begin soon enough. Successive US governments, whether controlled by Democrats or Republicans, did what they could to speed up and spread the processes; no matter what. What the TNCs wanted and got was easier access to the raw materials, markets, and cheap labor of the powerless of other countries, plus subsidies, tax breaks, and expanding sales and profits.

The human consequences may have been positive for a small minority, but they are negative or utterly disastrous for the rest. The main negative processes for workers in the rich economies are due to "downsizing and outsourcing." What was "sized down and sourced out" were the good jobs in a string of industries;

most notably, in electronics, cars, metallurgical and machinery products, and all forms of clothing.

US companies relocate their high wage and benefits jobs here to the opposite in the poorer countries, where wages are a small fraction of those here: $2 versus $30 a day; no health care, no pensions, no paid vacations, no eight-hour days, no sanitary provisions; no political power: Altogether now, and it's back to the cruel days of the industrial revolution in Britain. (See Bluestone and Harrison, 1982 and also 1988.)

And for the US economy? To be sure, globalization has meant: fatter bottom lines for businesses both large and small, and, for a while, a rise in good jobs for a few; however, it has meant worse jobs for most.

Item: Since 1970, General Motors has reduced its factory workers by more than 80 percent and (along with Chrysler) now faces bankruptcy and begs for (and gets) tens of *billions* from the government. Meanwhile, where are the dumped workers now? Are they working at all? And how are the not-yet-dumped workers doing, as their health benefits and retirements (and jobs) are trembling?

The trouble began as early as the 1970s. As will be shown in Chapters 7–11, when earlier good times hit the road bump of the 1970s' "stagflation," the stage was set for still another trans-formation; namely, speeded up mergers and acquisitions, always tighter whirlpools of downsizing and outsourcing, and increasing fragility. That is trouble enough for the US; but in that it is the "consumer of last resort" for the world economy, almost all other economies depend upon a "favorable balance of trade" (exports more than imports) with the US. Thus, as the US backs itself into a corner it takes others along. For its own socio-economic "health" the US must run an always rising deficit in its balance of payments as, at the same time, the people of the US must buy more and more as, like their country, they also sink into bottomless indebtedness.

That "trip" began in the 1970s. When the 1960s ended, the US was exporting much more than importing; but by 2008 it had a *trillion* dollar trade deficit and had accumulated a net debt of more than a trillion to both China and Japan. Many non-US economies (if not most of their people) were thriving from "globalization." But as I write this in early 2009, lenders have been shivering and worrying about how they will be repaid with the US economy struggling in a recession that is all too likely to become the first step toward global depression. (See Chapter 7.)

For purposes of perspective, note that Great Britain in *its* heyday *also* imported more than it exported, and lived well accordingly. But its "balance of payments" (trade, plus or minus all other inflows and outflows) was always positive and high: they were lending to, not borrowing from the rest of the world. So was the US, up into the 1970s. When Reagan took over the White House in 1981 the US had been and was still the world's largest creditor nation ever. Now the US has broken another record: largest *debtor* ever.

Keeping in mind the need for and reality of the always rising mountains of the domestic debts of households and of businesses, you'd have to believe in the tooth fairy to be relaxed about the future; even *without* war and/or environmental disasters; even *without* further socio-economic surprises. How or whether the welcome "Obama surprise" will change that cannot yet be known. (See Chapter 7 and Epilogue.)

Back to inequality and globalization. "Downsizing and outsourcing" shipped out the good jobs of strong union-achieved wages and benefits; this has worsened the already deep inequalities of income and wealth of most of the rich economies. That was compounded in the US after the 1970s, as conservatives took over the White House and Congress and reduced or cancelled what few socio-economic gains and regulations had been provided after the 1930s. Indeed, it was in the Clinton presidency that the financial protections created earlier were overthrown and when the ways in which the always understated unemployment rate were disgracefully made worse.

Item: Before the 1990s, unemployment statistics had included discouraged workers who had given up; since the Clinton years they are not included, and neither are once full-time workers who are now part-time workers. In short, if the US official unemployment rate were calculated as in most of Europe, it would be *doubled* and the present 8–9 percent would be inching toward 20 percent. (See Carlton Meyer, "America's 20% Unemployment Rate," Sanders Research Associates, April 6, 2009.)

But hasn't globalization helped workers in the poor countries? Are not the workers in those countries now able to find jobs where none existed before? Are not their economies stronger, more stable? Yes, for a small percentage; for the majority, no. They are working hard, but almost all have dirt wages for their hard labours. Jobs are sought and taken by the millions who once worked the land, or worked in country villages supplying those who did. Life was not easy before, but it was neither as hard nor as hopeless as now. Let's take a look at Mexico, as an example.

It is one of the *least* poor of the poor nations. The hordes of their desperate people making auto parts, etc. at the border *maquiladoras* for US companies, are there *only* because the job seekers have lost good lands to giant (mostly foreign) "agribusinesses." They must choose between working in a foreign-owned factory or, illegally and dangerously, to try to cross the border. Almost all come from the agricultural lands of Mexico, a repeat of their unfortunate "enclosure" predecessors in the Britain of the early industrial revolution. (See Chapter 2.) Few had earlier lived lives of luxury, but all had lived very much better than now; in terms of food, clothing, shelter, and dignity.

What the earlier history of the twentieth century did to most of Mexico's agricultural population was made considerably worse by globalization in the 1990s through the North American Free Trade Agreement (NAFTA). Its promises were many, but its results made a disaster into a catastrophe. (See Cypher, 2002a, 2002b.)

NAFTA has caused the loss not only of *good* jobs in the US but also some of all jobs; nevertheless it continues to have its praises sung by the relevant giant corporations and their sweetheart governments (Cypher, ibid.). What is now true of Mexico has been pushed to ever more horrendous depths; as, meanwhile, TNCs have shifted to even cheaper labor in Asia.

Globalization has also caused increasing starvation for countless millions of the people of "emerging" economies. The poor in such countries have often been on its edge; we have shoved them over the edge.

Item: Between 2005 and 2007 the cost of the cereals maize, rice, soy and grain, the nutritional staples of survival for poorer populations, rose 31 percent, 74 percent, 87 percent and 130 percent, respectively. India has forbidden further exportation of rice, whose cost has become prohibitively high for its own people. (*La Repubblica*, Italy, April 3, 2008)

The above focus has been on the increase of starvation for the poor; but globalization has also transformed what was once a level of relative wellbeing for workers into a desperate search for jobs. Those and other problems were supposed to be dealt with by the "free market's" processes of "decoupling." That is, if globalization is causing troubles, why, just "decouple"; get something like an economic divorce. But like divorce, that's easier said than done. Yet there is also a major difference: people *can* get a divorce; but nations, or, more accurately, particular industries in nations, are stuck with what globalization gives them. Consider just these headlines on two consecutive days in early 2008: "Exporters Across Asia Brace for US Downturn," "Decoupling: Theory vs. Reality; Big idea becomes smaller when put to test" (*International Herald Tribune*, January 25 and 26).

Those troubling headlines referred to the *companies* of both rich and poor exporting nations, *not* the *workers* in either the poor or once-comfortable skilled workers of the rich countries. There are so many cruelties and injustices of this sort for so many countries that to go on with it would seem to verge on caricature or masochism. (See Greider, 1997; Klein, 1999; Cypher, 2001; and Stiglitz, 2003.)

But there is more. All of the "ex-colonized" countries have found that at the slightest sign of troubles in their economies, instead of their place at the table of globalization "helping them," it swiftly transforms trouble into disaster: The International Monetary Fund and the World Bank come marching in with demands for *reducing* already meager social programs, or else loans will be cut back. The IMF and the Bank are at the beck and call of the conservative business world, so the smaller countries have a sword hanging over their heads. If and when the supporting rope is cut, the whole economy collapses, as in Thailand; or, as in Korea, where once healthy companies had to sell out at cheap prices to "vulture capitalists" (Henwood, 1997).

The foregoing economic "by-products" of globalization had by the 1990s brought a major set of transformations into being; notably, the first stages of financial domination of the economy. As will be seen in some detail in Chapter 7, that domination has taken the entire world economy into a financial crisis which could force economic life down to its knees. Here is one look at why (with more later). As international trade accelerated from the 1960s on, companies everywhere had to become conscious of and concerned with the relationships between their own currency and those with which they were trading (and/or investing). Such concerns had existed earlier, but as those relationships tightened and multiplied all companies had an increasing need to take into account the relative values of currencies; which in turn meant not only the stimulation of, but the need for, currency speculation – whether to increase profits or protect from losses. (See later discussions below and in Chapter 7.)

That set of developments was a vital part of the larger – and dangerous – trend toward the financialization of national economies; most fully and dangerously that of the US, with its always rising foreign trade, the domination of production by finance, and the domination of finance by speculation. Taken together, these have been the roots of the troubles now shaking the entire world. That's enough for now on the *economic* consequences of globalization. Let's turn to its blood brother.

Political Consequences of Globalization

The once colonized, imperialized societies are now formally independent, but that "independence," like political democracy, provides a cover story for subjection to the power of giant corporations and their political friends: the World Trade Organization, IMF, World Bank and, in the Western Hemisphere, NAFTA. Imperialism in modern dress. Those developments took hold as ex-colonial countries moved toward independence after World War II. (See the excellent early analyses of Cockroft et al., *Dependence and Underdevelopment*, 1972.)

The "dependence" in their analyses refers to the combination of indebtedness and subjection to foreign companies' policies. Although rich in natural resources, the ex-colonized countries were bereft of capital and had to borrow in order to develop their own economies; thus allowing new and old companies from abroad to lend and to own and to function as in the past; or worse, function as a social cancer.

When the "emerging economies" fell into recession or worse, they had to borrow more and, at the same time, to shape and reshape their socio-economic policies in accord with orders from the IMF and the World Bank, led by the US. Revealingly, when Argentina refused to obey "the Fund and the Bank" in the 1990s not only did its economy begin to flower, but its earlier quasi-fascist political system was ended. Much the same was true for Venezuela, when, led by Chavez, the country rebuffed a CIA-assisted coup d'état. (See Lebowitz, 2006.)

Stringent though outside controls may have been in the 1950s and 1960s, they became even more so after the 1970s, when what had been governmental grants and low interest loans from the US and others were transformed into loans from private finance. That shift was a consequence of Wall Street's inability in the 1970s to find sufficient demand for their capital from the richer countries, all foundering in the decade of simultaneous rising prices and rising unemployment (stagflation). Not only was borrowing by the poorer countries increased drastically, but the terms of the loans – especially from the US – were altered for the worse. Thus it was that the 1970s constructed the basis for what has taken both rich and poor countries to the present.

Interest rates rose in tandem with inflation, and oil payments, which virtually all countries had to make, had to be made in dollars (see Stiglitz, 2003). What the poorer countries required was the opposite: abundant cooperation among and between them and between them and the rich countries. What was received, instead, was uninterrupted coercion from today's imperialists to suit *their own* wants. The reality became and remains the national counterpart of worker exploitation: the poorer countries were and remain used and abused by and for outsiders – outsiders who, whenever troubles develop, leave the poor behind.

Given the policies of "free marketry" imposed upon the previously colonized societies, it should not be surprising that the political lives of those countries have also become corrupted: broader and deeper dirty dealing and an open door for dictatorships, with barely a scent of democracy. Many newly-independent countries sought to do otherwise, with hell to pay: for example, Nicaragua, Guatemala, Cuba, Chile, El Salvador, the Congo. All of their struggles for democracy were crushed by US CIA and/or military force; directly or indirectly; but always cruelly. (See Hochschild, 1999; Hersh, 1970, 1983; Jonas, 1991; Uribe, 1975; Everest, 2004.)

The costs of plutocracy in a rich country such as the US or the UK are high; for the poorer countries, they are deadly. Adding insult to injury, the major powers criticize the desperate nations for not behaving more responsibly. It is vital to remember that *all* of the major powers rose to economic strength in small or large part because for centuries they were able to make great gains from their ruthless exploitations of lesser nations. Those still-poor countries have only each other to colonize, imperialize, and exploit: slim pickings. Injustice rules, and inequality thrives.

Globalization's Cultural and Social Costs

The damages done to the peoples of imperialized societies have been immense, not least by the virtual destruction of their cultures.

Marx and Engels put it succinctly in their 1848 *Manifesto*, when imperialism and industrial capitalism were still learning to walk. It is relevant here to repeat one of their famous observations:

Constant revolutionizing of production, uninterrupted disturbance of all social conditions, ever-lasting uncertainty and agitation distinguish the bourgeois epoch from all earlier ones. All fixed, fast-frozen relations, with their train of ancient and venerable prejudices and opinions, are swept away, all new-formed ones become antiquated before they can ossify. All that is solid melts into air, all that is holy is profaned, and man is at last compelled to face with sober senses his real conditions of life and his relations with his kind.

The "uninterrupted disturbance of all social conditions" that first took hold in Britain and the other rich nations was a slowly moving river compared with the socio-cultural tidal waves that overcame "all that [was] solid..., and all that [was] holy" in Africa, the Americas, and the vast area extending from China to Persia. The Europeans had undergone slowly changing lives for millennia, due to internal developments. That was not to be so for the rest of the world.

From the sixteenth century on, the victims of colonialism and imperialism had change ruthlessly *imposed* upon them: to their harm and to the benefit of murderous outsiders. There never was and there is not yet any meaningful respect for the cultures and societies which, at an always faster pace from the sixteenth century until now, have been flattened, corrupted, distorted, enfeebled, and ridiculed. Billions of people now live in material desperation, with their cultures twisted, spat upon, and crushed.

Today there are many ways in which "the sins of our fathers" are coming back to plague and terrify us as, insanely, we continue to pile on more crimes and troubles. (See Chapter 8.) They are worsened by today's always more potent technologies of transportation and communication, as they penetrate all nooks and crannies of the lives of people in all countries, most devastatingly in the weaker nations. *Their* basic needs for health, nutrition, water, education, and shelter are so little met that, at least *15 million children* die of malnutrition every year.

The US and other rich countries have much to answer for. Time is running out, not only for the exploiter, but for the exploiters; most pressingly as regards our next focus:

Globalization and the Environment

Under this heading, much that is relevant here has been noted earlier and will be again – in Chapter 11 and the Epilogue. Here I note only that the environmental damages (like the economic, political, cultural, and social damages) to the peoples of the "emerging economies" have been considerably higher than for those of the rich countries; up to now. Given present tendencies toward the irreversible destruction of our "earth, air, and water" by "fire," we are rapidly approaching the time when environmental disasters will have only one home: the world. That tendency is fed all too well by militarism.

Globalized War

Historians have long argued over "Which came first, the flag or trade?" The answer is that flag and trade both strode into the weaker areas sword-in-hand. The partnership was habit-forming, from Columbus to the Puritans in "America" to Cecil Rhodes in Africa to Admiral Perry in Japan, to the US "Mission Accomplished" in Iraq, to the suicidal war in Afghanistan (where in 2009 Obama increased US involvement, as the Europeans steadily withdraw).

In the many centuries of its history, militarism has become not just a habit, but an addiction. Having been brought to their knees by it in World War II, most Europeans and Japanese would like to break that addiction, but the US, never having undergone such massive destruction on its home soil, marches on. The sustained militarism of the US will be examined at length in Chapter 8.

In Sum

Globalization has been neither only nor mostly an economic phenomenon. It may or may not be seen as mostly economic for transnational companies; but for the ordinary people of both rich and poor countries it has gone well beyond the economic into all quarters of their existence, most especially for those of the poorer countries. Whatever globalization's presumed benefits (until now?) for the rich countries, the harm already done especially to the poorer countries, has so many dimensions and stimuli it is difficult to see an end other than full disaster; for them, it has meant the loss of much they took as life itself and the worsening of a horror story that began with colonialism. (See Barber, 1996.)

That is the globalization we have. But there is another globalization: that which the "No Global" people seek. It proposes what many of us hoped the US was going to work for after World War II; namely, a set of processes understanding that the welfare of one depends upon the wellbeing of all; that wars must *never* occur again; that a world economy based upon mutual interdependence rather than exploitation is not only ethical, but the only safe and sane path. Only such a world economy *could* allow *all* of us, in both rich and poor nations, to be better off than *any* of us have been before. Instead, led by the US, the global economy is in the first steps of the worst economic disaster ever. Turn the page.

7

FINANCIALIZATION: LAS VEGAS, INC.

Today's financial world stands in sharp contrast with its past. Much of the difference has to do with the evolution from trading to industrial economies, but the changes since the 1970s and especially since the 1990s had both different origins and always more cataclysmic consequences. For purposes of perspective on the present, we'll first take a short look at the years just after World War II, when the US became the unchallengeable ruler of global finance. As it did so, the US dollar took over the role earlier played by the British pound sterling, but with several vital differences.

1. Britain's prominence had been due to its role as the leader of the industrial revolution. As it came to preside over the largest and strongest empire ever, it also became the "lender of last resort" to the other industrializing nations, including Germany and the US. But, as noted in Chapter 6, as the twentieth century opened both of those countries were overtaking and outdoing Britain's industrial strength using those borrowed funds. However, although Britain slowly fell behind in industrial strength it remained the financial king of the world as it took in the continuing large flow of interest on its loans. But then came two world wars.
2. As World War II ended, the US was Number 1 in all socio-economic-political terms, and the dollar became the unchallengeable currency of world trade and investment.
3. In the 1960s as US industrial strength came to be challenged by principally Japan and Germany, globalization took hold, spread, and deepened and, combined with "downsizing and

outsourcing," gave rise to always more frenzied consumeristic debt in the US. In the process:

4. The US became the largest *borrower* ever; and the dollar, rather than staying as king, became a nervous watcher of its decline in terms of the euro and the UK pound. When the euro became the currency of the leading European economies in 2000, the dollar and the euro exchanged equally; but already by 2007 the euro cost almost $1.50; today's wild financial crisis has pushed the euro down. Tomorrow?

5. As the current financial crisis began to spread, among the many nerve-wracking stories have been those from the oil countries. In September 2007 we'd already begun to read headlines such as: "Wealthy Nations in the Gulf Rethink Peg to Dollar" (*Wall Street Journal*), "Seven Countries Considering Abandoning the US Dollar" (*Journal of Currency Trading*). In 2009, that "abandonment" has yet to occur. In 2010?

6. The focus is on the oil countries; but why should they worry? Because since World War II their oil has always been sold in dollars; so, as their many *billions* of $$$ buy less, oil's dollar price must rise if the oil countries are to maintain their real profits. Until recently oil's price was ten times what it was in the 1990s; now it is pushed down by a sudden drop in oil demand because of the financial/economic crisis. So, another "tomorrow?"

In sum, we are in a time of deep financial uncertainty. Nobody can say what the future will be for the dollar (or for much else). In late 2008, the euro went down and the dollar inched back up, but for how long? The current jumpiness of the dollar signifies a major shift in the structures of economic and political power away from it; but toward whom? China? China + India + Japan? (Except that Japan is also in real trouble in 2009.) What we do know is that a *very* different and unstable future looms, the product of a global economy dominated by unregulated finance and speculation; mixed in with oil. For purposes of understanding, a comparison with the past is relevant.

A Look Back

In medieval Europe, capitalism was in embryo. Its birth was quickened by always growing inter-*regional* trade which, as nations came into being, became inter-*national* trade. Each step along the way was dependent upon receiving financial support from what ultimately became the banking sectors of national economies. It is worth noting that until well after World War II (except for a belch in the 1920s) banks were accurately seen as the stuffy center of "conservatism." Over recent decades they've become rodeo riders.

When capitalism was young, its financial world was dominated first by foreign trade, then by industry. Since the 1980s, finance has dominated not only industry but the entire business world and a dangerously high share of heavily indebted households. Consider this excerpt from an insightful 2007 article from *New York Times* financial reporter Gretchen Morgenson ("Financial Sector Slump a Threat to the Economy," December 12):

> Last week's ugly action in the stock market was caused in large part by fear about how badly banks will be hit by loan and securities losses. You know it will really be time to worry, however, when top regulatory officials start referring to the banks' problems as "contained." That was how they described the subprime mortgage mess in the preceding two years, even as it devoured homeowners throughout the nation... [But] we do know that because of its enormous and growing role in the US economy a financial services downturn is likely to have graver economic consequences than ever before.

What's so "enormous" about the role of finance? Begin with its profits: profits from the financial sector now account for 31 percent of *total* corporate earnings. In 1950 their share of profits was a bare 8 percent; by 1990, up to 20 percent. Here is a comment of a major bank director: "No one knows how big the challenges in the financial sector are; what I do know is that we have never had a more highly leveraged household sector than we have today" (*NYT*, ibid.).

The US economy and the globalized world interact 24 hours a day in a tightly interdependent "financialized" world economy. In itself that development should raise serious problems, but it is *not* "by itself":

- As the economy has come to be dominated by finance, finance has come to be dominated by sp*eculation* which, as such, contributes nothing to the economy except the means for a self-chosen few to make money.
- Finance and its layers of grossly over-paid executives (see below) are adding another form of exploitation to the capitalist process, paid for by those who are not among the leaders either of finance or the rest of the economy; feeding inequality all along the way.

Until very recently the financial sector served a merely "lubricating" function, much as simple loans once did in the pre-capitalist era. As the twentieth century moved on, economies came to be inconceivable without networks of financial institutions. In the twenty-first century transportation and communications technologies have made intricate financial "instruments" common, very "intricate," and *very* dangerous: more like bombs than "instruments."

Today we live within a "financialized" economy whose aims and means have come to dominate our lives as, meanwhile, its own functioning has come to be dominated by always wilder speculation. Now those aims and means have carried us to the edge of socio-economic disaster, to the point of self-destruction.

Financial domination (as distinct from agricultural, trade, or industrial domination) existed earlier in a few national economies: for the Dutch in the eighteenth century, and for the British as the nineteenth century ended (Boxer, 1965; Feis, 1930). There was a vital role for finance in both cases; but that was centuries before the era of consumerism and globalization, with their always tighter internal and external interdependencies. Never before recent decades have the leading economies *and* the entire global economy been so utterly dominated by finance; let alone by 24-7 global speculation.

The processes taking us from the 1970s to where we are today (and along with other dangers) have become always broader, deeper, more fragile; more explosive. The "subprime" and related collapses that began to surface in 2006 could and should have served as a warning siren; but, as with the Crash of 1929, the siren sounded too late. As George Soros, one of the most successful financiers of our time, put it in 2008: "We are in the midst of a financial crisis the likes of which we haven't seen since the Great Depression" (Soros, 2008; and see Foster, 2008). That depression began soon after the 1929 crash. As will be seen later, its record-breaking unemployment was still at 10 percent or more until a year *after* the US entered World War II.

Item: As we grunt and try to wiggle through the "subprime" and related financial crises that began to rear their ugly heads in 2006, it is worth recalling the so-called experts' responses to the 1929 crash. Year after year journalists, economists, and presidents told us that "Prosperity is Just Around the Corner." (See Soule, 1947; Mitchell, 1947.)

There are many dimensions, problems, and prospects in today's financialization; what follows will deal at length with only three of them:

1. How and why the present situation came to be
2. Its ongoing importance and functions
3. Its already great and always increasing fragility, as of early 2009.

I. From Banks to High Finance to Gambling Casino

For capitalism to come into existence at all two conditions had to be met: the creation of a property-less and therefore powerless working class (see Chapter 2), and the birth and maturation of trade and finance; the latter, dependent upon their interaction with colonialism and Europe's economic and expansion *outside* Europe noted earlier.

As the content, volume, and geographic scope of trade expanded from ancient to medieval to modern times, trading companies were created. The best known of those were the "East India Companies" of the Dutch, the British, and the French. Their risks and costs could be spread among the traders but ultimately needed financial assistance from *banks*. At first, banks specialized in borrowing others' savings in order to lend to other borrowers.

It is in the economic sectors of agriculture and industry that production occurs. Although traders and financiers may (or may not) perform a useful function, they do not *produce* anything. In the capitalist world nothing ever stays the same: financiers changed from being "intermediaries" to *controlling* others for whom they had once "mediated" in trade and production. For present purposes, it is important to note only that over time those processes accelerated, most markedly from the 1970s on. They did so partially because the leading nations entered a prolonged slowdown in the realms of profitable production, marked by "stagflation." The latter began to repeat a few years ago, but since 2007 with deflation and recession in some countries, with inflation and recession in others (for a while). It was in the 1970s that speculative finance began its march toward sheer dominance. (See Phillips, 2002; Dowd, 2004.)

Those broad generalizations were partially supported in the preceding chapter; now we probe further. Among the many important matters soon to be discussed, the following deserves a comment before we proceed.

Given that traders and bankers provide a service but do not *produce* anything; does that suggest that those in agriculture and industry *do*? Yes, but almost all production is done by workers, not by owners. That might be seen as a "Marxian" observation; but the owners would agree with it; indeed, they demand it. It is of course true that there are numerous decisions that must be made, and that those who make them are contributing to production. But the incomes of CEOs and other executives and owners are only in tiny degree in accord with that "work"; their incomes are stratospheric, even when the companies they have ruled over have suffered severe financial losses. Thus (as noted in Chapter 2), when in 2007 jobs were already being lost and average incomes decreasing, the US Congressional Budget Office announced this:

> The increase in incomes of the top 1 percent from 2003 to 2005 exceeded the total income of the poorest 20 percent of Americans: the total income of the top 1.1 million households was $1.8 *trillion*, or 18 percent of US total income, coming from investments and capital gains... In 2003, taxes on capital gains were *reduced*. (*NYT*, December 17, 2007)

The early capitalist Richard Arkwright and those a century or more later were indispensable to the technology and/or the creative nature of their enterprises. But the "creative" functions of the industries following them (textiles, communications, cars, etc.) are more accurately seen as those of "operators," adept at putting together giant companies by any means at hand, barely distinguishable from the military general or the Mafia leader who lets others do the "work." That takes us to today's financialization.

II. The Functions and Importance of Contemporary Finance

Our focus is mostly upon the US, but in this as in so much else, ways and means of finance (and the consequences) have been "globalized." Today's financialization took its first big jumps as the prosperous 1960s ended. They were also the years in which the West European and Japanese economies' reconstruction had made them not only competitive with US production (dramatically in autos, then steel, now much more) but had done so in a world economy slowly but surely moving into global excess productive capacities. Those developments gave rise to the most dazzling round of mergers and acquisitions (M&As) ever; until, that is, the 1990s and since. In doing so, they also reduced the incentive for *real* investment in new or existing production facilities. Unsurprisingly, the financial world was the prime beneficiary and ultimate home of M&As. (See Chapter 4.)

The incomes of financial companies fall under the categories of both "interest" and "profits," but what is more important are their quantitative and qualitative meanings. In that connection, the statistical tendency after 1949 is both illuminating and shocking. In 1949, corporate profits (of *non*-financial companies) were *ten* times as high as interest (for financial companies); in 1959, ten years later the ratio was *five* to one; in 1969, that had dropped to two-and-a-half times; by 1979..., it was less than double; however, since 1989 non-financial corporate profits have always been *less than* interest (*Economic Report of the President*, 1995).

As that process was taking hold, the traditional role of interest in the economy was abandoned. And in doing so it signified a major transformation in the overall functioning of capitalism; something like the difference between having a glass of fine wine to round off a dinner and downing a quart of gin. For example, from the 1960s on, corporate profits themselves have included large gobs of interest, not only because the number of financial corporations as a percentage of all corporations has risen greatly, but because an always rising percentage of the giant producing corporations have themselves merged with or created their own large financial institutions (e.g., both GM and GE are giant money lenders). Along the way, Wall Street has increased its size, its scope and, greatly, its political power since the 1970s, in leaps and bounds. So it was that:

In the early 1970s...the financial sector was subordinate to Congress and the White House, and the total of financial trades conducted by American firms or on American exchanges over an entire year was a dollar amount less than the gross national product. By the 1990s, however, through a twenty-four hour-a-day cascade of electronic hedging and speculation, the financial sector had swollen to an annual volume of trading *30 or 40 times greater than* the dollar turnover of the "real economy"... Each *month*, several dozen huge domestic financial firms and exchanges trade electronically a sum in currencies, futures, derivative instruments, stocks, and bonds that exceeds the entire annual gross national product of the United States. (Phillips, 1994; his emphasis)

Also, and in addition to the stimuli noted earlier, the financial sector grew mightily in response to the following and interacting set of changes: the emerging importance of money, equity, and pension funds, the enormous increase of household, business, and governmental debt, the spread and strengthening of insurance companies and their mergers with other financial companies, the expansion of amateur and professional financial speculators, and the rapid growth of international speculation in the explosive derivative markets. (Henwood, 1997)

Then, disgraceful as much in their origin as in their consequences, were the US Savings and Loan (S&L) scandals of the 1980s. The S&Ls were first legislated in the 1920s and flowered from the 1930s into the 1960s. (See Chapter 9.) Their original and stated purpose was to create regulated neighborhood "thrift banks" which, through ceilings on their interest charges, would enable middle-income/working-class families to purchase a house. With the help of a buoyant economy after World War II, the result was as hoped, so that by the end of the 1960s, two-thirds of all US families were "homeowners," most (myself included) having financed their homes by an S&L. However: enter Ronald Reagan, stage Right. One of his first triumphs was financial de-regulation. That served as an invitation to reckless financial practices by both households and all financial institutions: and the door was opened wide for the ongoing "subprime" disaster (among others) as financial activities were increasingly taken over by sharpies, fools, and downright criminals.

Consequently, by 1984 one after another of the S&Ls had collapsed and the basis for today's collapse was set. What had been socially-useful banking became one of many gambling casinos. However, the Reagan government saw to it that those who *caused* the debacle were not to lose any money for creating the basis for a disaster. In what should have been a warning for today the perpetrators of the disaster were "bailed out."

The cost to US taxpayers over time for the S&L wallop will be $200–500 billion; subsequent fun and games will add a *trillion plus* to "bail out" the Wall Street multi-millionaires who took us here. (See below.) For the S&L crisis, a new government agency was created composed of lawyers and accountants from the financial sector. The lawyers were paid $600-plus per *hour*. (See Soros, 2008 and Pizzo et al., 1989.) But the $700 billion bailout of November 2008 was just a first step. (See below.)

What is most ominous is that the 1980s should have served as a warning of financial hocus-pocus and fragility, but it didn't. The presumed "disciplinary function of free markets" would have left reckless financial institutions to drown in their own failed investments; just the opposite:

The national power structure bailed out the shaky financial sector, and on a large enough scale that in the end the banks and S&Ls rescued through federal insurance payouts represented a higher share of the nation's deposits than the institutions forced to close their doors in the economic hurricane of the late 1920s and early 1930s... Financed by massive borrowing and further enlargement of the federal deficit, the bailout served largely to safeguard bank investors and assets. The result was not just to prop up the stock market but to allow it to keep hitting new highs, while Wall Street firms achieved new record earnings...and the financial economy continued to eat the real economy. (See Phillips, 1994 and 2008.)

Sound familiar? The foregoing, taken together with the mountains of all kinds of debt and the need for them to go higher if national and global economic collapse are to be avoided, becomes fraught with dire meanings when we recognize the highly speculative quality of the entire financial system. Those "dire meanings" need not be imagined; they are in the headlines every day. Today's whirlwind financial world has come as a shock; it shouldn't have. Back in the 1980s, Michael Lewis, after graduating from Princeton, took a job working in Wall Street's "hedge funds" and related ventures. He left in disgust and wrote a revealing book telling what was going on: *Liar's Poker* (1989). In 2008 he put together a set of articles by himself and others, *Panic: The Story of Modern Financial Insanity*, in which you can find the comment below, taken from his article entitled "The End." The

1989 book was entertaining and enlightening, he notes, and had sold well. However:

> [Although] I had no great agenda, I had hoped that college students trying to figure out what to do with their lives would read it and decide that it's silly to phony it up and become financiers... Somehow that message failed to get across. Six months after *Liar's Poker* was published, I was knee-deep in letters from university students who wanted to know if I had any other secrets to share about Wall Street. They had read my book as a "how-to-do" manual... In the two decades since then I have been waiting for the end of Wall Street.

III. Altogether Now: Speculators of the World Unite!

They united all too much, if only for a while. Finance was once seen as the conservative corner of the capitalist structure; from the 1980s on, gung-ho speculation has been a thinly-disguised or hidden part of all financial instruments and commodities. Until the late 1920s, almost all speculators were "pros"; then the "innocents" jumped into the ring. After many being bloodied almost fatally then, it was foolishly assumed it wouldn't happen again; but in the 1930s the Glass–Steagall Act was passed to make sure. However, from the 1980s on and especially in the Clinton years (1993–2001) *all* such rules were cancelled in a process led by Clinton's Treasury Secretary Robert Rubin (now, worrisomely) a main advisor to Obama. With the total junking of financial regulation the stage was set for today's explosions, and the collapse of virtually *all* major financial giants: Lehman Brothers, Citigroup, AIG... (see below).

A tidal wave of "new innocents" e-mailed their way into the casino, prodded along by a group of pros both more numerous and wilder than earlier. Speculation became the biggest game in town, sucking in countless hopefuls, most tenuously (at first) in the housing market. Some were "subprimers" previously unable to get a home loan; others were better off who took out second mortgages on their homes in order to buy another and later get rich selling at a *much* higher price. Sitting in the wings of that show and humming to himself was that new devil called Mr. Housing Bubble.

From 2006 on the bubble was puffed up and up and up, bringing to mind the "tulip mania" of the seventeenth century in Holland (see Clark, 1947). But the "tulipers" were like kids playing marbles: today it's pro football played out in a globalized Wall Street (see Henwood, 1997; Shiller, 2008; and Stiglitz, 2006). Now a closer look at that "merry-go-round of Wall Street."

How did we get from financiers being fuddy-duddy stuffed shirts who wouldn't lend a dime to their mothers, to the financial circus that has been going on in recent years from the US all the way to Iceland and India? The fun and games began most contagiously with speculation in foreign currencies in the 1970s, after Nixon had ended fixed exchange rates. It was then that currencies began to exchange freely and that the door was opened wide to always rising speculation.

The Bank of International Settlements keeps track of the buying and selling of all currencies. Already in 1986 the Bank was startled to find that *daily* foreign exchange transactions amounted to $186 *billion*, and that less than 10 percent of that was for trade and investment; the rest was for speculation. Wow? Peanuts! Five years later the daily $186 billion had jumped to $800 billion, only 3 percent of which was for trade and investment. Now it flits back and forth between 1.5 and 2 *trillion dollars* in *daily* transactions, with barely 1 percent for trade and investment; that is, 99 percent is speculation. (See Phillips, 2008.)

After 1986, what should have served as warnings for the lords of speculation was the following string of financial collapses: Wall Street plunge of 1987, S&L plunge of 1989, East Asian financial collapse of 1997, Long-Term Capital Management (LTCM) collapse of 1998, the Enron collapse of 2001–02; then the "subprime" disaster of 2006, and so on. Despite all, the dice kept rolling. In Barnum's time, a sucker was born every minute; now one's born every nanosecond.

Some speculation is merely functional. For example, enormous transnational companies must deal in various foreign currencies every day to buy and sell this and that and pay for it. If they don't speculate (that is, buy and/or sell more than their ongoing trade and investment needs) they stand to lose and/or to forgo a profit they might have made by guessing right. But most other speculation is sheer gambling. For instance:

Item: Baring Brothers of London was one of the most respected and longest-standing banks in the modern world. It was the most important creditor for all the nineteenth century, and very conservative. But ten years ago it joined the speculators' parade. The activities of its Singapore man, who was certain that the yen was going to go down greatly, ended up leaving a $1.4 billion hole in Baring's balance sheet, and sent the bank into bankruptcy.

Nowadays that gaming is non-stop and global, as evidenced in the 1997 Asian financial crisis which started in, of all places, Thailand. From there, it spread like measles throughout the East, bringing otherwise healthy economies like South Korea's to their knees; in doing so it caused many Asian companies to sell out to always observant "vulture capitalists" from the West (Henwood, 1997). Now the whole world is infected.

Much of the whiz bang talk about the need for and benefits of "free markets" has as its center the virtues of "transparency"; for which finance has taken the prize, as it is the least regulated and most accessible to instantaneous communications and instant buying and selling, *and* the most "globalized," the most competitive, and the most integrated: the model of a "perfectly competitive market." But for the second and third tier economies those markets have meant something like handing thieves the key to the front door. Led by the US, the finance thieves functioned with the help of the US-created IMF, World Bank, WTO, and NAFTA. Revealingly, in its own pre-dominant period the US would *never* have allowed any such institutions to darken its door. As for speculation, the "Roaring Twenties" were, in comparison with the "new economy" of the 1990s and since, as a kitten is to a tiger (see Soule, 1947 and Stiglitz, 2006). Keynes, writing in the 1930s, was famously alarmed even by the kitten of the 1920s:

Speculators may do no harm as bubbles on a steady stream of enterprise. But the position is serious when enterprise becomes the bubble on a whirlpool of speculation. When the capital development of a country becomes a by-product of the activities of a casino, the job is likely to be ill-done. The measure of success of Wall Street, regarded as an institution of which the proper social purpose is to direct new investment into the most profitable channels in terms of future yield, cannot be claimed as one of the outstanding triumphs of *laissez-faire* capitalism – which is not surprising: the best brains of Wall Street have been in fact directed towards a different object. (Keynes, 1936)

Since the 1970s, at an always accelerating rate, the "enterprise" feared by Keynes has become became a roaring reality, with Wall Street the home of "the bubble on a whirlpool of speculation" which has thrown the US and the global economy into its present crisis. Question: Is today's financial crash 1929 all over again? No. It's likely to be much worse.

What follows will begin with a long examination of the causes and consequences of the US financial crisis that became evident in 2007 and that exploded globally in 2008. That done, we will turn to the policies created to deal with this crisis both before and since Obama's presidency, with a comment on their defects and better possibilities.

As the first discussion unfolds, it will be seen that despite several causal similarities between 1929 and the present there is reason to fear that the substantial differences between them are such that we must anticipate global economic difficulties considerably deeper and more severe than in the 1930s. Nor is it irrelevant to note that in the first few *years* of the 1929 crisis, the analyses of the "experts'" were all falsely optimistic and pursued wrong-headed policies: until shoved aside by FDR in the mid 1930s, after he finally ceased to take advice from Wall Street's "experts" (Phillips, 2008). As this is written in early 2009, it appears that Obama is learning to go against the reasoning of his initial experts in late 2008. (See below.)

The Nature and Causes of the Financial Collapse

Today we all live in "the house of global capitalism." Most of the world's people do so in the dirtiest and most dangerous part of the basement, but all of us live on terms set by the most powerful companies of the US, Europe, and Asia. We do so in the tightening grips of the inequalities suiting capitalism's aims, means, and power. In our time both capitalism's powers and its needs have sped up and increased in breadth and depth as, accordingly, so has inequality. The associated social dangers have been many; and today's financial collapse is "only" one of them, if also a big one.

First, an editorial note: what follows will be a mere summary of current financial processes and problems and their worsening. In 2008 the White House assisted most those who had profited most from what caused the crisis. It is to be hoped that the Obama administration will do what is needed, although he began in ways that are not encouraging, when his appointees in the financial realm were among those responsible for what brought the crisis; notably Robert Rubin, of Citigroup, Timothy Geithner, head of the Federal Reserve Bank, and Lawrence Summers, Treasury Secretary under Clinton in the 1990s and who presided over the financial deregulation which made today's mess inevitable (also see the note on Summers in Chapter 11). As will be seen below, it appears that already by the spring of 2009 Obama had changed the latters' minds for the better.

The first rumblings of what could become an earthquake were felt back in the 1980s (see S&L etc., above). Yet, the door remained and remains all too open for their continuation: the financiers who *caused* and profited from the crises were coddled by Bush's Secretary of the Treasury, Henry Paulson, whose previous job was head of one of Wall Street's giants, Goldman Sachs. Neither the crises of the late 1980s nor of the present could have occurred had not the Reagan administration abolished *all* financial regulation. The LTCM crack-up of 1998 was noted above but it is worth a closer look, for it was representative of today in two ways: its "risk principle," and its belief that if any real trouble came to be, those responsible would be "bailed out" by the government. LTCM was correct on the second "principle." The ways and means of LTCM intersected with "derivatives" and "hedge funds"; and the "risk principles" of both depended upon spreading risk ("slicing") in such a way that a problem in a particular investment would be resolved by there being no such problems in the thousands/millions/billions of other "slices."

The two professors who invented those ways and means (as noted in Chapter 6) were "free market" economists of the University of Chicago (and who had won the Nobel Prize for being *very* smart). When LTCM began, it was open only to those who had least $1 million to gamble and it was the only hedge fund of its kind; then there were eight. But *after* LTCM was bailed out so nicely, there came to be eight *thousand* such crapshoots. As they became "the game," Wall Street rang with flash new words like "derivatives," "hedge funds," "collateralized debt obligations," "credit default swaps" and other fancy ways of gambling (and OK'd by Obama advisor Rubin). Taken together these schemes created today's global collapse. (See Soros, 2008; Foster, 2008; Phillips, 2008; Pizzo et al., 1989; Shiller, 2008.) So it was that the Nobel Prize winners turned out to be dangerous fools; the economic version of the film character "Dr. Strangelove" who, as some oldies will remember, convinced the US Air Force to use complicated communications and carry nuclear weapons to serve the noble ends of the US. But damn! A communications screw-up with just one plane led to the end of the world. (Go get the DVD; it's funny as hell, until the pilot's "bailout" carrying the bomb.)

For about a dozen years in which the ground was cleared for today's crisis, the US's economic Dr. Strangelove was the head of the Federal Reserve System: Alan Greenspan. A sensible nation wouldn't have allowed him to enter the Fed's door: his position was and remains that the best government is *no* government: let Wall Street do as it wishes and, if there's a problem, let Uncle Sam pick up the pieces and go away again.

The post-1970s rightward lurch being what it was, Greenspan became the Fed's master and opened the door for finance to run wild. His position on the financial regulations created after the 1929 crash was simple: *no* regulations are needed, "unless," he in fact added – in just these words – unless there are *greedy* people; and he didn't know any. When Alan was brought before the Senate Finance Committee in 2008 and asked to explain himself, after much pressure he (reluctantly) said "I was mistaken."

He would have loved to have been in the audience the day a fellow economist gave the UCLA business school's graduates a speech whose title was "Greed is Good." Greenspan, the speech maker, the two LTCM profs, and Treas. Sec. Paulson should be forced to stand in a corner and repeat a *billion* times: "I am a horse's ass."

Nothing to be ashamed of, Alan et al.: in the fall of 1928, the leading economist of the US, Prof. Irving Fisher, announced that "The American economy is on a high plateau of endless prosperity." Just like you, Alan et al., Irving was both famous and "mistaken."

Now we dig more deeply into today's crisis. It was brought into view in 2006 by the "subprime crisis." As the twenty-first century was coming over the horizon, financiers on the lookout for new money-makers decided to set aside their historic conservatism regarding eligibility for loans (i.e., ability to repay) and they invented "subprime loans." Definition? Simple: subprimers were those who want a loan but who had never been eligible for one. So, the reasoning went, because the economy is going to expand forever, it would be OK to let these folks get a mortgage without the usual need (1) to make a down payment, (2) to pay interest on what's borrowed, or (3) to make monthly payments until…much later.

However. Among the many consequences of the ongoing financial crisis has been what has happened to the 6 *million* US families who were encouraged to obtain mortgages to buy homes as "subprimers," more than two-thirds of whom were not eligible for a normal home loan. There was, of course, an understated catch: In a few years, the borrowers would face interest rates up to triple the 5 percent of the S&L days, plus much higher monthly payments. Why not? The good times are gonna just keep rolling, no? The news in 2009 shows that at least two-thirds of those 6 million families have homes whose present market prices are lower than their debt, families who can't make their monthly payments, who are going to lose their homes, and be broken financially and emotionally. (The "other third" are middle-class people who bought a second house for speculation in what was seen as an eternally rising market.) The latest statement from Treas. Sec. Paulson is that the better-off third will be eligible for some kind of US assistance. As the other two-thirds lose their homes, *and* as the economy contracts and unemployment rises, how and where will the poor two-thirds live? And those financial execs who pulled down big bonuses even after their companies went broke, what about them? Will they have to pay back even a dime?

The entire housing industry and its customers were entirely different in the 1920s: one didn't even *think* about buying a home unless one was nicely up in the middle-income bracket. (Hard to believe, there weren't even credit cards then!) Related to that is another set of consequences that differ from 1929; it has to do with pensions and will affect all of us sooner or later. Only a very small percentage of the people were *directly* hit by the 1929 crash; but today, whether we know it or not, no matter where we bank, or what our job or income, we are *all* involved, and importantly so. We await a pension, gained through our company or a governmental agency and/or our personal contributions. But *all* pension funds are "in the market." *All* funds place their incoming pension contributions in investments of one sort or another in order to earn interest: in today's world, all of us are directly or indirectly involved in the world of stocks, bonds, derivatives, hedge funds; it's a "financialized" world. In the 1920s, it was the families of only the top 15–20 percent of the US population. (See Soule, 1947.)

Prof. Fisher's optimism in 1928 notwithstanding, about half of US families were at or below the poverty level in most of the 1920s (see Soule, 1947; Ryan, 1976). Today it's very different, under 20 percent are in (official) poverty, but almost all of us are in *debt* up to our chins. We got there prodded along by the consumerism that is absolutely essential if the US economy *and* today's world economy are to "flourish." The US consumer debt accumulation (for cars, credit cards and mortgages) was and is essential for both US and global "prosperity." Given the ways in which the US and world economies now function, it is easy to see that today's reversal and slowdown were unavoidable. Unfortunately, given the nature of those now in power in the capitalist world, it seems all too probable that the recessions now underway in the US and almost every other nation will deepen into a global depression.

Some of its likely meanings have already jumped up for what used to be the pride of the US economy: in April 2009, GM was given an ultimatum by Obama to straighten up fast: if the $30 billion-plus help wasn't enough, you're on your own. And countless others companies, whether in industry or finance, large or small, are facing the real possibility of joining the bankruptcy parade, with or without a "bailout." The whole bailout process has many problems and questions. However, it is also troublesome to note that although $700 billion-plus was granted without any reservations to a few giant financial companies, the Congress were then able to slow down the much smaller bailout for GM and Chrysler, even though in doing so they were also dooming tens of thousands of auto workers to be unemployed (plus many more in dependent industries). That prompted a *New York Times* article by Gretchen Morgenson, "Let's Treat Banks Like Automakers," and her comment that "most of the banks only needed a large hat in hand to share $700 billion" (December 15, 2008).

Already in 2008 the list of companies of all sorts needing governmental assistance to avoid bankruptcy was long, and lengthening by the day. That is subtly but revealingly represented by what is happening in the shipping industry, as noted in the UK *Independent* ("Shipping Holed Beneath the Waterline," November 6, 2008):

> The index which tracks the price of shipping bulk cargo..., an unparalleled barometer of the global economic trade in economic building blocks like iron ore, coal and grain is telling a worrying tale: the scale of daily charter

rates has fallen nearly 98 percent. The chairman of a major ship brokers said "The scale of change in rate is utterly staggering; the market has come down from super-boom territory to pretty close to bust, effectively in two months." Others in the business remarked "People are waiting for prices to fall further..." "It's anybody's guess how long it will take for money to start circulating again."

That's only one industry, but given its function, it is a major reflection of what is – or isn't – going on in world trade. Multiply that one industry by others whose stuff was being shipped, add the jobs lost, look in the mirror and...yell for help.

But won't the Obama White House reverse current tendencies and take us toward a saner and more decent political economy? That may be a reasonable hope, made all the more so by the program placed before Congress in February 2009 (see below). However, his presidency and the new Congress will increasingly be confronted by a set of problems both deeper in kind and broader in consequence within the US and over the globe.

Assuming Obama has the ability and will to take the substantial steps required, the question arises as to whether or not those with power in the business communities of the US and elsewhere can be persuaded to support the needed policies. The behavior of the Republican Party in Congress up to now (not one vote in favor in the House by the Republicans) suggests that their strategy is to block the road at least and paralyze at worst; probably with the 2010 congressional election in mind, with the GOP's reasonable assumption that a worsened economy will be blamed upon Obama. That said, if there are to be the necessary economic policies there will have to be a great deal of political support and pressure "from the bottom up"; as there was for Roosevelt in the 1930s and up into the 1940s.

In the US, with rare exceptions, the business community has never accepted the desirable and useful reforms of the 1930s into the 1960s. By the 1970s a "neo-conservative" movement was taking hold, and the business world had gotten its political muscles back. Together they started the work that allowed them to have the government do or *not* to do what they wanted. Their triumph was symbolized in the two administrations of George W. Bush.

Chapter 12 shows that after World War II Western European business, squeezed by relatively strong left unions and parties, acquiesced in many decent policies. What the EU will do as this crisis continues is unknown; but it must be noted here that in recent years the "politics" of its member states has come to resemble that of the US more closely than during the 1950s and 1960s. What the Bush administration did as the present crisis began was more likely to prolong (or provide the basis for a repetition of) the ongoing financial crisis. Such policies must be reversed and replaced. That is seen most clearly in one awful and typical example; namely, what the Bush administration did as regards AIG (American International Group). It is worth examining, so as to assure that what happened will not be repeated or, even better, that it will be undone; what was done for AIG (and others) was not only to *rescue* but to *reward* at least partially those responsible for our financial fragility. It deserves a closer look:

AIG's presumed function is to *insure* the investments of others. That came to include the "securities" called "collateralized debt obligations" and/or one of the family of crapshooters noted earlier (hedge funds, derivatives, et al.). In September 2008 AIG was set to go into bankruptcy from taking care of those already in deep trouble whom it had "insured." So, the Fed and Treas. Sec. Paulson *loaned* (make that "gave") AIG $85 *billion*. Not enough, so it got another $38 billion. Not enough; so another $40 billion from the US purchase of their valueless stock. Not enough; another $100 billion is just around the corner. (See *International Herald Tribune*, March 28, 2009.)

Nor is it by any means irrelevant to note that after AIG got all that help it gave two *very* expensive parties at luxury resorts for its execs; first in September, then in November. The September party celebrating the bailout will cost us taxpayers $500,000; they've kept secret the cost of the November celebration in Arizona. As I write in early 2009, their new debts to you and me exceed $150 *billion*. They will *never* pay them. We will. (See www. democracynow.org.)

That's sickening, but the numbers in the following table should turn your stomach. They are of two kinds, regarding the dance of bonuses to the execs and government bailouts for 2007–08, but not including the $50 billion in bonuses of 2009.

Company	Senior Officer Bonuses/ Total Bonus Pools	US Bailout Money
Merrill Lynch	$85 million / $9.5 billion	$10 billion
Bank of America	$36 million / $11.3 billion	$15 billion
Goldman Sachs	$313 million / $12.1 billion	$10 billion
Morgan Stanley	$64 million / $9.9 billion	$10 billion
Citigroup	$54 million / $20.7 billion	$45 billion
Wells Fargo	$40 million / $8 billion	$25 billion
JPMorgan Chase	$91 million / $13.6 billion	$25 billion
Total	$683 million / $85.1 billion	$140 billion

Source: see Frank Rich, "Has a 'Katrina Moment' Arrived," *NYT*, March 22, 2009

The AIG collapse and its above-noted blood brothers rewards represent all to well "the heart" of the financial disaster and its spoiled brat rescues. From the 1990s on, Wall Street, the government, and consumers joined a parade whose flags said "It's up and up and up and up…no problem, no limit, it's each for himself and God for all! Jump aboard!" We and millions of others will be paying for their fun and games for life. All of that is bad enough, but given the marriage of globalization and financialization worse is on its way.

What follows will focus mainly on the US, but globalization being what it is all other societies face or are already undergoing related dangers (if in different ways and degrees). After much chatter, and with GDP having fallen to just under 7 percent in the last quarter of 2008, the experts have finally recognized that we are in a recession; as at the same time, official unemployment is at 6–7 percent and rising.

It is worth repeating here that measured accurately (instead of politically) the latter rate would be more than doubled. Why "accurately"? Because, since the Clinton administration those who have despaired looking for jobs because they cannot find them are *no longer* counted as unemployed. One reads in the news that tens of thousands have lost their jobs on Wall Street, but little or nothing is said of the millions who were once in factories, in department stores, or grade school teachers, and so on, who have already or will soon lose their jobs. Non-measuring was normal in the depression of the 1930s also; until public outrage led to official (and still understated) measurement. Question: if and when GM, Chrysler, and/or Ford close down, will those who worked there be seen as unemployed or just more of those damned drifters? As noted earlier, if the unemployment rate were to count those who have given up hunting for jobs out of despair, or those who are half-time but want and need full-time jobs, then the rate would be doubled.

Today and Tomorrow

Since winning the 2008 election – thank goodness! – Obama has been much occupied with assembling his advisors and his cabinet. There are many serious problems facing us, including not only a desperately sick economy, but ongoing and potential wars, a seriously threatened environment, and deep needs regarding health care, education, and housing. I did what I could to see that Obama be elected, and wept with joy when he was.

However, a look at those whom Obama initially chose to have work with him in the White House does not offer us much encouragement, least of all in the realm of finance. His financial team centers upon Timothy Geithner, Robert Rubin, and Lawrence Summers. Rubin and Summers (plus Greenspan) were the financial team that "rescued" us from the LTCM financial crisis of 1997–98. In his *New York Times* article "Lest We Forget" (November 27, 2008) Nobel economist Paul Krugman recalls that "*Time Magazine* named Greenspan, Rubin, and Summers 'The Committee to Save the World who prevented a global meltdown,' forgetting to ask how we got so close to the brink in the first place…" Remember that it was Rubin and Summers who advised Clinton to get rid of financial regulations; that Rubin and Geithner were the brains behind the giant gifts to the giant financial companies, AIG only the most disgusting.

Behind all of that is a set of realities that are more than disgusting; they should be seen as criminal. Whether or not it is criminal now, it should be made so as soon as possible. I refer to the role of highly-paid lobbyists and those in both Houses of Congress who owe their seats to bribing campaign finance. Read these numbers and think about them: in the years 1998–2008, the – reported – lobbyist expenditures by financial corporations were $3.4 billion and the – reported – campaign contributions were $1.7 billion. That adds up to more than $5 billion (*Multinational Monitor*, January/February 2009).

Although Obama probably has good ideas about much of that and more, what he did in his first few months was far from promising. However, as things went from bad to worse between his first month and spring, he had begun to shift gears and go in a wiser direction. In his speech to Congress in late February 2009 Obama announced plans for domestic purposes which included a substantial set of policies favoring badly-needed governmental health care and educational programs, and also much-needed policies to protect the environment by reducing our wild use and dependence upon oil.

As the national economy continues to shrink and jobs continue to disappear, as health care costs continue to rise and health care benefits (already inadequate) fall (most notably in industry), and as states reduce already meager expenses on education, it may be expected that, even so, those in and out of Congress who have supported Bush will oppose every attempt to reverse the disasters of his presidency. It seems apparent that in doing so they realize that no problems will be resolved and many will worsen. So what? So Obama and the Democrats will be seen as responsible. Therefore, for the GOP it's good politics to sabotage any policies the Obama presidency proposes, in and out of Congress. They will get away with that unless the rest of us activate ourselves politically to see to it that the US can move toward becoming what it has always seen itself as being, but has only rarely moved toward becoming: "The land of the people, by the people, and for the people."

It may be noticed that the foregoing praise of Obama's domestic efforts has said nothing concerning his foreign policies. That will be done critically in the next chapter and again in Chapter 11 and the Epilogue, along with discussions of both the need and possibilities for his administration to turn us away from disaster and toward peace and social decency.

In Chapters 8, 9, and 10 it will be shown just how far the US has strayed from its cherished ideals, as regards both social decency and safety: As matters now stand, the never-ending wars of the US have all too long combined with a systemic neglect of the poor, of health and education, and of housing, and hunger. The latter tragedies have come to be seen as "natural," given our long-standing tendencies toward prejudice, discrimination, and greed. The election of Barack Obama as president was a surprising and most welcome first step in a much to be desired direction.

Now there are many more steps for him to take, but he cannot walk alone: we must be marching both ahead and behind him. In the election of 2008 we surprised ourselves by voting for a black man; we must continue to surprise ourselves by becoming involved in politics going beyond simple voting for Tweedledee or Tweedledum if Obama is to be able to keep his promises, and if we are to keep the promises of our birth as a nation. We awakened for an election; let's stay that way. We must stay that way; for those who voted against Obama are counting on us to let the worst in us take over again. It would be wonderful to show them how wrong they are; dangerous not to. (Of which, more in the Epilogue.)

8

MILITARISM AND INEQUALITY

Inequality's first form was very probably that between men and women. In the prehistoric era, men undoubtedly used physical force both against each other and against women. (See Veblen, 1899 and 1914, and Childe, 1951.) That may also be seen as the beginnings of militarism; that is, long before "civilization" emerged, inequality had become "normal," becoming always more complex as one form or another of "brute strength" emerged and took on different ways and means.

What follows is an analysis of the complexities, breadth, and depths of the many relationships between inequality and militarism in three historical periods: colonialism, imperialism, and the decades since World War II. First, however, it is appropriate to make explicit what is meant here by "militarism." It may be thought of as a giant octopus, whose powerful tentacles wreak always greater damage to all elements of our existence: physical and social, economic and political, cultural and ethical (plus, now, its assault on the environment). The following is a look at those "tentacles," separately and especially as they interact:

1. Militarism has always been and remains a means for getting what is wanted by the use or the threat of organized slaughter. Once used, it has almost always maintained its grip; even when it leads to disaster, as with drugs, its "cure" (if any) is temporary.

2. For many nations, militarism grew out of a necessary and successful war for gaining or maintaining independence; as with the US and other ex-colonized societies, as when, for example, Cuba's had to remain militaristic after its presumably

successful revolution against Spain, as the nineteenth century ended. Why "presumably" successful? Because the US entered late in that struggle on the dubious grounds that the Spanish had sunk the USS *Maine*. From then to the 1960s, the US controlled the economy and politics of Cuba directly or indirectly, aided by its fascist appointee Sgt. Fulgencio Batista. Not until, the 1960s did Cuba's independence became in any way real. (See E. Williams, 1984.) The US's history of was of course quite different. From its birth, it possessed the seemingly contradictory characteristics of being among the most militaristic of nations *and* the least threatened. It was safe, self-sufficient in all major resources and protected by two by very broad oceans. After 1900 it moved swiftly toward becoming both economically and militarily the most powerful of all nations, never challenged or challengeable until Pearl Harbor; and until made to seem so by the "spin" of Cold War. (See Wittner, 1978; LaFeber, 1976.)

3. Colonialism and imperialism were squarely dependent upon brute militarism; as was the damage, destruction, and enslavement of the colonized peoples up to and including their globalized and still distorted lives, whether in their home countries or in the lands where they had been enslaved.

4. To the human damage imposed by force upon the peoples of the colonized/imperialized lands, add the robbery of their societies' rich resources. Of the six and half billion people in the world today, less than a third live decently; all others live in where the land was stolen for the purposes of the well-armed nations. In consequence, the native peoples have had to live in despair, poverty, illness, and fear; as they facilitated the much higher level of material wellbeing of the industrial capitalist nations.

5. When we later briefly examine what has happened to the politics and the cultures of the victims of militaristic colonialism, we find sustained corruption, violence, and demoralization; always blamed on the character of the victims. But surely the European culture and its US variations are superior to what was lost by the colonized? As measured by the victors, yes;

by the defeated not at all, and with some reason. (See Wright, 1992; Mander, 1978; Nordholdt, 1970.)

6. Then there is the major role played by the "political economy" of militarism, a matter so important in so many ways in its multiple relationships with inequality that it will occupy a central role in Section III of this chapter. Its principal references will be the analysis of "the iron triangle," by Cypher (2002a), a leading expert on that tentacle of the "octopus."

7. Later we will emphasize two of the most subtle and socially damaging ways in which militarism's power structure has institutionalized inequality for its own purposes and,...

8. ...much assisted by racism and poverty, has provided its military with voluntary killers and victims who enlist principally because of few alternatives.

In the following three sections, we now turn to the foundations, uses, and consequences of militarism in the main periods of capitalist development.

I: Colonialism, Capitalism, and the Birth of Modern Militarism

The stark contrast between what has been and what could have been took hold as the modern era began, with an always greater and devastating degree of divergence between the realities and the possibilities. Militarism and its wars have been both cause and consequence of those tragedies. They have been a major component of the economic and social irrationality of the social order which has allowed and caused such gaps between need and possibility to persist and deepen. Tawney long ago understood both the initial and ultimate meanings of the modern beginnings of that evolution:

> Applied to the arts of peace, the new resources commanded by Europe during the first half of the sixteenth century might have done something to exorcize the specters of pestilence and famine, and to raise the material fabric of civilization to undreamed of heights. Its rulers, secular and

otherwise, thought otherwise. When pestilence and famine were ceasing to be necessities imposed by nature, they re-established them by political art. The sluice which they opened to drain away each accession of superfluous wealth was war. (Tawney, 1926)

The starting point for colonialism, modern militarism, and capitalism was much the same; all three depended upon and worsened the lives of the peoples of both the invading and the invaded societies. In the colonized societies, the initial and subsequent consequences were diverse, but all depended upon force, and all were horrifying:

- Whether in Africa, Asia, South or North America, formal or *de facto* enslavement and mass murder by the colonizers was the rule.
- In the colonized continents, virtually all pre-colonial social and cultural institutions were effectively destroyed or fatally crippled.
- The peoples of all the colonized areas lost control and/or use of their agricultural, mineral, forest, and water resources.
- Their populations were drastically reduced and/or crippled by hunger, warfare, and severe demoralization.

These consequences could not have been "achieved" without the superior weaponry of the Europeans and, after 1776, by the ex-colonized people of the US. Colonialism's crucial birthing elements were guns and ships that could go great distances and effectively carry cargoes of slaves and "spices." When he reached the Bahamas, Columbus thought he was in India (thus, ever after: "Indians"). He wrote in the ship's log that he was pleased to see that "They do not bear arms and do not know them; they have no iron and would make fine servants. With 50 men we could take them all and make them do whatever we want" (Zinn, 2000).

Neither the slavery initiated by Columbus in the Caribbean nor its exponential expansion in North America could have been born, let alone have become the early modern centuries' main element of trade, without enduring militarism. The same must be said for the theft of millions of acres of agricultural and mining lands and the thefts also of the dignity and humanity of the colonial lands' peoples. (See E. Williams, 1944.) In one manner or another, thus were the foundations established for what would become industrial capitalism: classic slavery for those stolen from their lands; "work slavery" for those in the UK whose lands were stolen in other ways to pave the way for the industrial revolution (see Chapter 2). Long ago, Marx succinctly underlined the vital role of colonialism in those and other achievements:

> The discovery of gold and silver in America, the extirpation, enslavement, and entombment in mines of the aboriginal population, the beginnings of the conquest and looting of the East Indies, the turning of Africa into a warren for the hunting of black-skins, signalized the rosy dawn of the era of capitalist production. (Marx, 1867)

Although such massive thievery has changed its clothing over time, it continues all over the globe. For centuries the colonized peoples have been robbed of their lands, their independence, their dignity, and their morale and have had to struggle endlessly to retain or regain the humanity stolen from them at the point of a gun, whether literally or by disguised alternatives.

By the mid eighteenth century, "the sun never set on the British flag" in either the military or the economic arenas: thus was laid the foundations for what became Britain's "industrial revolution."

Thus it was also that as the eighteenth century ended the stimuli for the other "civilized" nations to go and do likewise was compelling; and they did so, usually financed by Great Britain. That was dramatically so for both the US and Germany, both of whom would surpass the UK as the twentieth century opened (Veblen, 1915).

II: Imperialism, Capitalism, and the US

The Europeans and the Japanese imperialized globally because they had no alternative. The US would begin its global expansion as the nineteenth century ended, but began to enrich itself by just "expanding west" (and seeing itself as "an anti-colonial imperialist") (see W. Williams, and below). That takes us to an explanation of the differences between colonialism and imperialism, and their different historical contexts. The enabling difference in all cases was and is that of technology.

The industrial revolution took hold between the last years of the eighteenth century and the middle of the nineteenth. It meant an enormous increase in the productivity of all sectors of economic activity: in agriculture, industry, finance, trade, and at the center of all that, transportation. As both land and sea transportation were transformed by improvements in the steam engine, endlessly new needs and opportunities opened up; and colonialism steadily became imperialism. But:

> Imperialism required, as the colonialism of earlier centuries did not, a large measure of political control over the internal relations and structure of the colonial economy. This it requires not merely to "protect property" and to insure that the profit of the investment is not offset by political risks, but actually to *create* the essential conditions for the profitable investment of capital. Among those conditions is the existence of a working class sufficient to provide a plentiful and cheap labor supply, and where this does not exist, suitable modifications of pre-existent social forms will need to be enforced (of which the reduction of tribal land-reserves and the introduction of differential taxation on the natives living in the tribal reserve in East and South Africa are examples). Thus the political logic of imperialism is to graduate from "economic penetration" to "spheres of influence" to protectorates or indirect control, and from protectorates to military occupation; thence to annexation. (Dobb, 1937)

Each step of that evolution required an always deeper and stronger military. That has been altered in the present era as, year by year, place by place, direct political control by the armies of the imperialist powers has been replaced by the more indirect (and at least as harmful) controls achieved through international institutions such as the World Bank, WTO, and IMF and the almost universal corruption of the "independent governments" of the previously imperialized societies (see Chapter 6).

The people of what became the US have been "anti-colonial" idealists ever since being under British control; however, we have been against imperialism only when practiced by *others*; as, for example, when the US sought to remove a European power from an area it wished to control, whether nearby (Cuba), or thousands of miles away (the Philippines). Back in 1823, lest there be any misunderstanding, President Monroe issued his "Doctrine": "Be it understood: this hemisphere is *ours*: hands off!" (see Zinn, 2000). The US's geographic expansions in North America began while still a colony of the British; once a nation, they continued until the US extended from ocean to ocean: east to west, and south to north from the Gulf of Mexico to Canada.

It was done with little or no interruption, as it became the richest, most compact and (until the late twentieth century) the safest *empire* of all history (W. Williams, 1980). For the people of the US the word "empire" would seem not only wrong-headed but unpatriotic: "This land is *our* land."

Although that position has been convincing for all too many of us, it never was for the native tribes whose lands were stolen, who were forcibly brushed aside and/or robbed and slaughtered; those people whom we – but not they – have always called "Indians" and who (themselves and their descendants) became and remain deeply exploited and painfully unequal with their "civilizers" (Mander, 1978).

If the people of the US would wish to count the number of its interventionist activities from their beginnings in 1798 up to the outbreak of World War II, they may find it in W. Williams (1980). He provides an annotated list of 154 "undeclared wars" by the US, ranging from the Caribbean to North Africa, to the Mediterranean, to Central and South America, to China, Korea and Japan, and even to Soviet Russia, 1918–19, soon after its 1917 revolution (see LaFeber, 1976). All of those "undeclared wars" involved naval and/or infantry warfare and landing parties; some (especially in the Caribbean and Central America) were the first steps of what became a constant US presence, continuing with or without interruption to this day (if also with rising difficulties). The list of Williams ends at 1941; if continued from 1945 on it would be much longer (excluding *declared* wars): Undeclared were Angola, Cambodia, Chile, the Congo, Cuba, El

Salvador, Honduras, Nicaragua, Laos, Panama, and Vietnam. Our intervention there began in 1945, but we didn't "declare" war for another 20 years, and then with a blatant set of lies, asserting that we had been attacked by the North Vietnamese: with barely a belch from Congress (Young, 1991). All of the foregoing were acts of US imperialism, never acknowledged as such.

Only World War II may be seen as defensive for the US, unless one sees "the Cold War" as defensive; which it was not (as will be explained at length below). Up to here, the concern has been mostly with the nineteenth-century imperialist activities of the US. Meanwhile, the other capitalist nations were also seeking to establish or to expand their empires. For all concerned such activities depended upon sustained military force and the strengthening of militarism as a way of life. That was certainly provided, in one way or another. So what is "militarism"? For present purposes the term has two imperatives: A nation's economy must be structured and function to produce in substantial quantities what its military needs for attack and defense; its politicians *and* its people must be willing to support military costs in terms of taxes, possible shortages and dangers and, not least, to provide a substantial number who will volunteer or be forced to serve in the military forces and suffer the consequences. The US has been and remains more enduringly successful than any other nation in meeting both of those imperatives.

In its entire existence as a nation the US has suffered severely from only one of its many wars: the Civil War. Other than that, both economically and politically US wars have had positive consequences, and not only because other countries were greatly weakened as the US strengthened. There have been negative consequences of course, for those wounded or killed, for them and their families; but they have been relatively slight, whether as measured in terms of civilian or military casualties, when compared with those of others.

As the industrial revolution spread and strengthened, it had substantial consequences in the realms of foreign aggressions by the capitalist powers, most especially because of its accompanying strengthening of both transportation and weaponry. The main

European beneficiaries of early colonialism were Spain and Portugal. Both depended upon sailing ships, swords, and rifles. But as the nineteenth century moved toward its middle and end, these countries lost their ability to maintain control in far off territories. Their colonial rule was destructive and murderous to the natives, but what followed in the era of imperialism would carry those horrors to greater depths. Two examples are sufficient; one from the smallest of the imperialists (Belgium), the other from the largest (the US):

Belgium and the Congo

The Congo is not only the richest in resources in all of Africa, but one of the richest in the world, equal both in size and resources to the US east of the Mississippi. It was initially taken over in the late nineteenth century by Belgium's monstrous King Leopold II: for himself, not for Belgium. He did it with various lies and tricks, beginning with use of an organization posing as a beneficial institute. For many years his "institute" disguised enslavement and the selling of millions of Congolese, as the King gained easy access to the Congo's rich ivory, rubber, and mineral resources. The proceeds made him a billionaire of his day; but the process caused the death of at least *10 million* Congolese. His personal rule ended when Belgian's business community realized how much they were losing to him; their takeover enriched Belgian businessmen but the Congolese continued to be slaughtered. That history is carefully and fully documented in the fine book by Adam Hochschild, *King Leopold's Ghost* (1999); but also see the haunting novel of Joseph Conrad, *Heart of Darkness*.

The US and the Philippines

US involvement in this archipelago began at the close of the nineteenth century and ended only after World War II. The "Spanish-American" war had two locations: Cuba and the Philippines. As the Cubans fought for their independence, so did the Filipinos. Both came close to achieving it, but the US slammed the door shut on both. The story began in 1898, when Spain and the US signed a peace treaty. Imperialist brashness being what it is, Spain not only left Cuba, but also "officially" turned over to the US its control over Guam, Puerto Rico, and the Philippines (for $2 million); without consultation with the Filipinos. It is more than a little interesting to see some of what President McKinley (the Bush II of his day) had to say about Spain's offer to the US:

> The truth is I didn't want the Philippines, and when they came to us as a gift from the gods, I did not know what to do with them. I walked the floor of the White House night after night..., and I am not ashamed to tell you, gentlemen, that I went down on my knees and prayed Almighty God for light and guidance more than one night. And one night late it came to me this way: 1) That we could not give them back to Spain – that would be cowardly and dishonorable. 2) That we could not turn them over to France or Germany, our commercial rivals in the Orient; that would be bad business and discreditable. 3) That we could not leave them to themselves – they were unfit for self-government. 4) That there was nothing left for us to do but to take them all and to educate the Filipinos and uplift and civilize and Christianize them... And then I went to bed and went to sleep and slept soundly. (Quoted in Zinn, 2000)

Funny? The not so funny thing was that within one year Filipinos (like the Yankees in 1776) got the idea that they *were* fit for self-government. They held the US off for three years, suffering 300,000 dead; the US lost 70,000 with many more wounded, despite its greatly superior military strength. Those casualties were much multiplied by the two world wars, and by Korea, and Vietnam. Despite all, too few people of the US have ever learned to hate war enough. Instead, because of the economic lifts given to the US by World Wars I and II and the Cold War, all too many have come to see the militarization of the US economy and US domination of the world as having created jobs and (for some) as having saved the world from fates worse than death.

III: Militarism and the "Iron Triangle" of the US

It is the US habit to see ourselves not only as a peace-loving country but as *the* peace-loving country. Doubtless a meaningful percentage of us do in fact love peace. But, as noted earlier, our acts of enthusiastically supported warfare have had very little opposition from 1776 to the present. Worse, the long-standing militarism that resumed in Korea soon after World War II has not only increased but has done so within a socio-economic-political context that has made warfare "as American as apple pie." Why?

The answer to that has many elements to it, some touched upon earlier. For understanding the period after World War II to the present, it is essential to realize that since 1939–40, the US has had a militarized economy, in which a large percentage of industrial companies have been and increasingly are dependent for their profitability upon our huge military expenditures ("milex").

The milex companies are not alone: economists estimate that $1 of government spending adds $3 to overall spending and the national income. The tens of thousands of firms and hundreds of thousands of workers involved in military production know where their profits and wages come from. Add to them the innumerable other producers and retailers and workers whose incomes and jobs and purchases are indirectly involved, and the result is an ultimate threefold increase of that amount in the national income. Economists call that "the multiplier effect."

Consciously or not, a substantial percentage of businesses and workers support militarism for fear of a "subtraction effect" if the US were ever to "de-milex." But there has been little effort to show that the ways in which "milex" add to the national income would have at least the same "multiplier effect" on the national income from badly-needed governmental expenditures for decent education, health care, housing, and environmental protection: a lack of understanding which the emerging depression makes all the more harmful (and which is being acted upon by the Obama administration). Now some details, using the analytical framework of James Cypher's analyses of the "iron triangle" (Cypher, 2002a) and the earlier path-breaking book of C. Wright Mills, *The Power Elite* (1956).

The three members of the "power elite" and the "iron triangle" are closely-related. Mills designated his elite as "the corporate rich, the political directorate and the warlords." About half a century later, Cypher's "triangle" consisted of two governmental groups (civilian and military) and one private (the tens of thousands of business contractors who, only since 1946, have received the $12–14 *trillion* spent on "milex."

In those decades the world's many changes have caused differences between the "power elite" and the "three sides" to be blurred and to meld with global changes in all realms: economic, political, social and, especially, military. The result, especially in the US, has been to expand and strengthen the military realm and to "militarize" the society as a whole. The "Cold War" was sitting at the center of that dynamic. Its very name was an artful Orwellian device, given that in its first decades 6–10 million civilians and soldiers died in the very "hot" wars of Korea and Vietnam alone. So, before proceeding further, it is essential to examine the Cold War's duplicitous origins, nature, rationale, and effects. Although it lost some vigor after 1989 regarding both Russia and China, its militaristic spirit has been revived by "the war on terrorism" with renewed strength and heightened dangers, hand in hand with what has become worsening inequality over the globe.

Now an extended look at the related families of "Cold" and "Anti-Terrorist" wars, in their origins, rationales, and results. Why and when did the Cold War begin? What are the similarities and differences between it and the "war on terrorism"?

The Cold War

The popular belief, indeed the "official" position, is that it began in 1946, when Truman and Churchill stood side-by-side in Independence, Missouri, and Churchill, ignoring that the Soviet Union had been flattened both economically and militarily by World War II, declared that:

America stands at the pinnacle of world power... Opportunity is here and now... America should not ignore it or fritter it away..., for it faces a peril to Christian civilization... An iron curtain has descended across the European continent...from the Baltic to the Adriatic. (See Wittner, 1978; LaFeber, 1976)

However, if what is meant by "cold war" is the need to "face the peril to Christian civilization of the iron curtain," then for Churchill that threat was triggered in 1917 by the Russian revolution. With the smoke from World War I still in the air, both British and US troops were dispatched into the territory of what became the Soviet Union: US troops to Vladivostok on the Pacific, the British to the western borders of Russia. At least as important, the "Allies" supplied the White Army and the Cossacks with war's materiel in their prolonged fight against the Red Army; a war that began in 1918 and in many forms went on through the 1920s and into the 1930s; including everything from economic blockades to the secret support of Nazi Germany. (See Wittner, 1978; LaFeber, 1976.)

Less than a year after Churchill's 1946 prompting, Truman and his political allies in government and business began the selling of the "iron curtain" theme and stepped-up militarization. Here's a simple listing of the first steps in the US in the mid 1940s: The National Security Act created the National Military Establishment (its official name); the Departments of the Navy and the Army became the War Department and its US Air Force. And, Mr. Orwell, did you know that in 1947 what had been the War Department from 1800 until then was re-named the Department of *Defense*?

Add this: during World War II the Office of Special Services (OSS) did good work in gaining information behind the lines in both the European and Pacific wars: for example, on German economic and military capacities and the extent of bomb damages; and, in Southeast Asia, the assisting of behind-the-lines air-sea rescue efforts (with whom, in 1944–45, I worked as an air-sea rescuer in Vietnam). Then, in 1947 the OSS was converted into the CIA. It was more than a change in name.

It is customary to divide the world into several geographic regions: Africa, Asia, Europe, the Middle East, and the Americas (Central, North, and South). To one degree or another, since 1947 the CIA has operated in all of those regions (including not just Canada in North America, but also (illegally) in its own US. CIA operations have always been covert, ranging from illegitimate to criminal, from snooping to killing, from informative to misleading and counter-productive; and from Korea to the 1961 Cuban "Bay of Pigs" disaster to Vietnam to Chile to, most recently, Georgia, to...? (See Blum, 2004; Powers, 2002; Young, 1991.)

The position being taken here is not meant to overlook the crimes of the USSR to its own and other people (including many thousands of those who had made the revolution and were imprisoned or executed for their efforts to realize its aims); it is rather to argue that the Soviet Union was *never* a military threat to the US, but its revolution *was* of concern, for it served as one of many stimuli for anti-capitalist movements throughout Europe. Setting aside the "iron curtain" speech, the starting-point for the Cold War may be seen as the famous 1946 cable of George Kennan (then the US State Department man in Moscow). In that message (and subsequently), Kennan did indeed see the Soviet Union as a threat; but not as a military but a political threat whose basis was not the Soviet Union, but Western Europe's pre-war history (Kennan, 1998).

Why that threat? Because those who had presided over the pre-war Europe had either been fascists (Italy, Germany, Spain, the Vichy government of France, and the smaller Eastern European countries) or they had been tightly conservative. Their leaders and their political parties had tainted themselves too much to find popular support after 1945; in all of those countries, before 1939 there had been significant anti-capitalist (and anti-fascist) movements – many of whose supporters became the heroic muscle and brains of the military resistance to the fascists, the best-known of which were the *maquis* of France and the *partigiani* of Italy (Kennan, 1998).

The "left" movements were even more popular after the war; and understandably. Their rightwing and conservative opponents were at least as *un*popular. In short, Western Europe's anti-imperialism, anti-capitalism and anti-militarism constituted a serious problem not only for their own traditional "power elites" but for those of the US. The popularity of both the US and the USSR was high after the war, but with one huge difference, a difference never acknowledged by the US in the Cold War; namely,

US military strength was overwhelmingly the greatest of any country in history, both relatively and absolutely, and the Soviet Union's was at *its* weakest (LaFeber, 1976).

In sharp contrast, the US had incurred "only" 450,000 military and few or no civilian deaths, and its economy had risen to its and the world's greatest and strongest heights and there has never been a significant challenge to US capitalism. From the 1890s on, the business-dominated US "used any and all means" against the few reform/radical efforts to increase the power and improve working conditions (whether led by anarchist, socialist, communist groups or non-political unions); and their powers were used effectively until the late 1930s. Those powers came to include even the lynching of some radical union organizers by the conservative AFL, firing squads for at least one union organizer (Joe Hill), prison and/or expulsion from the US for suspected communist sympathizers during "Red Scares" from 1917 through the 1920s and 30s.

Taken together all of that paved the way for the "House Un-American Activities Committee" of the 1930s and fertilized the ground for the McCarthyism that became strong in the late 1940s, muscled up in the 1950s, and which, thinly disguised, continued through the Bush years. It was an all too successful "scare" program presumably focused on internal affairs; but from the 1950s on, it was in response for what was claimed as an *external* crisis. However, if there was any real threat (assuming that term was justified at all) it was the possibility that significant chunks of the ex-colonial world might break away from the world business system, to adopt some form of socialist economy. That possibility was transmuted by the governing class and its enthusiastic accomplices in the media into the "Soviet threat." (See Schiller, 1989.)

From its beginning, as noted above, the Soviet "threat" was put forth as military, not as political, but even its political element, despite what the Soviets might have wished, was never at all significant even in its political dimensions in the US. Much more could be said of the deep and persistent damages of the Cold War; up to here we have been concerned only with its beginnings, with little more than a glance at its "hot" consequences in Central Asia and the Middle East.

Although the US has never been a peaceful nation, neither has it been as persistently militaristic as it has been since 1945. A major element in helping to take it to that condition has been an all too cooperative media (see Chapter 5). One of the media's strongest "weapons" has been the always more effective use of "spin"; itself a "spin" of "euphemism." Now, as we contemplate the present, we are confronted by the murderous and potentially suicidal substitute for the Cold War: the "war on terrorism." (See Mayer, 2008.)

The US "war on terrorism" has many dimensions; most relevant for present purposes are its effects on inequality and its threats to the survival of democracy. The accepted view is that the Cold War "ended" in 1989–91, as the USSR faded away. It was in that same period that China sped up toward becoming what it is at present; a ruggedly nineteenth-century capitalist nation using modern technologies and ruled over by a ruthlessly anti-democratic Communist Party. Compared with China, US democracy is strong. However, as China changed somewhat for the better (prodded there by the 2008 Olympic Games) the US continued to worsen; interrupted and potentially reversed, it may be hoped, by Obama's presidency. The critical decisions for better or for worse in China's "Communist capitalism" are made by its "political elite"; such decisions for the US economy and politics have long been made by *its* "power elite."

Sitting at the hot center of that US elite is the "military-industrial complex." Ruled over by its most powerful industrial corporations, they are annually identified (if not by that name) in *Fortune Magazine*'s "500." One doesn't have to be a believer in "conspiracies" (I am not) to see that the emergence of "terrorists" was manna from heaven for many of that 500. Why? Neither least nor only, because of the economic costs of that new war plus Iraq and their associated profits for the "500." A summary examination of the recent monetary costs of war shows "why."

We start with few facts about the *trillions* of milex dollars spent before the war in Iraq (which officially began in 2003).

The "basic budget" for October 2002 to September 2003 was $437 billion (about the same as at the height of the Vietnam war). But that ignores important "add ons" such as foreign military sales, military space programs, veterans' benefits and retirement, foreign military aid, and interest on the national debt attributed to military spending (see Cypher, 1987, 1991, 2002a, 2002b). Adding all of that up, Cypher estimates the real military budget would rise by two-thirds in a given year: that is, not $437 billion but $700–900 billion (excluding the cost of covert CIA and other governmental units).

The total cost of official military expenditures from 1946 to *before* 2003 was about $12 *trillion*. Since then? Note the title of Nobel laureate Joseph Stiglitz's new book (which *excludes* the "add ons" of Cypher): *The Three Trillion Dollar War* (2008). Nor does Stiglitz include the payments to the 100,000 private contractors working in Iraq, some 50,000 of whom are the "private security" operatives of Blackwater US (now Blackwater Worldwide), assigned to protect US diplomats (but presently on trial for killing at least eight Iraqis, including an infant). They (and all US military) are granted immunity from prosecution under US/Iraq law. Some were involved in the abuse of prisoners at the infamous Abu Ghraib prison. (See "Subcontracting the War," *International Herald Tribune* editorial, October 2, 2007.)

Having sidled into the Iraq war in the previous sentences, it is appropriate to bear down and focus on the ongoing wars of the US in Iraq and Afghanistan, with the all too strong possibility of a war with Iran. In one way or another, all of those are put forth as part of the "war on terrorism," along with suggestions of "democratization." Those wars are complex in nature and origin; none have occurred (or will) because of the stated grounds put forth by the US. If only for that reason, they require a serious look, neither least or most because of their role as rationalizations for the "hyped-up" militarism of the US and the vital role of *oil* reserves. The ongoing or potential wars to be discussed are, first, Iraq, then Iran, and lastly Afghanistan. But first an introductory note on the rocketing costs of militarism.

The current *reported* costs (as distinct from real costs) of militarism were given useful attention in the *International Herald Tribune* on November 17, 2008: "The Pentagon's budget, including spending on the wars in Iraq and Afghanistan, reached $685 billion, an increase of 85% in real dollars since 2000 and equal to the rest of rest of the world's defense budgets combined; the highest level since World War II." That spending is part of what Phillips (2008) calls "the politics of evasion" by which the US government functions, with both political parties dependent upon campaign money from "special interests."

Militarism and the "War on Terrorism"

The Middle East is high on the always lengthening list of the regions now seen as wracked by terrorism; but "terrorism" didn't start there, let alone with "9/11." (See Barber, 1996; Everest, 2004; Klare, 2001.) Its usage began in the period of the French and American revolutions, and whose participants were called terrorists by those in power: terrorism, like beauty, "is in the eyes of the beholder, " or, for today, "one man's terrorist is another man's freedom fighter."

Doubtless the term was used at other times and places, but it was *the* term used again in the twentieth century by the British against the Irish who sought to regain the independence stolen from them in the seventeenth century; used again by the British in the 1940s as their rule over Palestine was being challenged by the post-Holocaust Jewish "Irgun" who sought a reborn Israel by any means necessary. Nor is it amusing to note that a word used by the British against both US revolutionaries in the eighteenth century and against militant Jews in the 1940s is now used by the Israelis against the Palestinians and their allies. Now the US uses it against Muslims. And it works.

In short, whether in past or present, there have been "terrorists." Some have deserved admiration, others the opposite. That the terrorists who blew up the Twin Towers killed indiscriminately should not mean that anything the US now does (or has done, as in Korea, Vietnam, Japan, Iraq, and Afghanistan) in the name of freedom and democracy was/is/or ever should be acceptable.

Nor does it have anything to do with "freedom and democracy"; nor can one believe that Cheney and Bush ever gave a hoot about either freedom or democracy. Still, the Bush administration cleverly chose to portray the 9/11 attackers as "hating America" and all the fine things "for which we stand." Hate us the "terrorists" surely do; but their focus is neither upon our freedom nor our democracy, it is upon the past and present harms done to their societies by imperialists. There is little understanding in the US of why there is so much resentment against us, little comprehension that the ways and means we and others have used over the globe which *we* see as emblems of our superiority, *they* rightly see as having demolished their cultures, their economies, *their* lives. Nor do the US and other "Christian nations" acknowledge that we all consciously used "terrorist tactics" against each other during World War II, with considerably more devastation in mind and in consequence than al Qaeda could even consider:

Item: The Nazis were quite consciously "terrorizing" when they bombed England; so were we and the British when we set fire to Dresden and Leipzig; as we did against Japan with our prize-winning terrorist act of burning Hiroshima and Nagasaki "to the ground" – despite that we had already won the war and Japan was seeking a peace treaty. If we were seeking to "terrorize" anyone with those "nukes" it was our World War II ally the Soviet Union. (See Wittner, 1978.)

None of that makes it easier to accept the tragedy of 9/11 or the loss of thousands of lives and the sadness and difficulties of their families. Still, those losses were tiny in comparison with the terrorist actions of the US in, say, North Korea while destroying its main city. (See Cumings and Halliday, 1988.) 9/11 was the first time the US had suffered death and destruction from abroad, except for the attack on Pearl Harbor (Hawaii was then a US colony). However, what followed the bombing of Pearl Harbor was very different in detail from 9/11, except in one vital respect: both bombings allowed the existing White House to enact otherwise politically impossible domestic and foreign policies. On the other hand, post-Pearl Harbor policies were either cancelled or much moderated after World War II. The cancellation or even the moderation of post-9/11 policies would also require a clear "victory" over today's "terrorism"; a "victory" that is out of the question because neither side *can* win. Why not?

Answer: Because each seemingly successful action by either the "terrorists" or those against them increases both the anger and the numbers of the designated enemies and heightens animosities, while providing bases for intensifying and increasing both "terrorist" and "*anti*-terrorist" efforts. To say that the militarized government of the US does not want to win means that it wants the war to continue, not to lose it. That argument will be extended and supported below and will refer not just to the Bush White House, but, all too possibly, to those likely to follow: It is hopefully conceivable that the Obama presidency will at least seek otherwise; although Obama's program includes that US troops leaving Iraq should be used to *increase* US troops in Afghanistan – where, it should be understood, outsiders have lost wars for centuries.

In all probability the powers of the past in the Middle East and Central Asia saw their countries (and their bank accounts) as having been blessed from above by the emerging importance of *oil* as the twentieth century unrolled. If our species manages to go through the twenty-first century without another world war – and we won't last the century if we don't – perhaps that might be seen as an appropriate position; if, that is, one ignores the wars and imperialist devastations associated with that oily "blessing." Going back no further than the medieval era, that entire region has suffered continuous attempts on the part of "westerners" to control them: initially for their importance as trade routes, then as military outposts, now *oil!*, the worst "blessing" in all of history given the many wars over its extraction and its impact on the environment.

As noted earlier, Iraq entered the gates of hell already as World War I was being born; as did Iran and Afghanistan, if with somewhat different reasons and enemies (see below). Now, that entire region has become subject to the struggles between the major post-World War II powers; notably over oil, of course, but that also ties in with strategic military positions: and let the "natives" be damned, as indeed they have been in Iraq, Afghanistan, and Iran (the short list). (See Blum, 2004; Barber, 1996; Everest, 2004; Klare, 2001 and Bacevich, 2008 as bases for above and what follows.)

It is not possible in a work such as this to provide an adequate history of these ongoing tragedies. However the insanity of what will now be noted as regards the US may be seen as a useful starting-point for what has already become a disaster. It occurred in 1979.

It was then that President Carter's National Security Advisor (Zbigniew Brzezinski) persuaded him to sign the first of several directives to have the CIA provide weaponry to those who became and *remain* the Taliban. Having been declared as defeated many times in recent years, the Taliban is now clearly defeating the US (and its allies) in Afghanistan. How do we know that the 1979 tale is true? Because "Zbig" (as he likes to be known) told us so in a boastful interview with the French *Nouvel Observateur* on January 15, 1998. This is what he said:

> Our stated intention in arming the Taliban in July 1979 was to draw the Russians into the Afghan trap. We didn't push them to intervene, but we knowingly increased the probability that they would.

He had that right: three months later the Soviet Army entered Afghanistan, guns firing. On that day, Zbig wrote to President Carter: "Now we give the USSR *its* Vietnam war." He had that right also. And three years later the USSR exited in defeat. However, US assistance very much increased the military strength of the previously weak Taliban, and what had been the main force resisting the USSR is now the main force defeating the US (despite ongoing claims by the US that it has been knocked out). To which this needs adding: the Taliban's main support now is its control over rapidly increasing opium production by poor farmers. Congratulations Uncle Sam! Question: Has Afghanistan become the US's *second* Vietnam? Thanks, Zbig. Beware, Obama.

Now we jump back to the US involvements in Iraq and Iran, thence back to Afghanistan. It will get the most sustained treatment because it also threatens to become the longest and worst of those wars; unless, that is, we also blunder our way into a war with Iran (see below).

The US and Iraq
Critics of the Cold War have said that if Stalin had not existed the US would have invented him. The same can be said for Saddam Hussein. There were similarities between the two leaders: both were monsters who wrought much harm upon their own people; both were seen as military threats. But there were also differences: Stalin's USSR was viewed as a threat to Europe and, in one way or another to the US; Saddam's Iraq was represented as a key element of al Qaeda terrorism and the possessor of "weapons of mass destruction." Question: If horrendous dictatorship was truly a concern of the US, what then of its 30-year support for Mobutu in the Congo, of Syngman Rhee in South Korea, of Pinochet in Chile, of Batista in Cuba, et al.?

As the Iraq war continued and worsened after 2003, it also became clear that Iraq did *not* have those "weapons," and that Osama Bin Laden's terrorist network did *not* function in Iraq. Yet the war continued and deepened, with many thousands of US soldiers dead and many, many more wounded and lives ruined. Multiply that by a factor of ten-plus for the Iraqis:

Item: At least 2 *million* have left Iraq in order to survive; the tens of millions who did not leave continue to suffer, their lives ruined.

We are told that the US will leave Iraq – sort of – in a year or so. Don't bet on it, unless you redefine the word "leave." The US will never exit fully, unless by force. There is too much to be lost: *oil*, strategic location, national pride...and? The catastrophe of Iraq will never end for its people. Its full nature has only been touched upon here, and it will be left at that (but see Everest, 2004 and Blix, 2004). Now we move on to Iran, also briefly, and thence to the steadily increasing horrors of Afghanistan.

The US and Iran

For Iran, World War I was a bloody interval between what preceded and what would follow. Soon after the war (1925) Colonel Reza Khan pulled off a coup and installed himself as "Shah." As with Iraq, Iran's catastrophe may never end. It was in 1925 that once fabulous Persia became Colonel Khan's Iran. In the 1930s the Shah was a fan of Hitler (Iran translates as "Aryan"). Interestingly, in the fall of 1941 (World War II in its third year for Europe) there was a joint Anglo-Soviet(!) invasion of Iran (re: oil and location, of course), which endured until 1946. Also in 1941, the Shah had dubbed his son "Mohammed Shah-in shah." Like his father, he proceeded to rule as an autocrat; until, under strong pressure in 1951, a free election was permitted. It was won by Mohammed Mossadegh. His aims were the overthrow of the Shah and the nationalization of Iran's oil resources.

However, by then the US had become pre-eminent, and in 1953 the CIA began its plotting to have Mossadegh arrested and jailed, after which the young Shah took over once more. (A process repeated with variations by the CIA in the Congo ten years later, when Lumumba was elected and murdered, with the CIA assisting.) (See Kornbuhl and Byrne, 1992; Kinzer and Schlesinger, 2003; Hochschild, 1999.)

But the tragic-comedy of US and Iran was not to end there: it would stretch out to bring Central America into the dirty game in the "Iran–Contra" trick and treat. The illegal "Contras" were seeking to overthrow the democratically elected new government which had recently replaced the Nicaraguan dictatorship. *Before* the 1980 US election of Reagan (vs. Carter) Reagan's people secretly made a guns deal with – of all people! – our "enemy" Iran, from which the US would secretly buy weapons while Iran and US ally Iraq were warring and Iran would free the US hostages it had taken during an earlier attempt by the US to do so. Complicated

– and dirty – world, no? (See Pitt and Ritter, 2002.) The deal was that the US hostages would be released *after* the 1980 election (which Carter would lose in part because of his failure to deal successfully with the Iran problem). Afterwards, not so amusingly, this is what the new President, Reagan, said: "I told the American people I did *not* trade arms for hostages. My heart and my best intention still tell me that is true, but the *facts* and the evidence, tell me it is not." Naturally he got away with that and much else, as his popularity broke all records. God Bless America. (See Wills, 1988.)

Unfortunately, although the relationship between the US and Iran has been worrisome enough in itself, it is made worse by our long-supportive relationship with Israel and Israel's hostile relationship with Iran; a hostility which has been made fiery by Israel's earlier attacks on Iran from the air, and its well-known wish to increase them – while, in recent years, anti-Israel sentiment in Iran has mounted (most notably from its present government). Not much more can be said here about that deepening anger except this: If a war between Israel and Iran, and/or a war between the US and Iran is to be avoided, it is absolutely essential that there be a reversal of recent policies. The US *must* convince Iran and Israel – and itself – that concessions are to be made from all concerned that assure all three nations: (1) that military actions will be shelved for an indefinite but substantial future; (2) that whatever the many controversies between the three parties they can and *must* be resolved, because (3) if the blustering on all sides is allowed to move toward and into war, all three parties concerned have already or will soon have nuclear weapons which they will be tempted to use. Which, not so incidentally, could well mean World War III, as other nations with such weapons (Pakistan, India, Russia, et al.) are unlikely to sit back and relax. In short, the time has come for all concerned to grow up (and that includes their peoples and ours). Now we turn to Afghanistan, an all too worrisome situation which reveals just how suicidal the major powers have become, led by the Soviet Union and the US. Obama is seemingly aware that US politics of recent decades have increased rather than lowered the danger of heightened warfare. Whether or not he will take moves to lessen conflicts can only be guessed at now; but his increase of US forces in Afghanistan does not bode well (of which more below).

The US and Afghanistan

Earlier, the folly of both the US and the Soviet Union has been discussed. Unfortunately, that folly not only continues but threatens to worsen. I am not an expert on Afghanistan, nor would be (as the saying goes). But I do read some of those who are. The two writers whom I will depend upon mostly in what follows *are* experts. Proof of their expertise may be found in a recent article in *The New York Review of Books* (February 12, 2009): "Pakistan in Peril," by one of them, William Dalrymple, in his review of the fine book by the other, Ahmed Rashid, *Descent Into Chaos: The United States and the Failure of Nation Building in Pakistan, Afghanistan, and Central Asia*. Taken together, those works are sufficient to show why the "war on terrorism" has backfired, and why the US should find its way out of Afghanistan as soon as possible. If and when we were to do that, *of course* there would be unwelcome problems of one sort or another; but if we don't we are tempting a major disaster.

As we begin here, it might be useful to refer back to the earlier discussion of "Zbig" and his foolhardy attempt to trick the USSR into harming itself. It is worth noting again here, that our arming of the (then weak) Taliban has had terrible consequences, both as providing an incentive for the Taliban successfully to sponsor the substantial enlargement of opium growing and trading (with much popular support from the otherwise very poor opium "farmers") and, in doing so, to add to the bases for "terrorism." President Obama evidently understands that the US (and allied) forces face defeat without an increase of "western" forces. Rashid and Dalrymple make clear that what will instead be "increased" will be the probability of an endless and always widening war, which *cannot* be won. Now, I hope not too awkwardly, I move toward dependence upon a few selections from Rashid's book and Dalrymple's review, beginning with a quote from the latter, writing from Lahore, Pakistan in early 2009:

> The situation here could hardly be more grim. The Talban have reorganized, advanced out of their borderland safe havens, and are now massing at the gates of Kabul, threatening to surround and throttle the capital, much as the US-backed Mujahideen once did to the Soviet-installed regime in the late Eighties... The Taliban already control over 70 percent of the country, up from just over 50 percent in November 2007. But they do succeed to some extent in containing the wave of crime and corruption that marked the previous [US supported] rule. This has become one of the principal reasons for their growing popularity and every month their sphere of influence increases.

Dalrymple goes on to note the problems, even the horrors, the Taliban have brought to the areas they now control, including strictures on women and education, and he also describes the increasing victories of the Taliban over various regions (including the vital Khyber Pass). That takes him, and us, to a prolonged quotation from Rashid's book, as Dalrymple points out how Rashid emphasizes "the degree to which, even since September 11, the US-led war on terrorism has left in its wake a far more unstable world than existed on that momentous day in 2001." Now, Rashid:

> Rather than diminishing, the threat from al Qaeda and its affiliates has grown, engulfing new regions of Africa, Asia, and Europe and creating fear among peoples from Australia to Zanzibar. The US invasions of two Muslim countries...[have] so far failed to contain either the original organization or the threat that now comes from its copycats...in British or French cities who have been mobilized through the Internet. The al Qaeda leader is sill at large despite the largest manhunt in history. Afghanistan is once again staring down the abyss of state collapse despite billions of dollars in aid, forty-five thousand Western troops. and the deaths of thousands of people. The Taliban have made a dramatic comeback. The international community had...several years of opportunity to help the Afghan people; they failed to take advantage of it. Pakistan has undergone a slower but equally bloody meltdown... In 2008 American power lies shattered... US credibility lies

in ruins. Ultimately the strategies of the Bush administration created a far bigger crisis in South and Central Asia than existed before 9/11.

And, Rashid importantly goes on to say:

> Serious analysis was swept under the carpet, making impossible any serious discussion or understanding of the "root causes" of terrorism: the growing poverty, repression and sense of injustice that many Muslims felt at the hands of their US-backed governments, which in turn boosted anti-Americanism and Islamic extremism... Bush did more to keep Americans blind to world affairs than any American leader in recent history.

The 9/11 attacks permitted the Bush administration to enact a set of domestic and foreign policies which, *before* 9/11, would have been out of the question but which gave the US government an effectively free hand to do what it will – torture included – both at home and abroad, both militarily and politically. To reverse those dangerous realities will be difficult indeed, and will require a determined, substantial, and enduring popular movement seeking a society in which peace and decency are taken seriously. It is plausible that Obama would be very much supportive of a substantial change in that direction, but only if he has clearly substantial support from the US public. That in turn requires that an always increasing percentage of our people understand the ways in which we have allowed ourselves to accept self-destructive policies that have nothing to do with either peace or decency, policies created and installed by and for an anti-democratic and militaristic minority.

That harsh assertion is fully and powerfully enunciated in a recent article, "There is No 'War on Terror,'" by Edward S. Herman and David Peterson. What follows is a deservedly long quotation summarizing their astute and frightening analysis of the deepening militarization of the US:

> The war on terror is a political gambit and myth used to cover over a US projection of power that needed rhetorical help with the disappearance of the Soviet Union and the Cold War. It has been successful because US leaders could hide behind the very real 9/11 terrorist attack and pretend that [our] own wars, wholesale terrorist actions, and enlarged support of

a string of countries (many authoritarian and engaged in state terrorism) were somehow linked to that attack and its Al Qaeda authors. But most US military actions abroad since 9/11 have had little or no connection with al Qaeda: and you cannot war on a method of struggle, especially when you, your allies and clients use those methods as well... al Qaeda was never the target of the Bush Administration; if it had been, the Administration would have tried much more seriously to apprehend bin Laden, and it would not have carried out policies in Iraq, Palestine, Pakistan, Iran that have played so well into bin Laden's hand... If Washington really had been worried at the post-911 terrorist threat it would have followed through on the 9/11 Commission's recommendations for guarding US territory (ports, chemical plants, nuclear facilities, airports and other transportation hubs, and the like). The fact that it hasn't done this, but instead has adopted a cynical and politicized system of terrorism alerts, is testimony to the administration's own private understanding of the contrived character of the war on terror and its alleged threats. Admittedly, the surge in power projection that 9/11 and the war on terror facilitated has not been a complete success. But the "war on terror" gambit did enable this surge to come about, and it should be recognized that the invasion-occupation of Iraq was not a diversion; its conquest was one of the intended objectives of this war.

That conquest may be in jeopardy, but looked at from the standpoint of its organizers, the war has achieved some of the real goals for which it was designed...; and has been a success: It has facilitated two US military invasions of foreign countries, served to line-up many other states behind us, helped to push NATO into new, out-of-area operations, permitted a further advance in the US disregard of international law, helped bring about quasi-regime changes in some major European capitals., and was the basis for the huge growth in US and foreign military budgets. While its destabilization of the Middle East has possibly benefited Iran, it has given Israel a free hand in accelerated ethnic cleansing, settlements and more ruthless treatment of the Palestinians, and the United States and Israel continue to threaten and isolate Iran. Furthermore, with the cooperation of the Democrats and mass media, the "war on terror" gave the "decider" and his clique the political ability to impose an unconstitutional rightwing agenda at home, at the expense of he rule of law, economic equality, environmental and other regulation, and social solidarity... [All this and

more] suggest that the shift to the right and to a more militarized society
and expansionist foreign policy may have become permanent features of
life in the United States. (Herman and Peterson, 2008)

It's Wake-up Time

It has been easy for us to blame it all on "W." I yield to none
in my contempt for him, but Bush was just one rotten apple on
the long-standing tree of militarism that has been a key part
of the people of our lucky country from its beginnings. Note,
for example, that *since* 1945 *all* US presidents and legislatures
have put us into and/or acquiesced in both open and concealed
militarist activities; all have had a hand in rubber stamping the
double-digit *trillions* of milex to "support" our huge armed forces
and send them to all quarters of the globe: all of that with slight
resistance in Congress and a much disdained and sadly weak
antiwar movement from the public.

There is an old saying to the effect that "those who ignore the
past are condemned to repeat it." If that "ignoring" were a game,
"we the people" of the US would win, for it fits us all too well,
even if "the past" refers only to the years since 1979 noted above.
So Zbigniew Brzezinski gave the Soviet Union "their Vietnam."
Now, wars in Iraq and Afghanistan go on and on and on, and
what once was "our Taliban ally vs. the USSR" defeats us time
and again in Afghanistan.

Recently it has seemed that *perhaps* "Zbig" may have learned
something from his cruel games of 1979 and thereafter. He wrote
an article in the *Washington Post* (March 25, 2007), "How
a Three-Word Mantra Has Undermined America." The three
words are the "war on terror," which, he adds, "have created a
culture of terror... which could now be used for preparing the
case for war with Iran." Slow to learn that, Zbig, but better
late than never.

Will Obama reverse that tragic course? He certainly has the
intelligence and decency to do so. But the Congress and all too
many of us have fallen asleep at the wheel, have been discouraged
by decades of corruption and cruelty, hardened to war by its

seeming permanence, softened by a false affluence and numbed and deflected by consumerism. Obama needs a great lot of support from millions of us to be able to dig the US up and out of the dangerous sewer we have let it become. If Obama is to help the US to climb up out of that sewer we must help him to persuade an almost entirely corrupted Congress that they must join the clean-up or find another job. Time is running out.

9

INEQUALITY'S CONSEQUENCES FOR ITS VICTIMS AND ITS VICTIMIZERS

I: Poverty and Health Care

Poverty

Whatever the many and dire harms of inequality, they are *all* suffered most severely by those in poverty. How many people live in poverty in the US? In the other well-off countries? In the poor countries? Why? What are poverty's consequences for the poor; and for society? Could poverty be reduced or eliminated in the US and elsewhere?

Compared with other rich countries, merely the ways in which the US government *defines* poverty has made it easier to give it short shrift. So, I begin with some definitions:

- *Relative* poverty exists within a particular society when, for example, those in the bottom third of the society's income distribution are likely to "feel" poor, even if they are living better than their grandparents and parents, but whose purchasing power is inadequate to meet the ongoing living standards of their nation; and even the middle-income people in a poor *society* (e.g. Bolivia) are likely to feel "poor" if and when they compare their lives with their counterparts in a rich society.
- *Absolute* poverty exists when people's health and life-spans are reduced by their inaccessibility to adequate nutrition, shelter, and health care; usually because they are also unable

to access the education and job-training that might lift them and their children out of poverty.

(More on these two types of poverty can be found in Sen, 1981.)

Research shows that "mortality rates are more closely linked to relative rather than to absolute income, with rising inequality meaning higher mortality." That could be explained by the probability that societies with higher inequality are likely to have lesser degrees of solidarity and, therefore, poorer health care (OECD, 2008; Osberg, 1991).

How many Americans are poor? In examining the two types of poverty as they exist in the US it will be seen that there is an urgent need to correct how the government *defines* absolute poverty. Despite our grinding and widespread poverty before the 1960s, we did not even have a definition of poverty until then, although subsequent research shows that at least *half* of the US were living in poverty in the "prosperity decade" of the 1920s, and many more so during the 1930s depression when, for the first time, breadlines and soup kitchens, etc. were created to assist the poor (Miller, 1971).

The 1960s turned out to be the longest and strongest period of sustained economic expansion in US history. It was also the decade of the Vietnam war when, in 1963, John F. Kennedy was assassinated, and when Lyndon B. Johnson took over. LBJ was a master of political dealing, for better and for worse. As his administration began in 1964, his better side took hold (if only to keep the worst of the Vietnam war in the background). LBJ hoped to put the US on the path toward becoming what he called "the Great Society."

In 1962, a startling book by Michael Harrington had become popular: *The Other America*. Until then, the "America" the US had been congratulating itself on was J.K. Galbraith's sardonic *Affluent Society* (1958). Both books showed that there were many millions of families and individuals who were poor and struggling in this, the richest society in history. For LBJ, what with JFK's assassination and the beginnings of protests against Vietnam and the draft, such books came to be a loud belch in church: so he declared his "war on poverty." But what was meant by "poverty" and how many "poor" were there? As you now read the official answers you may not know whether to laugh or throw up. LBJ ordered his Council of Economic Advisors to give him a "definition of poverty." After a long scramble, they did; and what a definition! Since it is still the official definition of poverty in the US, let's take a good look.

It was based upon a study by the Social Security Administration of the income needed to support a non-farm family of four. It established two standards for such a family, both based on estimates of dietary costs prepared by the Department of Agriculture:

(1) a "low-cost" budget, permitting the minimum diet consistent with the food preferences of the lowest third of the population and adequate to avoid basic nutritional deficiencies... The resulting budget stood at $3,995. But that called for a higher budget than welfare agencies were allowing for families receiving public assistance. To meet the administrative need of those bodies, the SSA prepared...

(2) ...an "economy budget" based on a deficiency diet designed for temporary or emergency use, setting the total budget at $3,165. On the basis of this figure, the Council adopted $3,000 as its family poverty line, and $1,500 for a single individual. It thus found some 35,000,000 people, a *fifth* of the nation, to [have been] in poverty in 1962. (Wilcox, 1969)

It is bad enough that both the $3,995 and the $3,165 were "rounded down." More important were two other matters, combining the absurd with the incorrect:

- "the emergency use diet" was itself put together by the Office of Civil Defense for a *post-nuclear attack* period
- the cost of the diet established ($1,000/year) assumed that food constituted one-third of a family's expenses; so multiply by three, and there you've got it.

That formula, altered in keeping with inflation over time, remains the US definition of poverty – even though the "post-nuclear attack" diet was ludicrous to begin with and has become even more so over time. Since 1962 the structure of household expenses has altered drastically: it is widely agreed that most poor families now pay at least *half* of their income for rent (Ehrenreich, 2001).

That's not all. Jared Bernstein (senior economist with the US Economic Policy Institute) pointed out that their formula "neglected rising costs of housing, health care and transportation for poor families, ignored important costs to low-income families, such as those many women with young children working and needing child care; that alone lifts the poverty rate to include nine million more families" ("Who's Poor? Don't Ask," *NYT*, September 26, 2003).

But are not other rich countries just as heartless as the US? Not quite. In Western Europe, for example, a family is defined as poor if its income is less than half of the median income. So, if half the population receives above $50,000 annual income and half below, then those with less than $25,000 are in poverty. By those measures the US poverty rate is *doubled*, as is the unemployment rate. (See OECD, 2008; Osberg, 1991; and Chapter 12.) Thus, of 19 European countries (plus Canada):

> The USA, with 16.9% of its total population living in poverty, has the highest level of overall poverty…; poverty is also more enduring in the USA [and] it has the highest rate of child poverty (22.3%). (Mishel et al., 2002–03)

Those who wish to know about and understand all of the dimensions of the distribution of income in the US will find the references in UNICEF (1996) and Ryan (1976) very useful. Now some more ugly figures from Mishel et al.: almost 14 percent of all US households live in poverty; about 25 percent of jobs provide incomes below the (understated) poverty line; 18 percent of all children live in poverty; 16 percent have no health insurance (see next section); over a third of all US non-marital births were from mothers in poverty.

There are over 190 countries in the world. UNICEF reported that as the last century ended most of the people in most of those countries were poor, a horribly high percentage of them *absolutely* poor, and that 15–20 million *children* die every year from malnutrition and live with a billion or so adults who are on the edge of starvation. And it gets worse every year. The cheerleaders for globalization like to say that "a rising tide lifts all boats." Most people in the imperialized world do not *have* "a boat"; many who had a little something saw it swept away by the tides that enriched the giant companies (see Chapter 6). Here is the effect of the great expansions into the "developing countries" facilitated by US after the 1960s:

> The gap in per capita income between the industrial and developing worlds tripled from 1960 to 1993...; by 1999, the wealth of the world's 475 *billionaires* was greater than the combined incomes of the poorest *half* of humanity (= 3 *billion* people). (Anderson et al., 2000)

But, surely, as that gap widened the bottom level was rising? Surely, but although the poor may have been relatively less poor, were they *absolutely* better off? Ask the people at work in the Mexican *maquiladoras* who make around $2 a *day*; or those making $1 a day in China and India. For that matter, ask people in Silicon Valley, with its hordes of minimum wage workers in the highest high tech companies of all.

Question: Given that agricultural and industrial productivity have increased at rates much higher than population growth in the past two centuries or so, why are so many more people living very badly, in both absolute and relative terms? Why so much poverty in the midst of so much prodigious plenty? There is no simple answer, but here's part of a larger one: The ideology we live by has "taught us" to think about the social process in ways that confuse and obfuscate rather than enlighten. Veblen called it "a trained incapacity" (1919). That "ideology" is hard to pin down, but it centers upon what we have come to mean by "individualism." A lovely word; one couldn't live decently without it (at least yours truly couldn't). But it has evolved from pointing to the high value placed on individuals' freedom and opportunity to refer almost entirely to what we have and can get. "Individualism" has become a euphemism for selfishness, a trait essential to the "healthy" functioning of capitalism. If you study hard enough, and work hard enough, *you* have the "right stuff"; "greed is good," good for you directly and thus indirectly for all.

Live an "individualistic life," so defined, and you'll "make it." If you don't make it, that logic informs us, it's because you don't have the right stuff. QED.

Given such reasoning, it is but a short step to "blaming the victim"; to discriminate against others because of their color, gender, or...something. We have an ingrained, well-socialized tendency to view the very rich as having "earned" and "deserved" their wealth and to blame the poor for being that way (Ryan, 1976). And after all, haven't some very rich people in fact risen from poverty? Sure, but even more striking is the continuation over many generations of maintained and usually increasing wealth along with less than average ability or any effort. Think of George W. Bush. (See Phillips, 2002.)

The Consequences of Poverty

Those in the top one-third of US incomes are more likely than not to have gained an understanding of what it means to be poor from the stereotypes provided by the media. Mostly, though not always, the picture given of poverty combines laziness with violence with crime with dissolute behavior in one mix or another; pretty much what we think of when we hear the word "homeless." Some of that may be accurate up to a point; but it is far distant from an adequate explanation, which itself has much to explain. (See Ryan, 1976.)

However: Almost all of those who are poor also have jobs; by official definition; but even by the understated official definition of poverty, their income is less than half of "a living wage" and is getting worse as I write in 2009. (See below.) Almost all who are poor work much harder than you and I do, under social and physical conditions that are usually more tiring physically and emotionally than most of us ever had to endure. Plato put it well when in ancient times (in his *Republic*) he argued that those with good jobs should receive the lowest incomes so long as they can be comfortable, and those with lousy (my word, not his) jobs should be compensated with the highest incomes. The reality is the opposite, of course.

Low wages for hard work are bad enough; being pushed around, treated like dirt, without security, without comfort, without... almost everything, makes life really difficult. Trying to support and enhance a family life can be a nightmare for worker and family; not least for the children as they undergo their disgraceful treatment in, usually, a lousy school, with predictable effects on morale and, among other matters, health. Just one example: "Research in the 1990s demonstrated how the paint and pipes of slum housing – major sources of lead – damage the developing brains of children...; a 1990 study published in the New England Journal of Medicine showed that youngsters with elevated lead levels have lower IQ's and attention deficits..." (David K. Shipler, "Total Poverty Awareness," *NYT*, February 24, 2004).

If one lived in a decent society, where those who are poor are treated as essentially unlucky human beings, it would be bad enough; however, to be poor in the US is to have insult heaped upon injury; to be treated despicably even, perhaps especially by people who themselves are not far from poverty; to have remaining elements of dignity shredded; it is to see yourself portrayed in the media, by politicians, even by teachers, as semi-human, as dregs. (For several fine studies, see Terkel, 1974; Gans, 1995; Piven and Cloward, 1971; Finnegan, 1998; Sen, 1981; Ehrenreich, 2001.)

The consequences for individuals and their families and the ways in which they are treated by society cannot help but have serious deleterious effects for the society as a whole: for example, by how crime is defined and how criminals are treated; by the corruption not only of government and business but of the people as a whole in terms of the withering away of decency; the disintegration of social consciousness; and the growth of fear, hate, envy, and violence. (See the books noted above for details.)

Is There No Way Out?

Of course there is, both in the US and abroad; but in the US, except for a brief period, we have not even sought one. Better ways of treating poverty require a major change in the ways the poor are viewed. The "American way" has almost always been to resent, scorn, even to hate the poor, as regards their homelessness, their hunger, lack of health care, poor education, welfare support, and anything else linked to an inadequate (or no) income; no matter what the reason – even when the reason is having been wounded (physically and/or mentally) in war, as is true for at least a third of the homeless veterans of our many wars: disgracefully, they are punished twice when once would be one too many.

The US welfare system functions with common attitudes and behavior. In confronting its agencies, the needy are almost always met with attitudes of suspicion, hostility, contempt, disdain, and/ or fear. *Of course* some of those in need are dirty, and/or lazy, and/or addicts, and/or something else unattractive. However: seldom, if ever, are they given the benefit of the doubt, where the "doubt" would refer to their being victims of parental abuse, of untreated disabilities, of terrible housing and educational conditions, of war-induced physical and/or psychological injuries, and/or having worked full-time but at wages that do not permit anything approximating a living wage (see below).

Clinton and his Congress in the 1990s prided themselves on having resolved this set of problems with their "workfare instead of welfare" programs and "earned income tax rebates." The traditional welfare program was sharply inadequate and, usually, rife with insulting treatment; but the "welfare reforms" of the 1990s took bad to worse. Suffice it to say here that in the "new economy" of the 1990s, of the 6 million-plus who were pushed off welfare after 1996, most did not have enough to eat. That says nothing of their housing, of what kind of work they got, with what kind of hope attached, what benefits; what dignity. The standard should be "a living wage" for all. What would such a wage be?

The Economic Policy Institute estimates that for a family of one adult and two children that would mean full-time work at $14/hour (= $30,000/year). That amount would cover health insurance, a telephone, child care, and groceries; but *no* restaurant meals, *no* video rentals or internet access, and *no* wine, liquor, cigarettes, lottery tickets, etc. However, *60 percent* of US workers earn less than $14/hour. The majority of households have two wage earners, a spouse or a grown child, and some are able to get food stamps. (See Ehrenreich, 2001; Gans, 1995; Piven and Cloward, 1971.)

When we consider what kinds of jobs the above-noted 60 percent have, a poll of their companies would doubtless tell us that they (the companies) could not function were they required to pay a living wage; and many or even most are speaking truly. So? So some things have to change; or, if we don't see to that, given that the US is the richest of all societies, we can face up to it and see ourselves as a cruelly and dangerously indecent society in which a small percentage lives in ridiculous and disgusting luxury at the expense of millions of others.

What about the US *minimum wage*? It is $5.15/hour, and up to now even attempts to lift it by 20–30 cents have been regularly defeated in Congress. (That may or may not change from 2009, but not so as to become a "living wage.") Working full-time at $5.15 or even $7.15 an hour leaves one below the official poverty level of $15,000 and only a bit more than half of a living wage for a family of three. The minimum wage must be doubled; in addition, universal health care and affordable and decent housing must be provided by the federal government. Also: those who are old and/or disabled must be supported adequately for all their needs, for which Social Security payments are notoriously inadequate; educational opportunities must be qualitatively and quantitatively changed for the better so as to stop the passing of both poverty and wealth from one generation to the next; and, as is so in much of Western Europe, child care must be made free.

All that, at least should by done if the US is to put an end to the disgraceful situation of the past and present. As will be seen in this chapter (and again in Chapter 12), all that is provided in almost all rich nations. In the US, it is the opposite. As Ehrenreich put it in 2008: "the working poor are in fact the major 'philanthropists' of the US, their own children neglected as the children of others are cared for as the poor live in substandard housing."

In a world that leans always more perilously toward self-destruction, changes for the better are difficult. It is even more difficult in the poor countries, both because any changes for their betterment depend upon outside cooperation (or the difficult breaking of ties), and because there are so many who are so desperately poor. Instead of doing what is needed, we do this:

Item: "Pentagon reaches for spending heights: Proposed 2009 budget (adjusted for inflation) would eclipse levels reached in World War II... but that does not include 'supplemental spending' on the war efforts in Iraq and Afghanistan or on nuclear weapons" (*International Herald Tribune* [*IHT*], February 4, 2008).

The record-setting poverty of the US hurts everyone; reducing or getting rid of it would benefit everyone. Why? Because poverty is greatly wasteful of human and nonhuman resources both for those who are poor and almost all others. But, it is said, if to change that would take more and better schools and more and better housing, it would also cost many billions. True; but better schools and housing require teachers and construction materials and workers and produce more and better incomes for the teachers and those who train them and the construction workers and materials producers and a significant increase of related jobs. All that costs just as much as "milex" (see Chapter 8); except that this is good for lots of people, and milex kills lots. The money for all that would come in part from the higher national and family incomes and the taxes made possible; a redoing of our tax system so as the rich would pay *much* more than now, and the rest of us accordingly less. What we've been doing in the US since the 1970s is increasing milex while reducing the taxes of the top 10 percent. As I write, in early 2009, President Obama has proposed sensible programs to meet the foregoing needs. Whether or not Congress will find a way to leave its lobbyists behind and act for the people is yet to be seen. (See Chapter 11 and the Epilogue.)

As matters now stand it is distressing – make that *disgusting* – to have to note: (1) the US's military expenditures are not only the highest in the world but also exceed those of all others combined; (2) of the 30 countries studied by OECD (2008), the poverty rate of the US is exceeded only by two much poorer countries: Mexico and Turkey. Shame on them, for they are not among the poorest countries; shame on the US, for we are the richest in world history.

Living still in the dark shadows of the Bush administration, it is hard not to think that having our nation take a turn toward decency and sanity is just a pipe dream. It was also a pipedream to have Bush voted out of the White House and Obama in. Critical to that becoming a reality instead of merely a dream was that countless thousands of mostly young people spent much time working for him, "ringing doorbells" and/or raising money. Once more: as we learned in the 1930s, improvement cannot become a reality unless there is pressure and support from the bottom; since the 1970s the pressure and lots of money had come from the top down. In consequence, the US, never close to being heaven on earth, did come always closer to becoming a living hell. That tendency was reversed by lots of people doing lots of work. Many more of us must do much more of such work. Obama cannot do it alone. And note this hopeful sign: Despite what was going on in DC in recent years, 16 major US city governments have recently adopted living wage policies for their employees, with more on the way. So, if city employees should have a living wage, why not non-city employees? Also, beginning with Maine, one state after another now seems bent on having its own health care system, moving in the direction of Canada's single-payer plan: where's there's life there's hope. But that "life" doesn't fall from the sky; it has to be built from the ground up, not least as regards the indecent and dangerously inadequate health care system of the US.

Health Care

Most of the people of the US see its health care system as the world's best. They couldn't be more wrong. This book has been replete with past and present US scandals, many of which should be seen as social crimes. High on that list are those concerning the cruelly limited availability of health care and its sky-rocketing costs. All too often those costs are not "only" about money; they are matters of life and death, including the premature deaths of children.

Item: "The USA ranks scandalously high on the list of infant mortality, right up there with the poorest countries: the American health care system, despite the highest expenditures in the world, is badly in need of an overhaul" (*IHT* editorial, October 22, 2008).

In support of that generalization, what follows will look at the many dimensions of health care needs *not* met, and at the major crimes and political power of the giant pharmaceutical companies. I begin with excerpts from the Harvard Medical School study by Doctors Himmelstein and Woolhandler published July 10, 2002 in the *Journal of Health Affairs* (emphases mine):

> Government expenditures accounted for 59.8 percent of US health care costs in 1999... At $2,604 per capita, governmental *spending* was the *highest* of any nation – including those with national health insurance.

Their study analyzes data on spending for government health care programs like Medicare, Medicaid and the Veterans Administration ($548.7 billion in 1999), as well as two categories previously overlooked in calculating government health costs:

- expenditures of $65.6 billion to buy *private* insurance for government employees (= 16 percent of the US workforce; e.g., members of Congress, firemen and school teachers)
- tax subsidies for *private* coverage – $109.6 billion in 1999, most of which went to the wealthiest Americans. The study found that the government's share of expenditures has nearly doubled since 1965, with tax subsidies and public employee benefit costs increasing fastest.

The essentially hidden government health spending has a major impact on family budgets. In 1999, a family of four with average health costs spent $7,016 for their own health expenses and premiums (including what their employer paid). In addition, they paid $10,416 in health care *taxes*: $1,578 for tax subsidies, $943 for government workers' coverage, and $7,895 for government health programs like Medicare and Medicaid.

Even many uninsured families pay thousands of dollars in taxes for the health care of *others* (who may well be better off). (Since 1999, those numbers have risen substantially; see below.)

One of the study's authors (Dr. Woolhandler) made this comment:

> We pay the world's highest health care taxes. But much of the money is *squandered*. The wealthy get tax breaks, and HMOs and drug companies pocket billions in profits at the taxpayers' expense. But politicians claim we cannot afford universal coverage. *All* other developed nations have national health insurance. We already pay for it, but we don't get it. It adds up to "public money, private control."

The other of the two authors (Dr. Himmelstein) noted:

> We spend over $209 billion each year on paperwork in insurance companies, hospitals and doctors' offices, at least half of which could be saved through national health insurance. We spend $150 billion on medications, at prices 50% higher than Canadians pay for the *same* drugs. By slashing bureaucracy and drug prices we could save enough to cover all of the uninsured *and* improve coverage for the rest of us.

Those observations were made in 2002. Later, in 2008, Dr. Woolhandler had this to say:

> More than 47 million Americans are uninsured; the Institute of Medicine estimates that there are above 18,000 excess deaths in the USA every year due to that lack. We spend about twice as much as other developed nations on healthcare; all of which have some form of nationalized health insurance. (Interview by *Multinational Monitor*, September 10, 2008)

Then, to see part of why our health system "is the most expensive in the world and getting more expensive," the editor-in-chief of the *New England Journal of Medicine* noted: "Physicians are paid largely on a fee-for-service basis, which gives them an incentive to provide more services for which they receive higher reimbursements; incentives that increase costs" ("McCain, Obama, and the National Health," *New York Review of Books*, November 16, 2008).

Most of the foregoing has been about US health care *spending*; but while spending more than any other nation, are we also providing decent *coverage* for our people? About 20 percent of us are completely without coverage; among the other rich countries, the worst rate is under *1* percent – and *all* those other societies have higher life expectancy and lower infantile mortality rates than the US (Russell, *Dollars & Sense*, May 1993). And: Number 1 in wealth and power, the US is Number 37 in terms of "overall performance" for health care systems. (France is first, Italy second and, far down on the list, the US is behind Colombia. See World Health Organization, 1997.)

And then there is the following horror story in "More Profit and Less Nursing at Many Homes" (*NYT*, September 23, 2007). The article is focused mostly on the giant firm Habana Health Care Center. In 2002 alone it purchased 49 *nursing homes*, each with about 150 beds:

> They quickly cut costs...; within months half of the clinical nurses had been dropped, as budgets for nursing supplies and resident activities and other services fell. While investors were soon earning millions of dollars from their 49 nursing homes, residents fared less well: Over a period of three years fifteen at Habana died from what their families contend [in court] is negligent care: Staff levels below mandatory minimums, malfunctioning fire doors, unhygienic kitchens, etc... [And:] The graying of America has presented financial opportunities for all kinds of businesses, including nursing homes, which received $75 billion in 2006 from taxpayer programs like Medicare and Medicaid. The typical large chain owned by an investment company in 2005 earned $1,700 per resident... The first thing owners do is lay off nurses and other staff that are essential to keeping patients safe...

Still, the people of the US are told (and most believe) that *because* our health care system is largely private it is therefore the most efficient and thus the best in the world: OK, maybe we pay more, but we get more and better health care; no? No. (See Chapter 11, where countries are compared on this and other matters.)

Much of the foregoing data concerned years in or close to the 1990s. Surely things have improved since then? Just the opposite.

Read what the *New York Times* had to say in mid 2008 ("US Spends Heavily on Health Care but Lacks Quality," July 17):

> The latest Commonwealth Fund study shows that although the US spends twice as much as other rich nations, its health care is in *last* place in providing timely and effective health care: 75 million are without adequate health insurance or altogether without insurance. [An earlier report (see above) saw "only" 47 million in that condition]

The main reason the US health care system is dangerously inadequate is quite simply because we treat health care as something to buy and sell – as though it were a cabbage, a video, a hamburger – not as an indispensable need. The richer you are, the more and better your health care. For the not well-off, it's a rocky road; not only is their life nastier and more brutish, but also much shorter than it need be (especially when we consider that, given their poor nutrition and housing, the poor are most likely to need health care; see next chapter). So it's tough for low-income people when it comes to steady health care; but surely they're OK when there's an emergency? Far from it: if you don't have health insurance – and many millions do not – you may end up taking that feverish child to an emergency room. And please don't think of ERs as socialized medicine for the poor. Among the awful facts is this one: the average cost of a visit – after waiting in line for an hour or more – is over $1,000, which is more than ten times what a clinic pediatrician would charge (Ehrenreich, 2001).

What does all that have to do with inequality? Seven answers:

1. Inequality limits accessibility to those who cannot pay the high costs and lowers the quality of treatment for most
2. It means that the special and unmet needs and problems of the aged, disabled, children, and the homeless will not be met
3. It means work dangers and the worsening inadequacies of work-coverage
4. It means high and always rising hospital costs for most, and high incomes and profits for the few
5. All this is worsened by the self-created shortage of nurses by profit-motivated hospitals

6. It has led to the perversion of medical technology
7. For most, the always rising costs of prescription drugs have allowed their health problems to deepen.

Now let's take a closer look at these "dirty seven."

1. The Inequality of Health Care

If you are among the top 10 percent of income receivers, you might receive the best health care in the world; if you are not up there you are likely to be badly off. When you need serious medical care you get what you and/or your insurance will pay, and increasingly these days, that will be much less than you need.

Health insurance has diverse sources. The US government insures those over 65 or officially poor (Medicare and Medicaid, respectively), and the military and other government employees; and/or you may have gained health care benefits as part of your job (of which, more later); and/or you may have purchased health insurance for yourself and your family on your own. Or, for over 47 million of our mostly very poor citizens, you don't have any insurance.

There are about 300 million of us, so 47 million doesn't sound too bad – unless you are one of them or, as is likely, your insurance covers much less than you need. That is happening always more to all too many innocents; of whom you may or soon will be one.

But what about those covered? First, although this is seldom if ever pointed out when people are counted as "covered," it is almost always *partial*; and, even dangerously so. Also, and even for the most fortunate among the *non*-very rich, the best insurance is still far from "free." I take myself as an example: I am among the well-covered, having both Medicare coverage and State coverage from a lifetime of university teaching in state universities. That combination provides what is probably the most generous health coverage in the country (except for those granted to themselves by CEOs, and by Congress to itself and to the military). So?

So this: the Harvard study above cited $7,016 for the average family of four, to cover its own health expenses and premiums.

Already back in 2001, according to my tax returns, I nevertheless paid out $9,784 for medical expenses (for a "family" of two), half of which was for "supplements" (payments required without any treatments or medications). This does not include the $10,000-plus for the "health care taxes" of the Harvard study. Those numbers were appalling; since 2001 they have doubled or worse.

If by the "average" family we mean "most of the people," then their coverage would be considerably weaker than mine, their "health care taxes" pretty much the same, and their health care much more inadequate.

Item: The poor who are not "poor enough" to have Medicaid (that is, poor enough to be a family of four with an annual income of under $17,000) are increasingly likely to find their hospital's emergency rooms closed, or doctors refusing to take Medicare or Medicaid patients.

What about the other rich countries? In the US we read of how inefficient or just plain awful the health care systems are in, say, Canada, or Italy, or the UK: "So much time is spent waiting in doctors' offices, long waits for surgery, and frequently incompetent medics." (Not so: see Chapter 12.) We too spend lots of time waiting in doctors' offices (while pharmaceutical lobbyists waltz by us); or often wait a month or two for an appointment, etc. Ah! But we have *choice!* We can always go to different doctors and wait for them in *their* office: "the free market" at work.

In the 1960s it seemed that long strides ahead were underway, through Medicare (for the old and disabled) and Medicaid (for the poor). But Medicare covers only 90 days of hospital care and a payment "supplement" is required to take care of doctors and drugs. That supplement began as $3 a month; now the "supplement" payment is more than 20 times that. Also, Medicaid covers only *half* of the poor; the rest still have to use open emergency rooms, if they can find one.

From the early 1980s to now, the average worker's family health care costs have gone from bad to worse, because of declining union strength, a conservative shift in US politics, the rising costs of physicians, hospitals and drugs, and HMOs (see below).

That's bad enough, but it's made worse by severe cutbacks or termination of employer-funded plans. Thus, according to a 1999 report from the Commonwealth Fund, in the years 1979–98, this is what happened to *employer*-sponsored health insurance benefits (much worsened since): two-thirds in the private sector had health coverage in 1979; in 1998, down to one-third. For workers in the lowest fifth of the wage scale, coverage fell from 42 to 26 percent. Of the top 20 percent of wage-earners, 80 percent received coverage, as compared with 25 percent of those with $7.00/hr or less. In 1983, 45 percent of employers paid the full share of premiums; in 1998, only 26 percent. In the ten years since 1998, all that has deteriorated further, so that the average family faces rising costs while benefits and wages both decline, and jobs are harder to find.

Item: Under the headline "Small Employers Severely Cut Health Care" (*NYT*, September 6, 2002), we learned that health insurance premiums had risen in double-digits since 1999. The *NYT* was quoting the report of the Kaiser Family Foundation, which showed that "Workers are paying more of the costs, as higher premiums deductibles and co-payments for prescription drugs, doctor visits and hospital charges outpace wage increases." In that same report, it is shown that for small companies the normal situation now has become substantial increases in workers' payments for insurance alongside *decreases* in services and drugs provided. Today? Those figures were from 1999. As this is written in early 2009, more than 6 million jobs have since been lost. It doesn't take much imagination to sense what that must have meant to those millions now "uncovered" (and who may well have been earlier, as well).

2. Special Needs of the Aged, Disabled, Children, and the Homeless

Despite the strong emphasis on "family" by our politicians and the media, the US is disgracefully indifferent to what happens to those who cannot pay for needed care, let alone for the even worse off homeless. There is something different about each of the groupings in the heading above; but they have increasing helplessness and misery in common. But didn't Medicare meet the needs of the old and the disabled? No. Medicare does not assist in the payments for prescription drugs, and the 2–3 million-plus Medicare patients whose HMOs (health management organizations) have ceased to cover them and who often find it difficult or impossible to find another HMO in their locality is high and rising. In 2002 "the Bush administration proposed deep reductions in Medicare payments for a wide range of drugs and medical devices used by hospitals to treat people who are elderly or disabled" (*NYT*, September 22, 2002). A well-kept secret is that Medicare, a governmental program, is now administered by for-profit HMOs. In Western Europe, considerably more often than not, to be old and/or disabled is either to remain "in the bosom of the family," and/or to be able to participate in the numerous facilities for old people in centers designed for just that. More to the point, when old people are ill, they are taken care of in degrees and ways not found in the US (except when the left-behind family is able and/or inclined to set them up in a home).

And the *disabled*? Only to the limited degree that they are part of a political lobbying group, can they achieve even minimal improvements in their "rights" not their *needs*. But *needs* as a basis for public policy is as "un-American" as *lasagna*. Perhaps in no country is all done that could be; but the gap between needs and possibilities in the US makes the gaps of others seem enviously narrow.

That is so also for US *children*. Perhaps 20 percent of families and their children in the US have easy access – whether taken or not – to basic needs; but the other 80 percent? Certainly not for the millions of US children who live in poverty. And as for those in between bottom and top, what then? It depends upon just how caught up in the hurly-burly of US socio-economic existence their parents are; how much real time the children have with their parents, as distinct from their TVs; how attentive their parents are to their diets, health, schooling; to the needs and possibilities of their *being* children.

3. Work Dangers and Coverage

Until very recently the matter of injuries and ruined health on the job has been more neglected than studied. The study by J. Leigh (1995) filled that vacuum, and I depend upon it in what follows. The data are for 1992, with more deterioration than improvement since:

- There were over 6,000 job-related deaths, over 13 million non-fatal injuries, over 60,000 disease deaths, and over 1 million contracted illnesses at work.
- The total direct and indirect costs associated with those injuries and illnesses were estimated to be $155.5 *billion*, almost 3 percent of GDP.
- Direct costs included medical expenses for hospitals, physicians, and drugs, as well as health insurance administration costs: over $51 billion.
- Indirect costs included loss of wages, costs of fringe benefits and loss of desirable parental home care, as well as employer retraining and work disruption costs: $103 billion.
- Injuries were responsible for 85 percent of all costs, and diseases for 15 percent.
- Workers' compensation covered roughly 27 percent of all costs. Taxpayers paid approximately 18 percent of the costs, through Medicare, Medicaid, and Social Security.
- The foregoing costs were borne by injured workers and their families, by all other workers through lower wages, by firms through lower profits, and by consumers through higher prices.
- The Bureau of Labor Statistics is the most reliable source for non-fatal injuries, but it misses over half of job-related injuries.

A major conclusion of Leigh's study was that "despite the size of these costs and the fact that so many people pay them, occupational injuries and illnesses do not receive the attention they deserve...; in the course of four years of medical training, the typical US doctor receives *six hours* of instruction in occupational safety and health."

Item: "In April of 2002, Bush unveiled a new workplace safety policy that calls for *no* mandatory steps by industry and instead relies on voluntary actions by companies to reduce injuries from repetitive motions on the job... [from which] there are more than 1.8 million injuries...that result from repetitive motions like lifting, bending and typing" (*NYT*, April 6, 2002).

4. High and Always Rising Hospital Costs

As noted earlier, the US has the most costly health care system in the world while providing the least coverage for the average inhabitant. The reason for this extraordinary gap between cost and benefits is a mirror image of the inequalities, extravagance, and waste that mark our entire socio-economic system. Here are some elements of a partial explanation:

Item: US doctors' incomes are the highest in the world by far, averaging $200,000: twice those of Canada and Germany, three times those in Japan and the UK. (See White, 1995.)

Item: Hospital staffs are bloated with non-patient care and financial and billing employees. There are at least 1,500 separate for-profit health insurers in the US. Their administrative costs are sky high and amount to 25–35 percent of total health costs. In contrast, Canada has only one insurer (the government), with fewer administrators and costs than the Blue Cross system of *one* US state, Massachusetts, which covers only 3 million people. In 1991, according to the US General Accounting Office (GAO), those administrative costs were $67 *billion* more than would have been required under the Canadian system (C. Gordon, 1995). In that same year the inefficiency exploded. According to a Harvard University Medical School Study: on an average day in 1968, American hospitals employed 435,100 managers and clerks while caring for 1,378,000 patients. By 1990, the average daily number of patients had fallen to 853,000, but the number of administrative personnel had grown to 1,291,600 (*NYT*, August 5, 1993).

Think of that while you are cursing your way through the many letters you get from your insurance system: "This is not a bill" or "This *is* a bill." *They* see that annoying paper as essential for their profits; but it does nothing for *your* health, and may harm it. And mind you, as we are told over and over and over, "a for-profit system" in health care is the high road to efficiency.

5. The Shortage of Nurses

Now on the edge of 90, and having spent time in hospitals as both a patient and worked for years as an orderly in surgery, I have learned that however important the doctors may be in critical moments, the nurses are the mainstay of a patient's successful stay in a hospital; they are simply vital at critical moments, with or without a doctor present. As this century began there was already a dire shortage of nurses: 12 percent of what was needed. By 2009 the shortage had doubled. It would be serious enough if the shortage were due to the lack of interest in such difficult work by sufficient numbers; but that is not the reason. Rather, "as the health care system shifted toward managed care, hospitals merged, and nurses were laid off to cut costs. Those who remained found themselves working longer hours and caring for more patients... and many nurses moved to work in other fields or other non-hospital jobs..." (*NYT*, May 28, 2002). In the same period, the *New England Journal of Medicine* found that "perhaps thousands of deaths each year are due to low staffing: nurses are the eyes and the ears of the hospital for judging whether a patient is recovering; problems cannot be spotted if nurses do not have time to observe their patients" (*NYT*, May 30, 2002). Then, a few months later, a sorry confirmation: in "Patient Deaths Tied to Lack of Nurses" (*NYT*, August 8, 2002) we learn that "the national organization that accredits hospitals reported today that the lack contributed to nearly a quarter of the unanticipated problems that result in death or injury to patients."

That rising shortage of nurses will be difficult to resolve. Even though hospitals are now in a "bidding war" to gain more nurses, it is not only that they are in competition for a pool that cannot be sufficiently refilled for some years, it is that the mere increase of nurses' salaries will not change the larger fact that nurses are now treated like workers on an assembly line; that is, those "eyes and ears" of the hospital will still have too little time to pay due attention. It may be assumed that it has been the most conscientious nurses who have left the hospitals: in disgust, despair, and misery.

In sum, in this and all the other elements of our wrong-headed health care system, there is an ineradicable conflict between providing sufficient health care and making sufficient profits. HMOs now rule over much of our health care system; since they and their managed care system began to take firm hold in the 1990s, the gap between care and profits has widened at an accelerating rate, producing a major crisis. Why? Because of the interaction between unnecessarily rising costs and the managed care "solution" to provide always less satisfactory health care. "Unnecessarily"? Yes, for the costs have little to do with health service, and almost everything to do with profits.

6. The Perverse Role of Medical Technology

In the health care sector, as elsewhere, technological change can be for better and/or for worse. Its negative role in the ongoing health care crisis may be seen as arising from the two main types of technological invention at work there: (a) "genuine improvements" in the invention of new technologies for existing maladies, and (b) technologies invented to "solve" equally invented "problems." However, in both cases, costs rise disproportionately to the contribution to improved health (Keaney, 2002). "Genuine improvements" are usually available only to those with the very best health coverage (and the highest incomes): need is not the main criterion nor success the common effect. Rather, the hospitals or clinics dispense such technologies where payment and profits can be gained. In such cases, a real need could be met. But in the case of "invented technologies for invented problems," not health but *only* the profits of patent holder and hospital are at issue. "Two-thirds of the drugs approved from 1989 to 2000 were modified versions of existing drugs or even identical to those already on the market... Some of the reformulated prescription drugs are now among the most heavily advertised" (*NYT*, May 29, 2002). "A major reason for a 'reformulation' is that a *patent* on an existing drug will expire. So Sarafem, identical with Prozac, comes out with a new name and differently colored capsules + a higher price + lots of advertising, on which Big Pharm spends $2.5 *billion* yearly." The report upon which the *NYT* article was based is from the National Institute for Health Care Management; it concluded stating that "pharmaceutical companies are turning more into marketing companies." Thus, and like so much else in our socio-economy, medical technology is driven more by greed than by any social or human use it might have. Occasionally, of course, such a use has existed; but more often there is no beneficial effect, or harm has been done.

7. High and Rising Prices of Prescription Drugs

The false "invention" of drugs is unfortunately not the worst element created by the drug industry; unfortunately, that honor goes to the problems created by extortionately high drug prices for those who are not rich; that is, at least 80 percent of the US population, hitting the old among them hardest. The problem is great for at least half of the US people, and worst of all for those who have been led to believe they are "covered," but in fact are not; namely, those dependent upon Medicare and Medicaid, the old, the disabled, and the poor. In a *NYT* op-ed by Senator Zell Miller (Democrat, Georgia), he pointed out that "If Medicare were being invented today, no one would think of starting it without a prescription drug benefit..." (*NYT*, June 1, 2002).

The good Senator might be wrong even about "today." In 2008, Congress haggled over whether or not Medicare should cover prescription drug costs for the old and disabled. The quarrel between the GOP and the Democrats is not whether or not, looking forward to elections, both say "Yes, but..." The "but" has to do with how much of a "deductible" must be paid by the patient. "Deduction" is another of those corporate euphemisms, for it refers to what the insurance agency does *not* have to pay, but the patient *does*. In the House, the GOP proposed that of costs up to $5,800, insurance would pay $1,100, the patient $4,700. The Democrats in House and Senate propose that after a $100 (or no) deductible, the patient pays either 20 percent of each prescription or a flat co-payment of $10–40, depending upon whether or not the prescription is for a generic product. The GOP, unsurprisingly, would have the government pay subsidies to private insurance companies to "induce them to offer insurance covering drug costs," while the Democrats say, plausibly, that "this is the first step in a GOP plan to privatize Medicare." The argument goes on. Perhaps it will be resolved more decently as the Obama presidency moves on; perhaps not: the lobbyists for "Big Pharm" have been at the top of the list of winners. And here is another apparent anomaly: the Veterans Administration buys drugs for its patients in the same way the Canadian government does, using the bargaining power of its large purchases to gain much lower prices on drugs. (The VA also provides health care for vets on the same footing as the Canadian single-payer system.) So we're not just talking about "principles" here.

So much for *Medicare* and prescription drugs. The law for *Medicaid* (for the poor) did provide coverage, but recent study has shown that even though Medicaid recipients have access to medical care about equal to those with private insurance, they have just as much trouble getting medications as those totally uninsured. The costs of drugs, whether for cancer control, asthma, high blood pressure, you name it, are very high and getting higher ever month.

The foregoing was for the old and the poor. What about those on the other side of the track? The CEOs of the nine biggest drug companies receive an average of $19 million annually (not counting stock options, etc.), and their industry (according to *Fortune*), is not only the most profitable of all industries, but its usual profit margins are nearly *four times* the average of the profits of the 500 largest US companies (*Multinational Monitor*, September 2001).

It has been stressed many times in this work that the current "bad times" concerning the consequences of inequality began to take hold from the 1970s on. If there was a critical turning point, it was in the election (and re-election) of Ronald Reagan, surely one of the two or three most popular presidents in US history. When he was governor of California he made his first big step toward becoming a national figure in what became a famous speech. I quote: "We were told four years ago that 17 million people went to bed hungry each night. Well, that was probably true. They were all on a diet." (See Wills, 1988.)

So it seems that the always inadequate and begrudged programs for the decent treatments of the "ill-clothed, ill-fed, and ill-housed" proposed by FDR in the 1930s had by the 1980s already become a cheap joke. But there's nothing amusing about Reagan's legacy; it continued and became always more disgusting up into this century. When, in October of 2007, Congress reluctantly passed legislation to expand the sickeningly inadequate State Children's Health Insurance Program (providing health insurance to almost 4 million children now with *no* health insurance), Bush vetoed it (one of only seven vetoes by him). One of his major advisors, William Kristol, is also a great joker, and funny enough to make Reagan dance in his grave: "First of all, whenever I hear anything described as a heartless assault on our children, I tend to think it's a good idea. I'm happy that the president's willing to do something bad for the kids" (quoted by Krugman, "Conservatives Are Such Jokers," *NYT*, October 5, 2007).

That may change with Obama in the White House; it certainly must. Here are two quotes from the *NYT* in 2007, the first from September 16, the second from November 25:

> The number of uninsured health care in the USA is approaching 50 million, the average cost of family coverage has risen 78 percent in the last six years, and more and more employers say they cannot afford to provide health care coverage and still compete in a global marketplace

The relentless decades-long rise in the cost of health care has left millions of Americans struggling to pay their medical bills. Workers complain they cannot afford high premiums for health insurance. Patients forgo recommended care rather than pay out-of-pocket costs. Employers are cutting back or eliminating health benefits, forcing millions more people into the ranks of the uninsured. And state and federal governments strain to meet the expanding costs of public programs like Medicaid and Medicare.

Among his first sets of proposals to Congress in the spring of 2009, Obama urgently asked for a substantial set of improvements in the US health care system. It may be hoped that what was asked for will be legislated and put the US moving toward decency. But there are two factors that must be dealt with: (1) in both the House and the Senate, most of the members of both the Democratic and Republican parties have long and successfully been "bribed" in many ways by the medical and pharmaceutical lobbyists, and (2) the people of the US have just as long been political observers (if that) rather than participants. If the US is to change for the better, we have to reverse both these factors. In the news March 6, 2009: "Obama Vows to End Health Care Stalemate." He'll need our help: soonest.

The foregoing discussion showed that about 50 million people in the US have *no* health care, except what they can get in an emergency room somewhere; and then, more likely than not, they'll have to pay up.

Item: In 1939–40 I was working on the night shift in surgery at the San Francisco Public Hospital (as an "orderly"). We were on the floor above Emergency, and when an ambulance came in with a serious problem it would get our attention by a loud siren; and I would go downstairs to get the person. It sounded, I went down, and what I found was a screaming man and a yelling official, the former, a poor man, having trouble understanding, the latter an official asking how much money he had. When it turned out, finally, that he had $300 in a bank, they put him back in the ambulance and took him to a private hospital. A week or two later, while pushing my gurney through a ward, there he was, pale and screaming. The private hospital had used up his $300 in a couple of days and sent him back to us. He died two weeks later. Broke. God bless America.

Recently, millions of workers who thought they were safe with the health benefits going with their job have discovered they had been taken for a ride: for example, those of General Motors, whose jobs have declined by about 50 percent in recent years. Their job losses are representative of the losses in much of US industry and other relatively well-compensated jobs, as the US economy has become dominated by finance and services.

Item: "4.4 million jobs lost just since 2007" (*IHT*, March 7, 2009), "Unemployment hits 25-year high in US; Obama describes loss of 4.4 million as 'astounding.'" "That's a lot of workers that are not coming back," said an economist. Also, note that the (finally!) broader official rate measuring unemployment and *under*-employment was then at 14.8 percent (instead of 8.1 percent). It counts also those who have given up looking, or are working part-time instead of full-time. Those who lost jobs also lost health care. "Obama vows to end health care stalemate."

He'll need lots of help from us. Down with the lobbyists, up with the people.

10

INEQUALITY'S CONSEQUENCES FOR ITS VICTIMS AND ITS VICTIMIZERS

II: Education, Housing and the Homeless, Nutrition and Hunger, Opportunity, and Dignity

Education

All agree that a good education is essential for a good life; but what is "a good education"; for that matter, what is "a good life"? However defined, shouldn't those "goods" be for everyone? And if so, what needs doing; and *undoing*? The answers to those questions have of course varied very much from time to time, place to place, and over time in any given place. We begin here by examining only the "non-good" educational system of the US in our time, from K-12 (ages 5–18) through the university.

In the educational realm, as with so much else treated in this book, the US has had the ability to develop an excellent system for all; yet never have we realized those possibilities, or even sought to do so. Even worse is that in keeping step with the general rightward political shift since the 1970s, our entire educational system, never "good," has gone from bad to worse. Support for those generalizations will follow, but we begin with an all too appropriate condemnation of our time – Vachel Lindsay's poem "The Leaden Eyed," written in the 1920s about *his* time:

> Let not young souls be smothered out before
> They do quaint deeds and fully flaunt their pride.
> It is the world's one crime its babes grow dull,
> Its poor are ox-like, limp and leaden-eyed.

Not that they starve, but starve so dreamlessly,
Not that they sow, but that they seldom reap,
Not that they serve, but have no gods to serve,
Not that they die, but that they die like sheep.

(cited in Rodman, 1939)

About 80 years later, as a discussion of Einstein's brain was going on, the late and much-admired biologist/paleontologist Stephen Gould observed that he was "less interested in the weight and convolutions of Einstein's brain than in the near certainty that people of equal talent have lived and died in cotton fields and sweatshops." In their different ways, the poet and the scientist agreed: a decent education could and should be available to all, but social powers have precluded it for almost all, everywhere; that the responsibility for mal-education or non-education of the majority lies in our social institutions, not in the genes of their victims (Gould, 2003).

That certainly refers to the plight of the vast majority of the world's people, living in societies (ours included) where access to what passes for a good education is effectively rationed in terms of income and wealth, color, and/or gender. But the reference also applies to those lucky enough to be exempt from such discrimination: the educational system is dreadfully inadequate for all; or worse than inadequate.

Indisputably, educational systems function first and foremost to strengthen the status quo, the core of which in the modern era, almost everywhere has been and remains capitalism and nationalism. Beginning in grammar school and lasting through the PhD the central point of reference is the maintenance or strengthening of that status quo; although seldom if ever is that made explicit. That the young – whether 7 or 17 – can and do have other needs and possibilities is given short shrift at all levels, except by an always small and now shrinking number of teachers, almost everywhere.

All US education, even for the well-off, is not only defective but mutilating; and to point out that 80 percent of the world's people would love to have access to our education is a reflection on how desperate *their* societies are, and were made to be so over the centuries by societies like ours. And for those *not* well-off in the rich societies? Whatever might be wrong with even the best schools when set against acceptable criteria, it may be said that everything is wrong with the schools for children in *poverty*; especially for girls and those not "white."

In 1967, Jonathan Kozol became a new teacher in a segregated school in Boston; segregated despite the 1954 Supreme Court decision calling segregation unconstitutional. In his first year as a teacher he wrote a book on children in US schools, focusing on children who were both poor and black: *Death at an Early Age*. Since then he has become a recognized authority on the tragic realities of schools throughout the US. Here is an excerpt from his *Savage Inequalities* (1991). For several years he had visited over 30 schools throughout the nation; these are the book's opening words:

> What startled me most was the remarkable degree of racial segregation that persisted almost everywhere. I knew that segregation was still common in public schools but I did not know how much it had *intensified*. Most of the urban schools I visited (all outside of the Deep South) were 95 to 99 percent nonwhite. In *no* school that I saw anywhere in the United States were nonwhite children truly intermingled with white children... The dual society, at least in education, seems in general to be unquestioned... In public schooling, social policy has been turned back almost one hundred years.

Kozol was referring to elementary schools. Let's now look at some of the defects of education at all levels, beginning with those for the youngest.

K through 12: Given what happens "at home," K-12 is where our "young souls are [further] smothered out," whether we are rich or poor. All three levels – elementary, high school, and university – are vital to us, but because we are more vulnerable and susceptible the younger we are, it is at elementary school where we can be hurt or helped most. If we are hurt sufficiently there (and setting aside other relevancies), we have to be very fortunate at the later stages to bounce back and go on toward becoming our realizable selves. Whatever today's defects, they are not unique to our times. Education for "all the people," or even for many of them, took hold along with industrialism, for it requires that workers can at least read "directions." Industrialism first came to be in England in 1815, when the first factory was born. Three years earlier, Charles Dickens was born. In 1854 he wrote *Hard Times*. Between his birth and that book, the industrial revolution had exploded. Vital to its functioning was a working class; and vital to industrialization's functioning was the growth of popular education. *Hard Times* was much concerned with the impact of industrial capitalism on people's lives, not least upon their early education. The first paragraph of the book is set in a classroom. The teacher, Mr. Gradgrind, standing next to the Schoolmaster, explains:

> Now, what I want is, Facts. Teach these boys and girls nothing but Facts. Facts alone are wanted in life. Plant nothing else, and *root out* everything else. You can only form the minds of reasoning animals upon Facts: nothing else will ever be of any service to them. This is the principle on which I bring up my own children, and this is the principle on which I bring up these children. Stick to Facts, sir!

In delightfully sharp contrast, note what the novelist Doris Lessing had to say as she received her Nobel Prize for Literature, in 2007 (as quoted in *NYT*, May 23, 2007):

> Ideally, what should be said to every child, repeatedly, throughout his or her school life is something like this: "You are in the process of being indoctrinated. We have not yet evolved a system of education that is not a system of indoctrination. We are sorry, but it is the best we can do. What you are being taught here is an amalgam of current prejudice and the choices of this particular culture. The slightest look at history will show how impermanent these must be. You are being taught by people who have been able to accommodate themselves to a regime of thought laid down by their predecessor. It is a self-perpetuating system. Those of you who are more robust and individual than others will be encouraged to leave and find ways of educating yourself; educating your own judgment. Those that stay must remember, always and all the time, that they are

being molded and patterned to fit into the narrow and particular needs of this particular society."

It is necessary to distinguish between being educated and *learning*. As the words are used here, the former is a "top-down" process suiting a curriculum delivered to the teachers who – and quite apart from having also been "educated" in the same manner – must follow the rules in order to keep their jobs. That done, both pupils and teachers are fitted into an educational status quo, itself accommodating the larger socio-economic system.

"Naturally," one might respond. Except that if there is any hope for this or other societies to wrench themselves loose from the "commissions and omissions" that constituted the past *and* that took us into the dangerous present, that hope resides in each generation having the opportunity to think for itself: to *learn*; to ask and to answer questions; to *change* their minds," *not* to prepare for college entrance exams, as is now so disgustingly common at the *elementary* level. The best that can be said for most contemporary "education" is that it prepares one for jobs, to become able to continue doing what is *being* done: no questions asked, except "How?" Hardly ever are the young taught to ask "Why?" or "For whom?" let alone "Are there alternatives?"

It is bad enough that the average youngster spends at least 4–6 hours a day watching TV, but something truly rotten has been added; namely, the commercialization of the school space, within and outside the classroom. Consider these data compiled by Michael Moore, quoting studies by the Center for the Analysis of Commercialism in Education:

The National Geography Spelling Bee now has a corporate sponsor; book covers are distributed free to students, with ads for various companies; sports shoes companies "sponsor" inner-city high school teams; two large companies have programs rewarding schools for getting parents to buy their products; for example, General Mills gives a school ten cents for each box top logo sent in, up to $10,000 a year (= 100,000 boxes of their product sold); in the 1990s, 241 school districts sold *exclusive* rights to one of the big three soda companies (Coca-Cola, Pepsi, Dr. Pepper), perhaps the grossest offender being Colorado Springs: the school district will receive $8 million-plus over ten years from its deal with Coca-Cola. And so it goes – ads on school buses, on school rooftops, even, in an inspired variation, GM's supplying to many schools the economics course GM writes and for which it provides the textbooks.

And then there are the electronic marketers in the classroom, the kingpin of which is Channel One Television. In the name of better education, 8 million students in 12,000 grade school classrooms watch Channel One – an in-school news and *advertising* program – every day. Of the daily 12-minute programs, *80 percent* is devoted to advertising, the rest to non-commercial matters. And Channel One is shown predominantly in low-income communities with minority populations, where the least public money is devoted to schools.

Item: "Neediest Schools Receive Less Money, Report Finds": "As schools enter a new era of tough federal demands to raise achievements among poor and minority students, a report [by Education Trust] shows that in most states, school districts with the neediest students receive far less state and local tax money – an average of just under $1,000 per student – than the schools with the fewest poor children" (*NYT*, August 9, 2002).

But what about the much-touted school voucher program, presumably designed mostly for poor and minority children? Referring to the recent Supreme Court decision upholding Cleveland's voucher program, heralded as "the second coming of Brown v. Board of Education," Brent Staples wrote: "The voucher program serves only about 3,700 of [Cleveland's] public school system's 75,000 children. Chosen by lottery, the children from the poorest families are provided a maximum of $2,250 – less than a third of the cost of educating a public school student – if they wish to move out of the public school program" ("School Vouchers: A Small Tool for a Very Big Problem," *NYT*, August 5, 2002).

The article went on to note that of the three possibilities for their attendance – suburban schools, non-religious private schools, and religious schools – "the religious schools enrolled 96 percent of the eligible students, with the other schools being too costly or too crowded" – thus intensifying the present tendency to violate the separation of church and state, while also intensifying the long-standing tendency to neglect public schools.

Many have given up on our public schools and many others never cared about them in the first place. Those who have "given up" include a lot of hard-working not very well-off people who scrimp and sacrifice to get their kids into a private (and costly) school that will (hopefully) give them a chance to have a decent life; and some few who simply have enough money without having to sacrifice. Most of the rest of us have to take our chances with the K-12 public schools. It is in those first years, K-8, that we spend the most time learning to be boys and girls rather than human beings; to be "good Americans," and (among other things) to think of what jobs we can get, rather than what life has been and/or could be, for ourselves and others.

Then it's on to high school: assuming, however, that the child's grammar school has met the requirements of the Bush administration's inaccurately labeled "Leave No Child Behind" legislation of 2002. The program required that the funded school have all of its students pass proficiency exams in math and reading by 2014, requiring an 11 percent increase every year. How does it work? Here's one example: "The law has had unintended consequences, including its tendency to punish states like California, that have high standards and rigorous tests, which have contributed to an increasing pileup of failed (and closed) schools... [According to a University of Colorado professor:] 'No matter how hard teachers work, the school is labeled as a failure; that's just demoralizing'" ("Under 'No Child' Law, Even Solid Schools Falter," NYT, October 13, 2008).

The heart of that law, as with so much of the entire educational process, is "passing exams." The pre-eminence of that standard succeeds most in "teaching" young people that education is coercive, teaches them to hate learning from childhood and into the next step up into high school. It is difficult enough to be an adolescent, but in high school fears and tensions are multiplied.

There, young people are considerably more prone to becoming conformists when faced with diverse punishments from their peers if they are "different"; there too, the damage done by assembly-line education has more fertile soil in which to flourish, as whatever individuality we had as a child is crushed. (See Kozol, 1991.)

To repeat, the fault is not simply or mostly that of teachers, whether for small children or adolescents. Some teachers, it may be assumed, *became* teachers in order to do something useful, interesting, challenging; even beautiful. But the bureaucracy wears them down, as does the working atmosphere where the children steadily lose the possibilities they were born with, as they become, instead, cogs in a dehumanizing machine. No wonder that the high school dropout in the US is 25 percent, six times that of Finland ("What Makes Finnish Kids So Smart?" *Wall Street Journal*, February 29, 2008). Now on to the next step up, with its own scandals: "the higher learning."

Veblen wrote a book with that title in 1918. Its original subtitle was "A Study in Total Depravity." The publishing company found that undesirable, but settled for something it did not see as equally derogatory: "On the Conduct of Universities by Businessmen." If Veblen were around today, he would find that the universities have degenerated so much since that he wouldn't bother to write on the subject. "Degenerated" in what ways?

Not least is the always deepening corruption achieved through "subsidies and constraints"; two sides of the same coin. The subsidies have been numerous, mostly in those realms which directly or indirectly contribute to the military strength given by chemistry and physics. The "constraints" are as subtle as they are important. For example, in a *NYT* op-ed piece "Power Over Principle: How the Military Bullied its Way into Law Schools" (September 7, 2002), Professor George Fisher of Stanford Law School stated that "this year there will be a new team of recruiters at many law schools: those from the Judge Advocate General's Corps of the United States military." Nothing totally new there, except that more than ten years ago most of the leading law schools forbade such "teams," because the military rejects qualified students who wish to serve if they are "openly gay or lesbian or bisexual: "Dishonesty is the best policy?" But now the universities are bowing and scraping, beginning with the two richest: Harvard and Stanford. So why have they and other US law schools changed their policy? The reason, Prof. Fisher reports, "is money":

> In 2000, The Department of Defense issued regulations reinterpreting federal law, stating: "If *any part* of a university denies access to military recruiters, the entire university will lose an array of federal funds." (Harvard would lose over $300 million, for example. They could afford it with their billions in endowments; other less rich schools could not.) For years law schools have stood in defense of the anti-discrimination principles they teach. Now the military is forcing them to bend their principles – and the cost falls not on the schools but on their students. (*NYT*, ibid.)

In the universities, as elsewhere, corruption spreads and thickens, taking so many forms it is barely noticed. The function of college professors is twofold: to teach, and to expand the frontiers of understanding and appreciation through research (and thus to become a better teacher and help others to do so). In "the good old days," by which I mean before the 1970s, to become a part of "the higher learning," one gained an MA or PhD, began to teach (and study further) and, if judged as competent, moved from being an Instructor to Assistant Professor to Associate Professor (with tenure) to Professor. In 1970, 78 percent of university level teachers had received tenure (which meant your job was secure, even if, for example, you were a social critic). But by 1999, those tenured had dropped to less than one-third (US Department of Education, 1999 statistics). In California, for example, over 70 percent of those teaching were "part-time temps." (In Italy, they are called "precari" or "adjunct professors" = shaky.) The shakies teaching two courses in California are paid at poverty income levels ($12,000–$14,000/year), usually with a maximum of $3,000 a course – with no benefits, no "*study*" in which to speak to students (or to "study"). And those were the "numbers" ten years ago. Now? Worse, of course; as it is also in Italy, where I now teach.

Whatever is true at the colleges and universities, it is considerably worse at community colleges – many of which, according to a Harvard University report of 1995, have *no* tenured teachers, and where over two-thirds are part-time temps (Taira, "All Quiet in the Classroom," *San Francisco Bay Guardian*, March 12, 2002).

So? So, the teachers thus affected (1) often must work at more than one institution at a time, which often involves commuting from city to city; (2) are made unable to even *think* of doing serious research or writing; (3) are thus deprived of even a slim chance at a permanent job; (4) learn to keep their mouths shut on any kind of controversial matter, within or outside the school; (5) are ruled over by the small percentage of tenured profs who got theirs 30 or more years ago (as I did); and (6) are stuck with their very low pay.

Imagine how little time (or thought) they are able to give their students; and imagine, also, how little time those with tenure give *their* students, if any. In short, the line between a university and a department store or a tool factory, as with any other business, has become hard to find: a business is a business is a business. (See Nelson, 1999.)

Along with much else, after the 1970s, education began to slide down. When the "downs" began, it was not from a high mountain, but from a low hill. The improvements made in the educational realm in years after World War II could be seen as only first steps, as was true also for other changes involving health care, housing, unions, and the like (discussed earlier, and below); the deterioration of education was part and parcel of a general deterioration toward always increasing inequality.

Seeking the prize among those sickening developments has been the decline of public moneys spent on *schools* and the meteoric rise of expenditures on *prisons*. Both sets of those public expenditures are largely financed by the individual states and must be approved, directly or indirectly, by voters approving bond issues (and the taxes to pay for them). Taxpayers must decide: schools or prisons. In California, voters made their choice in the 1990s: prison expenditures now exceed those for education. That "competition" is loaded in favor of prisons (and their staffs and those who build them) but at the expense of prison*ers*, many of whom would not be there had there been less racism, less poverty; less inequality, and *more* and better education.

In the decades in which the schools' loss and the prisons' "gains" have occurred there have been at least three background developments goading them on: a "flight to the suburbs" and to private schools for middle and upper income families, a continuing racist din about crime and violence from politicians and the media, and the intensification of the borrowing and spending habits intrinsic to consumerism. The consequences include a growing resentment of taxes for education and, at the same time, a grudging acceptance of always increasing incarcerations: in which, measured in per capita terms, the US has become Number 1. Here from the *International Herald Tribune*, November 20, 2008: "California State universities might turn qualified students away." "Might" is hardly the proper term, given that in that same story we learn that the system has "already informed 10,000 academically qualified students that it has no money and is faced by further budget cuts."

There is so much wrong with those realities, so much that is harmful not just to the system's victims but, as well, to its (conscious or unconscious) perpetrators and to the society as a whole, that it is difficult to know where to begin in response. But one indisputably major consequence is what we have lost along the way, and for the future: the terrible and probably permanent loss of positive, badly-needed human potentialities for all concerned.

This discussion of education began with the poet Lindsay's appeal "Let not young souls be smothered out," and the scientist Gould's lament concerning those who have lived and died and in the fields and factories, with never a chance to move toward, let alone reach their possibilities. Very few of us, no matter what our social circumstances, could ever become an Einstein or a Beethoven or a Picasso; no matter what. But all of our minds *could* be more fully and richly used and developed in a formal educational process devoted to just that, instead of being "educated" to adapt and to help preserve the status quo.

For centuries, the rich societies have had the ability to enable more and better education for all; but that has seldom or never been the inclination of those in power. Like health care, schooling should be designed to meet all humans' needs and possibilities; not only those of a small and privileged corner of the society (if that). In the US, public schools are financed mostly by individual states and the financing of educational budgets depends upon voter approval.

Even in "good times" an increase in educational budgets has been difficult to achieve; in today's "hard times" it would be considerably more so. A recent study by Washington University estimated that "the ongoing recession will lead to 547,000 teacher cuts without a stimulus" (see "Our Greatest National Shame," *NYT*, February 15, 2009).

President Obama is trying to get Congress to provide a national "stimulus" for education. Pressure on Congress from us is badly needed if he is to succeed.

Housing and the Homeless

This is written in early 2009. Say "housing" to almost any passerby in the US these days, and the immediate response would be "bubble" – unless, that is, the person passing is one of the millions of homeless. Millions? Yes. There are more than 500,000 homeless in just one state, one of the richest: California. Homelessness will be discussed and analyzed at some length later; but first, the "housing bubble." This always worsening problem was discussed at length in Chapter 7; here a few more words about what should be seen as the criminal doings of allowing a basic need to become just another room of the gambling casino with star players such as those of LTCM (Long-Term Capital Management), AIG, Enron, and their buddies all gambling on the principle that if you spread your bets you can't lose, but you *can* make a bundle.

Well, a decade ago LTCM *lost* the biggest bundle ever (up to then). But not really: as briefly mentioned in Chapter 7, LTCM was bailed out, with our taxes. It now appears and is fully expected by the big players that the Treasury Department (under both Bush and Obama) will go and do likewise for the popped housing bubble, thus encouraging another speculative folly a few years from now. If and when we recover, and if the lesson is finally learned. Don't hold your breath, and cough a little as you read the following extract from "A 'Moral Hazard' for a Housing Bailout: Sorting the Victims From Those Who Volunteered" (*NYT*, February 23, 2008 – months before the first $700 *billion* Congressional "bailout" of 2008, with $800 billion to follow):

> A confidential proposal that the Bank of America circulated to Congress this month suggests creating a "Federal Homeowner Preservation Corporation" that would buy up to $739 *billion* in troubled mortgages at a deep discount, forgive debt above the current market value of the homes and use federal loan guarantees to refinance the borrowers at lower rates." [Despite assurances in the proposal], the bailout would mostly benefit banks and Wall Street firms that earned huge fees by packaging *trillions* of dollars in risky mortgages without documenting the incomes of borrowers and often turning a blind eye to clear fraud by borrowers or mortgage brokers... Right or wrong, the arguments...are likely to be blurred with arguments for rescuing home prices. At that point, industry executives are likely to argue that what is good for Bank of America is good for the rest of America. [They got it: the S&L give-away all over again. See Chapter 7.]

It is thought that the housing bubble was created from the bottom up; that is, by borrowers who could not in any way afford to buy a house, but who found a new way to do it: "*subprime* mortgages" and ARMs ("adjustable rate mortgages"), with very low or no interest paid; until some years later at *very* high rates. But those fancy ideas were created at "the top." To repeat, the subprime borrowers, almost all of them low-income families, didn't have to make any "monthly payments" when they took out such a loan. But, 2, 3, 4, 5 years later, they would have to, and, just as the interest rate they must pay is higher than normal, so too are their monthly payments ("The Mortgage Overhang: Who Should Pay?" *NYT*, September 19, 2007).

Who should pay? It was not the borrowers, but the financiers who invented that new way to make a fast buck. "Subprime" sounds crazy, and is; but it was worse than crazy – it was criminal. Why? Because the subprimers' low incomes by definition would not earlier have qualified for a housing loan. Those who took out those loans, did so in the hope that, low-income though they were *then*, by the time they had to start paying that higher interest rate and that higher monthly payment, they would have a job paying enough…and so on. Instead, almost 2 *million* families have lost their homes: "Putting the brakes on foreclosures: 3.2 million homeowners will likely lose homes to foreclosure this year and next" (*NYT* editorial, October 23, 2008). And then what? (See below: "The Homeless.")

That rush to madness in the housing market began a decade or so ago and ended with a full crash by 2008. It was already wobbling on the edge well before that November 2007 proposal quoted above; a year later it was over the brink, taking other countries with it. "Financial bubbles" have popped all over the world, because of the links between financialization, globalization, and speculation, all taking place in totally unregulated financial markets. Taken together they made inevitable a replay of the 1920s and its crashed copy-cat gambling casino. But today's collapse is much broader and almost certainly will become deeper and more disastrous than the 1920s, thanks to globalization.

When the "surge" began, its participants were relatively sane compared with what they became as it continued. The reference there is not only to people, but to financial organizations of all sorts in the US and all over the world. (See Chapters 6 and 7.) Combined, they brought all economies closer together than ever before in history; and, in doing so, also tied together all of the different sectors of finance and laid the groundwork for unmitigated disaster.

A significant percentage of the subprime borrowers had low-paying jobs and might even have been on the edge of "official" poverty ($25,000 a year for a family of three); the majority had annual incomes of between $30,000 and $50,000. None were "homeless" in the sense in which that term is usually taken.

Saying that, I add that not all but many of those who *are*, literally, "homeless," as will now be seen, are both fully employed and badly paid.

The foregoing might well be seen as a complaint of an outsider. "Outsider" I am, but the person now to be quoted – George Soros – is Mr. Insider himself. He made *billions* by understanding what was going on in the casino. Here is what he thought as 2008 began: "[Earlier] periodic crises were part of a larger boom-bust process. The current crisis is the culmination of a militarily based and artificial super-boom that has lasted for more than 60 years" (*Financial Times*, January 23, 2008). Onward and downward.

The Homeless

In his 1933 inaugural address, President Roosevelt famously deplored the desperation of "one-third of a nation: ill-clothed, ill-fed, and ill housed." It was a fine sentiment, but a gross understatement. According to H. Miller (US Bureau of the Census statistician for 30 years), even using the understated measures of poverty, over *half* of the nation was in that fix as Roosevelt spoke (Miller, 1971). Then as now, those who are "ill" in one of those categories usually find themselves in all three, with each unmet need worsening the other two. That is especially so for those who are not only "*ill*-housed," but *without* housing.

When FDR spoke, both the US and much of the world were deep in history's worst depression ever (up to now). In contrast, the closing years of the twentieth century encompassed the most prosperous years ever – *if*, that is, you were on the top layers in one of the rich countries. But (as noted in Chapter 6) at least 4 *billion* living in poverty in the rest of the "globalized" world were impoverished. The focus here will be on the US, but neither there nor in the rest of the world are desperate conditions often due to natural calamities: they are "manmade," a consequence of economic policies combining greed, callousness, ruthlessness, and what may be seen as a cultivated ignorance.

There are explanations but no acceptable excuses for such human misery; least of all for the US: *Uncle Scrooge*. When confronted with those who live badly it is common for those who live well to "blame the victim," implicitly assuming that their own wellbeing is the consequence of some combination of ability and hard work, and that the harsh conditions of the badly-off are simply due to their lack of ability and/or their laziness. This is a comforting assumption for the comfortable, but a factual delusion. (See Ryan 1976.)

More often than not the homeless are viewed with scorn and rage when seen in the streets, and with anger when proposals are made to reduce their numbers and improve their condition; a condition which, when not taken to be a result of laziness and stupidity, is seen as one of self-indulgence: drugs, liquor, gambling...or something wicked. The facts are different. The homeless may be (1) physically and/or psychiatrically disabled, either or both cases requiring not just a shelter but special facilities; (2) and/or they have *problems* with alcohol and/or drugs; (3) and/or, often as not, they are "normal" people (often families) who work full-time and cannot find an affordable dwelling; (4) and/or, for all too many women, alone or with their children, have fled from a dangerously abusive father/husband/lover.

Those among us whose attitudes toward the homeless are prompted by disgust, fear, racism, attitudes of superiority or some mixture of those and other forms of prejudice should be ashamed of ourselves rather than scornful of the homeless, if only because at least a *third* of the US homeless men are veterans of our wars in Korea, Vietnam, Iraq, or Afghanistan. They have bodily and/or psychological damages from wars entailing the large-scale and indiscriminate killing of civilians. If you have done that and can come out of it inwardly unharmed, there may well be something wrong with *you*. (See Young, 1991.)

Whatever problems those on the streets have as individuals, they have been deepened by the "reforms" of the Reagan era (and worsened since then), which deposited them there, in the name of one artifice or another, including the policies of "benign neglect," coined and advocated by the much-admired "liberal" advisor to President Nixon, Senator Daniel Moynihan.

The California State Department of Housing and Community Development estimates that at least a third of its homeless are families, most with children; that about 50,000 of those sleeping on the streets are seriously mentally ill; and, that nearly 4,000 young people who "graduated" from foster homes are without skills, adequate education, financial security, or morale ("Homelessness Is *Our* Problem," *San Francisco Chronicle* [*SFC*], May 8, 2002). In the Los Angeles area, the proportion of families in some shelters has risen from a third to over a half because of the employment crisis. "The breadwinners can't find jobs, so they're losing their housing" ("No Work, No Homes," *NYT* op-ed, August 14, 2003).

Then there is the high percentage of homeless individuals and families *with* jobs, but with such low incomes they cannot find affordable housing. Add to that, since 2007, the greatly rising numbers of jobless people who quite simply cannot find a job, *plus* those who now work part-time and need the full-time job they lost through recession and/or downsizing; *plus* the cruel inadequacy of the "minimum-wage": what was always an inadequate wage and becomes always more so pushes a *fully*-employed recipient well below the official poverty level.

But doesn't the federal government provide assistance in the way of public housing or housing subsidies for those who need it? It did; or, rather, once it *almost* did:

> When the New Deal programs for public housing and subsidies took hold in the 1930s and were improved by the Federal Housing Act of 1949, they created livable rental units for poor and working-class people. That legislation was *deliberately* undone in the 1980s when the Reagan administration cut funding for the construction of low- and moderate-income housing and revised the tax structure in a way that made affordable multi-family units less attractive for investors to build." ("Facing Up the Housing Crisis," *NYT* editorial, July 5, 2008)

Nowadays such assistance as there is goes mostly to those who are happy to take it but who don't *need* it. The National Low Income Housing Coalition, taking its figures from the 2001 Budget of the US Government, found that 62 percent of all housing subsidies go to households earning more than $100,000 a year. So those with under $100,000 at least get the other 38 percent? Perhaps, but neither in terms of their need, nor in order of its severity. Consider these data, from the "good times" of some years back:

- The California Association of Realtors showed that in 2002 only 29 percent of all Californians were able to afford a home at all, and only 12 percent a median-priced home.
- The US Conference of Mayors, after surveying the 27 major cities of the US, listed the leading cause of homelessness as the lack of affordable housing.
- In California, more than 500,000 are on the affordable housing waiting lists.
- Already in 2002 more than 70,000 affordable low income rental units, like so many thousands before them, are "at risk of conversion to market rate units, driving low income families into homelessness" ("Myths About the Homeless Delay Solutions," *SFC*, July 5, 2002).

Much of the foregoing relates to California some years ago, in what were seen as "good times." As today's recession moves toward what could well become a depression, those difficult conditions in California have worsened, and throughout the nation. It is relevant to add that California, one of the richest states, was expected to go bankrupt in 2009. It must be expected that already weak assistance for the homeless will decline; that those who are and will become homeless there and in other states, will continue to lack adequate health care or decent clothing and, as will be seen in the section to follow, will remain dangerously hungry.

All of that is common in a country that prides itself on decency, on its concern for family and, contrasting itself with other countries, on its public-spiritedness. Meanwhile, many millions eat too much while many others seek handouts, almost all of whom would much rather line up for jobs doing something useful. (See Hartman, 1983.) That takes us to the next set of disgraces.

Nutrition and Hunger

If the Reverend Thomas Malthus were alive today, he would be jumping up and down with pride and joy; not because his wrong-headed "theory" was right (which it wasn't), but because his cruel policies have found a home in the US. Over two centuries ago he argued against what today is called "welfare" for the poor (then meaning the unemployed) with his "theory of population growth." Malthusian "theory" has been used by economists and politicians ever since he spat it out (not only by Reagan and both Bushes, but by Bill Clinton). The theory is that "population inexorably rises more rapidly than food supplies; therefore, do *nothing* to help the poor; to help them now means to have more of them around in misery later" (Malthus, 1798). He added that in addition to letting the poor wallow in their desperation, steps should be taken to force them to live under unsanitary conditions, so as to increase the death rates among them. Malthus himself is long dead and gone; but his ideas still rule, if more cleverly "spun."

Of course there are sensible and decent reasons to lower global rates of population growth, not least because most of it takes place among people who are poor and/or as a consequence of coercive sex for powerless women. Those causes can be alleviated, but only by pursuing the socio-economic measures opposed by today's Malthusians. The truth is that both the historical and contemporary facts of food supply fly in the face of Malthusian "theory." Since the eighteenth century food supplies in the world have almost always increased more rapidly than population. Thus, over the past 35 years, in which more people starved to death than ever, global food production outstripped population growth by a good 16 percent, "enough to supply every person on the earth with 4.2 lbs. of food every day" (Lappe et al., 1998).

That such a tragedy now marks the world is no accident; it is an outcome of the normal and natural working of an economic system driven by profit, not by need. Here is a fine analytical summary of the whys and wherefores:

> Capitalism presents us with the paradoxical reality of a rapid growth of food production and perpetuation of overproduction (relative to markets

and income distribution) on one hand, accompanied by the reinforcement of social exclusion and thus the growth of hunger on the other. The latter is not, as is sometimes thought, mainly a result of population growth (which has generally been surpassed by the growth of productivity in agriculture), but instead a consequence of the fact that the immediate object of food production is not human sustenance and well-being but the growth of profits. The coincidence of hungry mouths with overflowing grain silos may seem to be a paradox, but it is paradox not of our analysis of, but of capitalist agribusiness itself. (Magdoff et al., 2000)

Saying much the same thing, the Nobel economist-philosopher Amartya Sen has pointed out that "Starvation is the characteristic of some people not *having* enough to eat. It is not the characteristic of there not *being* enough food to eat" (Sen, 1981). One of the major political disputes in this era of globalization is that the free trade advocated by the richest economies, including the US's, is violated by all of them with their practices of encouraged and rewarded *restriction* of production which, despite all, leaves the immense surpluses maintained by subsidies and "dumping" practices. Such policies became common in the 1930s, the years of deepest privation of modern times: more than symbolized by the "bonfires" of oranges in California (which I saw) and of coffee in Brazil.

The "famines" of the present find their counterparts in the many "famines" of the past, best-known of which was Ireland's in the mid nineteenth century. The quotation marks around famine are meant to point to an ugly fact: In the same years that more than 1 million Irish died from malnutrition and starvation (1846–49), Ireland was *exporting* always more food to England (the US of the nineteenth century). How could that be? It was made not only possible but probable by the brutal colonization of Ireland from the seventeenth century into the twentieth. Among England's other social crimes, the colonization of the "Emerald Isle" meant that the best of its lands were taken over by English (and, later, Scottish) landowners, the hard work on the land to be done by the destitute Irish producing agricultural products for export at a profit to the oppressors. The lands left for the Irish themselves were the "peat bogs." The bogs produced potatoes, period. Thus, when in 1844 the potato blight took hold (and continued for several years), the average Irish family was left to starve or to emigrate. Ireland's population fell from 9 million to less than 5 million over those years, and it stayed there until just recently. (See Woodham-Smith, 1962; Cahill, 1995; Delany, 2001.)

What about the US? In its *Advanced Report on Household Food Security* (1999), The Department of Agriculture found approximately *36 million* people in the US without adequate access to food and, worse, about 20 percent of children from 5–18 living in "hungry homes" in the ebullient good years of the late 1990s. The same study found that 55 percent of US adults are overweight, and 23 percent are obese. Worldwide, a *billion* people are overweight, while several billion are malnourished, and every year at least *12 million children* die from lack of adequate food. (See "Bodily Harm," *SFC*, April 23, 2000.)

Serious though that problem is in the US, it is dwarfed by the catastrophic food shortages for at least two-thirds of the world's people. The main cause of always greater and more deadly hunger in the poorer countries in the world is quite simply that the ownership and control of their lands and water supplies have been stolen out from under them, along with their cultures and their dignity. In our time, the stage set by colonialism and imperialism is being danced upon in different costume by globalization. (See George, 1976, 1979; Klein, 1999.)

The realities of death-dealing hunger have been haunting most of the world's people now for at least a century. In recent years (mostly through the United Nations) well-publicized programs for alleviating that hunger have been announced and, once in a while, efforts have been made to put them into effect. Meanwhile the problem worsens and even those limited efforts decrease. In the article "UN Official Urges Food Aid For the Poor As a Priority" (*NYT*, June 9, 2002), we learned this:

> With about 810 million people going to sleep hungry, the head of the UN Food and Agriculture Organization [FAO] says that development experts mesmerized by international trade and high technology need to tackle

poverty first. We say that before [the G-8] goes to discuss the digital divide, you need to look at the three elements you need to live, which is to breathe, to drink and to eat... Among those living in perpetual hunger are 200 million children under age 5... Because of big subsidies to farmers in richer nations, at a cost of more than $1 *billion* a day there are huge stocks of food in developed countries... Yet there are still 800 million people who don't have enough money to buy the food they need. Over one *billion* live on a $1 day.

Why and how can such a horrifying tragedy persist? This is how:

Concentration and centralization and rural dispossession within this sector are being reinforced by new technological innovations, particularly in the area of biotechnology, leading to such developments as the proletarianization of the farmer, and to the appropriation of ownership and control of indigenous plants and animals in third world countries. The global commodification of agriculture has its counterpart in the destruction of peasant and small-scale agriculture throughout the world. Subsistence farming is in decline in the third world while the production of luxury crops for export to the rich countries is being expanded as never before. The result is a rise in world food supplies, together with an increase in world hunger..., [even] in the United States itself, at the very heart of the system... (Magdoff et al., 2000)

Although hunger is literally a life-and-death issue for more than a billion people and a life-and-misery matter for billions more, decent people in the US are held back from doing the decent thing about it by ignorance and confusion. Those weaknesses are fed by agricultural giants such as Archer Daniels Midland who profit from it. Meanwhile, through the media, bought and paid for politicians, and the difficulties for a decent public to know the realities, our policies continue to make a horrifying situation always more so; intensified by the growing (and profitable) use of grains for "biofuel" and the rising demand for foodstuffs in China, India, and other rapidly developing countries. (See below.)

Those who wish to combat these horrors with knowledge may be assisted by a powerful and readable book: *World Hunger: 12*

Myths (Lappe et al., 1998). The book is compact and worthy of reading; here is a mere listing of those *myths*:

1. There is not enough food.
2. Nature is to blame.
3. Too many mouths to feed.
4. Food vs. the environment.
5. The Green Revolution is the answer.
6. Justice vs. production.
7. The free market can end hunger.
8. Free trade is the answer.
9. Too hungry to revolt.
10. Foreign aid.
11. We benefit.
12. Food vs. freedom.

That listing indicates the many complexities and the many barriers to clarity for even well-intentioned people; all the more reason to get to work to break through those barriers, to save countless lives. Ah!, we like to think, but even though all those lands were stolen from various societies' lands, the technologies we are now using there will allow their more efficient, more productive use; and if it hadn't been for us moving into those lands, a bad situation would have continued and...so on.

That dreamy support of dangerous and destructive practices of globalization neglects two large facts. The first is that the thievery of lands in Africa, Asia, Latin America *and* North America ruined the lives of their peoples in many irreversible ways in order that the invaders could make a profit or gain military strength. That can never be undone. (See Wright, 1992 for the tragic details.)

The second large fact is that today's globalized usage of those lands to make money for giant corporations, as in the colonial-imperialist pasts, has not only disrupted whole peoples and their cultures and their economies, but it has also destroyed whole forests (contributing to global warming, among other crimes); their having changed the ways and means of agriculture allows "no turning back." The lust for profits has dangerously ignored the costs; most dramatically in its destruction of whole "ecosystems." Reporting the findings of two studies published in the prestigious journal *Science*, this is what the *NYT* had to say in the article "Biofuels Deemed a Greenhouse Threat" (February 8, 2008):

> These studies for the first time take a detailed comprehensive look at the emissions effects of the huge amount of natural land that is being converted to cropland globally to support biofuels development. The destruction of natural ecosystems – whether rain forest in the tropics or grasslands in South America – not only releases greenhouse gases into the atmosphere when they are burned and plowed, but also deprives the planet of natural sponges to absorb carbon emissions. Cropland also absorbs far less carbon than the rain forests or even scrubland that it replaces... Taken globally, the production of almost all biofuels resulted, directly or indirectly, intentionally or not, in new lands being cleared, either for food or fuel... These plant-based fuels were originally billed as better than fossil fuels because the carbon released when they were burned was balanced by the carbon absorbed when the plants grew... But [now it is known] that the process of turning plants into fuels causes its own emissions... The clearance of grassland releases 93 times the amount of greenhouse gas that would be saved by the fuel made annually on that land...; "So for the next 93 years you're making climate change worse, just at the time when we need to be bringing down carbon emissions" ... The world has to reverse the increase of greenhouse gas emissions by 2020 to avert disastrous environmental consequences.

The lands being discussed *had been* lands used to provide food for the native peoples. Dreadful news for a few billion people; but good news for those responsible: "Grain-processing giant Archer-Daniels-Midland Co. said its quarterly profits jumped 42%, including a sevenfold increase in net income in its unit that stores, transports, and trades grains such as wheat corn, and soy beans" ("Grain Companies' Profits Soar as Global Food Crisis Mounts," *Wall Street Journal*, April 3, 2008). Malthus must be whistling in his grave.

Opportunity

Among the phrases we have come to take for granted in the US is that ours is "The Land of Opportunity." Indeed, it may be said that for those numberless generations who left their countries to come to ours, that phrase was first on their lists, outranking even "Land of the Free and Home of the Brave." For a large percentage of those who emigrated, the US was in fact a "land of opportunity." But it was the opposite of that for the native tribes whose lands, lives, and "opportunities" were stolen from them, or for the millions of Africans who were forcibly enslaved; or for the countless Chinese who were "shipped" to the US to build the western railroad systems and who, once freed, found themselves facing the real possibility of being lynched by angry white workers in San Francisco (see Chapter 3).

"The land of opportunity" – it may well have been just that for those who went to the US voluntarily, eager to leave behind the problems, difficulties, even the threats, of their homelands; most especially those from Europe; although even they more often than not continued to have difficult lives, both economically and socially. But if the emigration was in the years after 1840 and up to 1917, the probability is high that their lives and, especially, the lives of their children, were full of many more and better opportunities than those in the lands they left behind. Those generalizations are meant to apply almost entirely to Europeans. They certainly held also for some from Asia, Latin America, the Middle East, and Africa; but, after World War I (and even more after World War II), they have not been so for most (Handlin, 1981).

The largest number of unwelcome emigrants in the US since World War II have been and remain those from Latin America, hundreds of thousands (perhaps millions) of whom have entered illegally. Legal or illegal, they do not find themselves in a "land of opportunity." Like many millions of "Latinos" born and raised in the US, they find themselves discriminated against economically, educationally, socially, and politically, with an unknown but large majority that remains poor, condemned to jobs with no future. Especially in Southern California, Arizona, and Texas, their lives have been "nasty, brutish, and short." But so far as lack of opportunity is concerned, that's the short list. The whole list of those facing very limited or no opportunity must begin with Afro-Americans and Native Americans ("Indians"), whether the focus is upon their education, a decent job, housing, health care, or the "opportunity" to live safely and be accepted, simply, as a human being.

Earlier the concept of "basic needs" was put forth; in addition to nutrition, education, housing, and health care, "opportunity" was cited as one of our basic needs. It is a very different need from the others. In addition to other matters discussed below, opportunity is essential if we are to have sufficient access to meeting all of our needs. But there is more to it than that.

Like myself, most who read these pages will have been fortunate enough to meet their basic needs to a comfortable or at least bearable degree. As such, we are not likely to be conscious of the ways in which we have had access to "opportunities"; just as those who have always had enough to eat do not think about starving. However, reflection leads one to understand that among the many social crimes of inequality, one of the most telling for most is the lack of opportunity; the inability to build a life in which one can meet both one's needs and, importantly, one's possibilities.

Earlier in the book, reference was made to some of the "positive" consequences of World War II for millions of people in the US; for example, to women and to blacks. Many millions of them were able to get jobs previously denied them *only* because they were of the wrong gender or "color"; add to them the veterans (myself included) who were able to further our education. A moment's reflection points to what this meant not only to them but also to their children; and, it may be added, what it meant not only to the economic but to the social and political life of the nation, in both quantitative and qualitative terms. Turn that around and ponder what earlier it had meant to the nation and with so many who could *not* have such jobs; what it meant not only in quantitative but in qualitative terms. "A job is not only a job"; it carries with it a way of life. And that carries us to the closing section.

Dignity, Morale, Self-Respect, and Family Life

The men and women who, during and because of World War II, were able to get jobs in, say, a General Motors factory, had not entered heaven, but they may well have at least taken some steps back from hell. Even setting aside for a moment how their own lives were improved in some degree at least in terms of basic needs, consider what it meant to the education and health – and futures – of their children; and what that must have meant to their own "dignity, morale, self-respect, and family life." Turn that around and, like John Lennon in one of his greatest songs, *imagine*...

Imagine it is the early 1940s; you are black, the mother of a 10-year-old boy; you live in a ghetto in a big city, you work as a house-cleaner, you never finished high school, and your husband also has a lousy job (or he is no longer around). Try to imagine what your "home life" would be like; how to make ends meet, the worries and fears about: your boy's education, what he does after school every day and with whom (if he is still going to school); imagine your exhaustion, your worries, your sense of hopelessness; your lack of dignity, your morale, etc. Then, all of a sudden, there's a terrible war. You and your husband (if not in the army) get jobs with decent pay, respect, and so on. What are the probabilities for your home life? For your hopes and fears for your child? For your morale, your dignity, your family life? Of course, there would still be problems; still...

There is no need to go on with this scenario, except to say that after World War II, whether in the US or in the other industrial countries, opportunities arose year by year that the average person had never experienced before. And standing there with opportunity was hope: "not heaven on earth; but no longer so close to hell." Therefore: bless war? No! *Damn* the system of institutionalized inequalities that *required* a war to bring about what could and should always be everywhere, for all, without having to bring about the sudden deaths of tens of millions.

Put differently, although few who read this will have lived lives of luxury and ease, many will have at some time been close enough to facing "not enough" to "imagine" what it must be like for those who are poor, who are discriminated against because of gender and/or "race"; how that would lead to despair and bitterness and anger and demoralization and dehumanization.

Almost all who read this will have lived their lives mostly or entirely in this, the richest nation in all history but, also a nation "rich" in inequalities; while, at the same time, seeing the US as the model of democracy, freedom, opportunity, decency..., etc. "Model" we may have in rhetoric; but in reality?

In closing this chapter, I refer the reader to its start – to Vachel Lindsay's lament of the 1920s: "Let not young souls be smothered out before / They do quaint deeds and fully flaunt their pride..." That we have "let" all that continue and, in recent years, to worsen, is not the world's *one* crime, but it surely is among its most heart-breaking, most tragic, and, ultimately, the most dangerous crime for one and all. For a comprehensive and readable description and analysis of the disgraces noted in this chapter, see Barbara Ehrenreich's latest book, *This Land is Their Land: Reports from a Divided Nation* (2008). ·

11

INEQUALITY'S INTERACTING CONSEQUENCES FOR THE ECONOMY, DEMOCRACY, AND SOCIAL DECENCY

Inequality and the Economy

Up to here the focus has been mostly upon the several impacts of inequality on "people," because of their class and/or their gender, "race," nationality, or religion. Now we broaden the focus to grasp inequality's serious damages to society as a whole, beginning with the economy. As we proceed, it will be seen that the harm done by inequality to its direct victims spreads as an infectious disease throughout all dimensions of our lives.

Inequality's seriously harmful effects to the economy as a whole are most devastating to those directly harmed, but the harms don't end there. All social life is in constant and significant interaction with all else in the society to some degree, with both intended and unintended consequences; the latter also harm even those responsible: a sliver of justice. As a basis for understanding the aims and the need for this study, note again that a fine place to begin is with Tawney's *Equality* (1931). In the Preface to its 1938 edition, he acutely summarized the economic "ravages of the disease of inequality." After showing that a tiny percentage of very wealthy people "year by year [took] nearly one quarter of Britain's annual output of wealth," he went on to note:

> The wealthy, far from being an economic asset, are an economic liability of alarming dimensions. They involve (1) a perpetual misdirection of limited resources to the production or upkeep of costly futilities, when what the nation requires for its welfare is more and better food, more and better

houses, more and better schools. (2) They mean that, for lack of these simple necessities, the human energies which are the source of all wealth are, in the case of the majority of the population, systematically underdeveloped from birth to maturity. (3) They result in the creation of a jungle of special interests, which stubbornly resist all attempts to reconstruct the economy on a more just and rational line.

That was written over 75 years ago regarding the birthplace of industrial capitalism; it applies with a vengeance to today's capitalism, most clearly to that of the US, aided by our long history of class inequality nourished by gender and intense "race" discrimination. To that it needs adding that the "price" of unlimited control by capitalist goals in our time has intensified and created crises well beyond those of Tawney's era. As is detailed in the following three sections, our "limited natural resources" are today even more "misdirected" and in ways earlier unimaginable; our *human* resources have been both dangerously distorted and "underdeveloped"; and although the corruption and the "jungle of vested interests" of his day were bad enough, compared with today's "jungles" they were like a neighborhood garden, not least when their related vested interests and bottomless corruption are taken into account. Now to Tawney's first reason why the wealthy are an economic liability.

Wasted Natural Resources

The capitalist class that exploits and misuses the working class not only controls what is and what is *not* produced and its ways and means, in the last century it also combines peacetime with wartime waste and destruction in ways and degrees surpassing all previous periods combined. In doing so, it has created the foundations for what may become an apocalyptic twenty-first century. (See my *Waste of Nations*, 1989.) Consider the following:

- Since 1945, there has not been a year without large or small wars. Although no single war since then has yet matched the 60 million deaths in Europe alone in World War II, the total for the "small wars" since then is appalling (in the Middle East, Central Asia, Central and South America and Africa; the Korean and Vietnam wars alone each claimed more than 3 million lives and millions more were wounded). Then add the staggering socio-economic damages and the displacement, demoralization, and social paralysis accompanying and following the wars, and add up the waste.

- The wars' wastes neither began nor stopped there. They must include the extraordinary wastefulness created by military production and use and, less obviously, what is lost to societies when a significant amount of their people's efforts and skills and creative possibilities are siphoned away by militarism and military operations. (See Chapter 8.)

That said, the "honors" for massive waste and destruction of resources, equipment, and lives do not go only to war and militarism. Setting aside the *trillions* of dollars of admitted military expenditures *after* 1945, the "non-war" functioning of the socio-economy has itself been responsible for at least as much waste and destruction; an always accelerating process. The official US military budget for just 2008–09 (adjusted for inflation) exceeds that for the *four* years of World War II, even if we ignore that the "official" budget is a set of calculated lies. (See Chapter 8 and Cypher, 2002.) That takes us to a set of related questions and answers, keeping in mind that each one discussed bears upon and worsens the others:

What is produced, and what is *not* produced, and *why*?
How are they produced, within what structures of control?
What is, and is not, *consumed* and by *whom*?
How well are *human* and *natural* resources used, when measured by the criteria of satisfaction, stability, safety, the environment, time, needs and possibilities?
How much of our wastes are *destructive*?

Implicitly or explicitly, those are the questions guiding what follows. I begin with what may seem to be a terminological matter, but it is much more than that.

Efficiency versus Waste

The US and its people waste so much in so many ways it is hard to know where to begin. But because we declare ourselves to be the very most efficient economy in the world, it is best to start with something like a definition of "waste," and its costly, deadly, and simply foolish components and consequences. Although the popular view has been that the US is Number 1 in economic efficiency, the reality is that we are the most wasteful of all nations – ever. That reasonable people can accept that reality in practice is partly rooted in the common confusion between *plant* efficiency and *economic* efficiency; where "plant" refers to the processes taking place *within* a factory, "economic" to the socio-economy.

The US was long seen as the world's leader in plant efficiency for autos, electronic goods, steel, textiles; almost everything. That was reasonably accurate up to about 1920, but in recent years it has often been considerably less so: the Japanese and Germans have long produced better cars with greater efficiency than our (now collapsing) "Big Three"; many countries produce steel more cheaply than we do, as is true for a broad range of manufactures, including TVs and ingredients of the computer world. But isn't that so because other countries' wages are lower? No. They are indeed obscenely lower in the "emerging economies" of the world (e.g. in Asia), with wages and conditions matching or even worse than those of the industrial revolution in Britain; but there we are referring not to efficiency but to labor exploitation. Also, money wages in the other industrial countries are more often *higher* than those of the US. (See Osberg, 1991.) Nor does that take into account our considerably lower "social wage"; the health insurance, pensions, paid vacations, public education and housing of *all* of the other rich societies are much higher than in the US (for the minority who receive – or used to receive – any at all).

Moreover, if the great efficiency of the US economy is the focus, it is difficult to explain why the average hours worked by US workers are so much *longer* than those of Japan, Britain, Germany, and France. Note also that although others worked more hours than US workers from 1950 through the 1980s, those in the US worked more from the 1990s on. (See below.) The reasons for that reversal since the 1980s are to be found in the realm of *political* economy more than in narrow economic considerations. (See Phillips, 2002.)

But there is another relevant and vital difference between the US and others, little noted or discussed; namely, the costs of what the late David Gordon calls "bloated management." What is "bloated" includes the exorbitant incomes of CEOs, plus the rapidly rising non-production costs in the largest companies, due to the inflation of managerial staffs (thus enlarging the "empire" of the top officers), and the enormous increase in the number of "supervisors" who are, in effect, "patrolling" the workers (D. Gordon, 1996).

As this is being written in early 2009, the leading (and non-leading) economies are sinking into a deep recession which could become a depression, some with still rising, most with stagnant or falling prices; all in deepening troubles. It now seems clear that neither in the US nor elsewhere are the "authorities" able to see how they can control the mad beast now circling the globe: all of the major capitalist nations have allowed their economies and their governments to bow and scrape to the spirit of "Las Vegas, Inc." – except, as noted earlier, Communist-capitalist China; which, understanding that its enormous exports to the US (inter alia) are seriously shrinking, has (ironically) already instituted its variation of FDR's New Deal program of public expenditures; wondering and worrying what will happen with the $2 *trillion*-plus the US owes it. Now, as the world writhes in crisis, "China realizes that the likelihood of a fall in the value of the dollar would mean a big capital loss for it" (Krugman, "China's Dollar Trap," *NYT*, April 3, 2009).

Oil is *the* product of our era, as steel was in the nineteenth century; only more so. Its importance neither begins nor ends with its price; there are also its serious relationships with war and peace, the economy and politics, and with environmental damage. As this is written, the financial crisis and associated global downturn have greatly reduced the demand for oil for all forms of transportation and much of industry; accordingly, its $140-plus per barrel has flopped. What will happen with oil in the near future cannot be known. What can be known is that over the long run oil will continue to be very much a major player on the stage of economics and politics. It deserves a closer look:

Oil! Its innumerable uses began their hold about a century ago for personal and commercial transportation, for vital uses in industry and agriculture, and for domestic life. In doing so, the oil companies moved toward always more substantial economic, political, and social power. It is arguable that our world would be both better and safer entirely without oil. Absurd? Only if we ignore oil's "importance" noted above and below, can we not be concerned with oil's influence and its prominence in the processes that maintain and increase inequalities. Oil's importance has led to a vast literature, some of which can be found in the following: Sampson (1975), Foster (1999), Klare (2001), Heinberg (2004), Tanzer (1961), Everest (2004), Sinclair (1926). What follows here is a mere summary concerning (1) oil and war, (2) oil and the economy, (3) oil, politics and power, and (4) oil and the environment...

1. Oil and War

Wars have been a constant in all of history; for the past century they have not only been more numerous but immeasurably and always more costly in all measures of existence. Moreover, and whether or not seen as such, they have had one element in common: control over agricultural and, especially, mineral resources with, in the past century, *oil* ranking always higher on the list as significantly causal. (See Chapter 8.) Most clearly and increasingly since 1945 that has been so for petroleum fields. When those wars flourished, oil was popularly seen as abundant. No longer. Ten years ago a barrel of oil cost $11. January 2008: $100/barrel; May 2008:

$135/barrel. Since then it has been falling (November 2008: $75/barrel). The price goes up as demand increases from both leading and "emerging" economies; down as recession takes hold. If and when we emerge from the ongoing recession/depression the price will rise again because demand will surely exceed supply: oil discoveries peaked about 50 years ago.

Item: Since 1984, world oil production has exceeded discoveries in a widening gap. "Normally," there is a widening gap between supply and demand with rapidly escalating prices of oil, gasoline, and natural gas. Given the direct/indirect control of oil resources, industry, and politics by a handful of companies ("the Seven Sisters") and a few nations (Saudi Arabia the strongest), are the prospects for "oil wars," greater or lesser than in the past? The books by Sampson, Everest, Klare, and Heinberg noted above give a worrisome set of answers.

2. Oil and the Economy

As with war, there are all too many reasons to worry about the economy's health and dangers without having to bring oil into focus. But, because the supply and price of oil affect so much of our consumption and production and, as well, our foreign trade and financial and service sectors, when oil is in trouble, so is the economy. The most recent "stagflation" resulted from always higher and rising oil and food prices for the US, and Europe, Japan, China, et al. Although oil and food are very different, they also have much in common. The demand for both is steadily rising because of the higher demands from industrializing countries like China and India and Brazil, and supply can't keep up for oil because we've used up so much and so carelessly in the past, and still do.

3. Oil, Politics, and Power

Given that both Bush and Cheney were "oil guys" before they got into the White House, oil giants could relax. But they don't take anything for granted: the oil and gas industry spent almost $20 million on congressional campaign contributions in 2004 (more than ever before); then doubled that amount in 2006. The money was well spent: recent subsidies for them are about $6 *billion* a year, a return on investment of more than 600-to-1. "The Best Congress Oil Could Buy" (*Multinational Monitor*, September/October 2007). And for the election campaign of 2008? See the *New York Times* editorial of March 3, "The Senate Shills for Big Oil": the 5 biggest companies cleared $145 *billion* in profits in 2007, and got $7 *billion* in tax breaks. More than coincidental with those developments was that in the 1990s the ratio of CEOs' incomes to production workers' incomes (led by those in oil) rose from 140-to-1 to 209-to-1; in 2007 it was 450-to-1. (The ratio in Japan for similar years has been 7-to-1.)

4. Oil and the Environment

In Chapters 4 and 5 this was discussed briefly. Suffice it to add here that both the search for oil and its multiple uses are destructive. The search itself batters the natural environment; for example, the physical harm done to the seas and land of Alaska by oil spills and endless pipelines. At least as horrifying is the irreversible damage done to the socio-political-economic lives of the native peoples of oil-extracting countries. It is both tragic and remarkable that those damages (and polluted air) are widely-known and yet, at the same time, the craving for more and bigger cars rises rather than falls (except as forced down by today's housing busts) – while, at the same time, the support for safer and much cheaper public transportation falls rather than rises: the "consciousness industry" has done its job all too well. "Climate change"? "Global warming"? No place to park? No problem.

Today, all nations are "in tune," but the songs being sung are in a minor key: casino capitalism, over-production, stagflation, recession, financial crisis, corruption, waste, wars and, last but by no means least, environmental disaster. If we were to work up "a dirty laundry list" of waste, it would have to include the horrendous wastes integral to war, consumerism, its advertising and associated wastes. But heading that list, and most relevant to the tragedies and self-destructive meanings of inequality, is the waste of human beings. The novelist Toni Morrison provided a dire soliloquy on such waste in her novel *Tar Baby*:

> That was the sole lesson of their world: how to make waste, to make machines that make more waste, how to make wasteful products, how to talk waste, how to study waste, how to design waste, how to cure people who were sickened by waste so they could be well enough to endure it, how to mobilize waste, legalize waste... And it would drown them one day, they would all sink into their own waste and the waste they had made of the world and then, finally, they would know true peace and the happiness they had been looking for all along...

Now to a less eloquent look at that closely related mixture of stupidity and criminality of our world: Because we are part of nature, we too are harmed when we abuse it and destroy it. So we turn to some of the details of harm we allow to be done to ourselves. That takes us to Tawney's second reason why the wealthy are an economic liability.

Wasted Human Resources

The harmful effects of inequality occur both within and beyond the economy. In the foregoing section, the waste and mistreatment of workers by "bloated management" was discussed. But such waste neither begins nor ends there. Add to that the cruel wastes of gender and "race" discrimination that limit the education and training of those discriminated against. Such prejudice not only restricts their life possibilities, it also systematically reduces the productivity of our economy and our social wellbeing as a whole.

As noted in Chapter 10, a dramatic confirmation of that was shown during World War II: because 16 million men and women were in the military, the normally available work force was drastically reduced just when the war demanded greatly *increased* production. So? So suddenly it was discovered that – behold! – the discrimination against women and blacks was holding back the entire economy's production. *Who* would have guessed it? They could drive a bus! They could even work on an assembly line putting tanks and fighter planes together! (And, come to think of it, might even be able – who would of thought it? – to teach, practice medicine, be an engineer! Wow!)

All of that and much more was made possible – for a while – by the FEPC (the fair employment practices laws) enacted during the war, prodded along, it is worth noting, by Roosevelt's wife Eleanor. FDR was a "conservative" when first elected, but Eleanor had spent much of her life quietly working for a decent society. The FEPC legislation was federal in origin and in its enforcement, and applied *only* to federally-financed production. It was objected to, fought against, and systematically violated, especially in the South; and, as time went on, it was supplanted or shoved aside at *all* levels of government. However, in much of the country, the war and immediate postwar work experiences with "fair employment" opened the door to considerably reduced job discrimination in the nation; until, that is, very recently.

An attempt to reproduce "fair employment" in the realm of, especially, education (see Chapters 3 and 10), was manifested in the "affirmative action" legislation of the 1960s. But, since the 1970s, in one way or another and in one state or another those efforts to lessen or get rid of discrimination have been watered down, abandoned, or reversed. It needs re-reversing.

There is much more to be said about wasted natural and human resources, comment on which will be found in other chapters. But first a focus on an instructive bright spot of our history since 1945; bright both as in "shiny" and as in "intelligent." It should be put in place for all, not just for veterans: the GI Bill. It provided that all of the 16 million veterans of the World War II were eligible for financial assistance to renew or begin their education at any level: grade school, high school, community college, or university. The financial assistance included not only tuition, but books and living expenses. It was what enabled me to attend university; and, more to the point, it made a full education possible for women and for black veterans, among others discriminated against. And inequality got a slap in the face. There is a "GI Bill" for our present wars; but it covers only tuition.

The post-World War II GI Bill was a vivid example of what a sane and decent society can and should do, and the socio-economic improvements of the ensuing years showed just how sane that legislation was. Not only did the – now shrinking – entire educational system expand and flourish as the lives of many *millions* were enriched, but, as well, the US economy entered a quarter century of what economic historians unanimously see as its strongest years *ever*. As depression looms – and even if it didn't – now is the time to put together a second "bill"; this time a bill for the education of *all* the *people*. (See Epilogue.)

However, as noted, from the 1970s on politicians at all levels shifted the US into reverse to take us back to the political economy of the 1920s, and to a "modernized' version of the discriminatory practices of the pre-World War II era; including an educational system in which money counts first, from kindergarten on. Not coincidentally, the anti-discriminatory laws of the postwar years were dropped in one state after another; as education worsens and as jobs decline. (See Chapters 7, 9, and 10.) Now we turn to Tawney's third reason why the wealthy are an economic liability.

"The Stinking Jungle of Special Interests"

The phrase is Tawney's, and he was referring to the politics of Britain. Were he alive and walking through US politics now he would need a gas mask. "Stinking politics" have not been confined to the capitalist era, but recently they have sunk to new depths and, among other vile results, inequalities have worsened and spread. What's so specially stinking of the US as compared with others? Recall that US capitalism and its democracy came into being accompanied by phrases such as "all men are created equal," and "one man, one vote." Rarely was there a comment that such language was odd in a slave society, or in a society in which "man" would be taken literally until the twentieth century (and, mostly, still). I have quoted Tawney before; here it is helpful to do so once more, and at length:

> Democracy is unstable as a political system as long as it remains a political system and nothing more, instead of being, as it should be, not only a form of government, but a type of *society*, and a manner of life which is in harmony with that type, which requires an advance along two lines: (1) the resolute elimination of all forms of special privilege which favor some groups and depress others..., and (2) the conversion of economic power, now often an irresponsible tyrant, into the servant of society..., accountable for its actions to a public authority... What that means in the conditions of today is to destroy Plutocracy and to set in place an equalitarian society. (Tawney, 1931; italics mine)

As Tawney wrote, the "special privileges" for capitalists were as common as London's fog and had been since capitalism's birth. But the "special privileges" of that past were minimal when set against today's corruption and wars. A second reading of Chapter 2 and its discussions of corruption, campaign financing, and lobbying is suggested as relevant for grasping their role in the ability of the business world to gain the "privileges" they seek and get. Those discussions will not be repeated here; we take a close look only at corruption of US local, state, and national government in order to "stamp out" regulation.

In the Driver's Seat: King Corruption

In the modern world there have been periodic moments of shock when particular corrupt activities have come to light, whether in the UK, France, Italy or, to end what is a long list, today's US. A recent and well-publicized scandal was when, after Senator Obama became President Obama, the governor of Illinois – Rod Blagojevich – used that power to sell that office to the highest bidder; was caught at it, and is no longer governor. The appropriate theme in a lead article by Frank Rich in the *New York Times* ("Two Cheers for Rod Blagojevich," December 15, 2008) was that "the governor of Illinois is a timely scapegoat for an era of corruption and profound lack of accountability," and he goes on to show the commonality of such practices, not least as regards Wall Street's Robert Rubin (economic advisor on "deregulation" to John McCain in the past, and now Obama's advisor). *C'est la vie.*

Item: "A Rich Education for Summers" (*NYT*, April 6, 2009): "Summers plays down his stint in the hedge fund business as merely a part-time job, but he earned nearly $5.2 million in...one year at one of the world's largest hedge funds [D.E. Shaw, a $12 trillion firm], working only one day a week 2006–08. 'This is what might be called contamination,' said Andrew Sabl [Professor of Public Policy, UCLA]." When Shaw was asked if Summers would run his own lucrative hedge fund, Shaw replied: "I don't know; I am really glad he's running this" (i.e. as advisor to Obama).

In Chapter 6 considerable attention was given to the successes of giant corporations and Wall Street in ridding the nation of the various protective socio-economic reforms instituted from the 1930s through the 1960s. But the post-1970s *anti*-reform efforts effectively sought to "*un-democratize*" the society as regards the "ill-fed, ill-housed, ill-clothed" and the efforts to diminish the racism accompanying those "ills." As those efforts proceeded and succeeded, they fed the also growing and spreading processes of what has become institutionalized corruption in all corners of society.

Most of that corruption has involved "big money": to set up rightwing research institutes, to feed an extraordinary growth of tens of thousands of lobbyists and highly-paid other "experts" involved in the direct and/or indirect control of the media in all of its divisions; and/or in the increasing corruption of universities (mostly in science and engineering departments); all have been involved in shaping the country in the interest of its *very* rich minority. Taken together, they have made the US and its politics into an always more "stinking jungle of special interests" in which *big* money has succeeded in bringing out the worst in us and our society. US politics have been altered to the point where all who run for office, whether on the local, state, or national level – from cop in the street to president – know that "money talks," and that they'd better listen: it goes with the political territory.

In the past, reform movements have had positive consequences in all quarters of our society. The subsequent and ongoing total corruption of politics has made it almost impossible for a socially decent person to be elected to office: "decent" as regards education, housing, poverty, racism, health care, and/or, peace. Instead, positive reforms seeking a better society for all have been shelved or stamped out; forgotten. Corruption and its consequences are "normal."

The massive lobbying and campaign financing that sped up after World War II have made all earlier successes of business in creating and/or stifling governmental policy seem as child's play. Those who specialize in the buying of government for purposes of the wealthy and powerful are also the prime beneficiaries, supporters, and/or practitioners of inequality; of course. The business world has never been alone in seeking and getting its way with the government, nor is it alone in using corruption, campaign financing, and lobbyists as handy "tools"; but from the dawn of the twentieth century, and much more in the twenty-first, those methods became *de rigueur* for those who wished to shape public policy.

They have now gone well beyond "buying votes" to finding direct and more usually, indirect ways of "producing votes." This has been so whether the aims have been negative or positive, racist or profit-seeking; whatever. It soon became clear that such ends, were they to be achieved, were costly in many dimensions. To have and maintain a politically-oriented organization or "research institute," and/or to pay for "publicity," and/or..., you name it: to gain the sustained attention and "cooperation" of legislators takes *lots* of $$$. That (tax-deductible) money has been there for the asking; and is used effectively.

The access to big money is of course most feasible for those who already have it: first and foremost, big business and the wealthy; plus groups representing the status quo as regards racism, guns, militarism, and religious fervor. Except for the just-noted enthusiasts, those who see themselves as the beneficiaries of inequalities are usually those best positioned to maintain and/or increase them: taken together they are sworn enemies of those locked in poverty, denied health care, decent housing and a good education.

The corruptors' gains were increasingly achieved from the 1970s through the 1990s, paving the way for two overlapping processes easing the way for today's dangerous trio of economic power, corruption, and militarism. The resulting increased inequalities now threaten an already fragile democracy. Note once more this telling comparison concerning the evolution of military contracts (as detailed in Chapter 8): during World War II new heights of concentration occurred – just 100 companies received two-thirds of *all* war contracts. They doled them out to tens of thousands of smaller companies who thus became beholden to them, and usually stayed that way after the war. But that was just a beginning. From the 1950s on, the process of concentration sped up, so that by the 1990s, always fewer companies received always more military contracts. From 1946 to 1996, "milex" had passed $10 *trillion*; by 2008 that expenditure had passed $13 *trillion*, as the number of companies granted them continued to decline. (See Chapter 8; Herman and O'Sullivan, 1989.)

A major, always more costly and dangerous result is the continuation and increase in US military splurging, with the rest of the world playing "me too" all too much. Thus, for the year 2006, *global* military spending exceeded $1.2 *trillion*, with the US's $529 billion accounting for 46 percent of the total. The US was also the biggest arms *seller* in that year, followed by the UK and China (*Multinational Monitor*, June 6, 2007).

Both despite and because of all, early in the twenty-first century the US economy had already fallen into the phenomenon called "jobless recovery"; a process in which as productivity continues to rise, jobs increasingly fall, landing in the poor countries at dirt wages. Thus: "Job Creation Remains Slow" (*NYT*, August 8, 2003). What was actually going on is indicated in the article's last paragraph: "Technology spending has been weak since the stock market bubble burst three years ago, and business investment over all has been the weakest segment of the economy for the last several years. Instead, companies have shifted strategy and hunted relentlessly for every possible way to squeeze more production out of the remaining workers." That was in 2003; since 2007 joblessness has risen always more swiftly, going from 550,000 a month to this: "No end in sight to job losses; 663,000 more cut in March" (*NYT*, April 4, 2009). It is expected that 5 million will be lost by the end of 2009, and with no recovery in sight.

In his excellent and readable new book *The Case for Big Government*, the long-time *NYT* economics commentator Jeff Madrick (2008) summed up some of the "low spots" of recent years and their consequences, as he answers this question: "How did the wealthiest nation in history come to believe it is not wealthy?"

> America has no free and high quality day care or pre-K institutions to nourish and comfort two-worker families... College had become far more expensive and attendance is now bifurcated to class... Transportation infrastructure has been notoriously neglected, is decaying and has not been adequately modernized to meet energy-efficient standards or global competition. America has not responded to high energy costs and global warming in general. America has a health care system that is simply out of control, providing on balance inadequate quality at very high prices... The financial system, progressively deregulated since the 1970s, broke free of government oversight entirely in the 1990s and early 2000s and speculation reminiscent of the early 1800s was the result with potentially equal levels of damage... These facts amount to about as conclusive a proof as history ever provides that the ideology applied in this generation has failed.

Now we must find the answer to another question: "Will the Obama administration be able to turn that massive deterioration around?" It could, but not unless it breaks the grip of corruption that strangles all efforts for reform, whether on local, state or national levels. The Nobel economist Paul Krugman – now also an almost daily and worried commentator for the *NYT* – had this to say in the spring of 2009 (also, see his recent books):

> Here's the picture that scares me: It's September 2009, the unemployment rate has passed 9 percent, and despite the early round of stimulus spending,

it's still headed up. Obama finally concedes that a bigger stimulus is needed. But he can't get the new plan through Congress because approval for his economic policies has plummeted partly because his policies are seen to have failed, partly because job-creation policies are conflated in the public mind with deeply unpopular bank bailouts. And as a result, the recession rages on, unchecked. OK, that's a warning, not a prediction. But economic policy is falling behind the curve, and there's a real, growing danger that it will never catch up. (March 10, 2009)

By the time you read this, Krugman's worries may well have been confirmed; or worse. If that is so, it is because the policies of government at all levels, not least those of the Congress, have been effectively bought and paid for by the very people who have taken us to these miserable conditions. There is of course a set of policies that would not only take the US out of its present economic pains, but also reverse the processes noted by Madrick above; reverse them and take us not only to a healthy economy but a sane society. Of which, a bit more below and more in the Epilogue. (A readable and strong analysis of what has gone wrong and what should be done about it may be found in the article by Arthur MacEwan, "Inequality, Power and Ideology," in the bi-monthly magazine *Dollars & Sense*, March–April 2009.)

Inequality and Social Decency

Make that "inequality and social indecency." Given what has preceded this page, it should be unnecessary to provide further details as to the sordid breadth and strength of inequality in the US. I have been a "left-center" critic for many decades. But the past few decades' socio-economic conditions have come to the point where distinct "centrists" in the US have become severely worried and critical of the right-wing shift of the "status quo." A clear example is Kevin Phillips. He has long been a self-described conservative supporter of capitalism, and, until recent years, an advisor to Republican presidents. In his books since the 1990s, however, Phillips has come to many of the same conclusions as "left-centrists"; if also with a different starting-point, expertise, and a more conventional set of goals. Although – or because – he is a devout believer in capitalism, Phillips is now among the most severe critics of, especially, US capitalism; as is illustrated by the titles of his most recent books. Note their titles and ascending dates:

1990 *The Politics of Rich and Poor: Wealth and the American Electorate in the Reagan Aftermath*
1993 *Boiling Point: Democrats, Republicans and the Decline of the Middle Class Prosperity*
1994 *Arrogant Capital*
2002 *Wealth and Democracy: A Political History of the American Rich*
2006 *American Theocracy: The Peril and Politics of Radical Religion, Oil, and Borrowed Money*
2008 *Bad Money: Reckless Finance, Failed Politics, and the Global Crisis of American Capitalism*

Taken together, these books represent a sustained and severe critique of the US political economy; all written by a self-styled "conservative." Much as I admire his books, I must add that Phillips wishes to "conserve" a substantially democratic capitalist nation, the likes of which has never existed anywhere in the capitalist world (although the Scandinavian countries are much more democratic than elsewhere). Phillips fears that in this precarious world, to function always more in the ways and means of US capitalism, is to race toward economic and political disaster. The following could have been written by a Tawney:

> As the twenty-first century gets underway, the imbalance of wealth and democracy in the United States is unsustainable... Market theology and unelected leadership have been displacing politics and elections. Either democracy must be renewed and politics brought back to life, or wealth will cement a new and less democratic regime: plutocracy by some other name.

It was written by Phillips in his 2002 *Wealth and Democracy*. Tawney was earlier quoted at some length from the Preface to the

1938 edition of his *Equality*. In 1939, as World War II exploded, the "capitalist democracies" of Italy, Germany, Spain, and Japan (soon to be followed by France) had all descended into fascism and militarism. These were Tawney's closing words to the British people a year earlier in his Preface (1938):

> If, in this country, democracy falls, it will fall, not through any fortuitous combination of unfriendly circumstances, but from the insincerity of some of its professed defenders, and the timidity of the remainder... If it stands, it will stand, not because it has hitherto stood, but because ordinary men and women were determined that it should, and threw themselves with energy into broadening its foundations. To broaden its foundations means, in the conditions of today, to destroy plutocracy and to set in its place an equalitarian society. It is [my] hope that this book may make some contribution to that cause...

Those words could well serve as the closing words to this book. Today the US economy is rushing into a deep collapse which seems likely to take the world economy toward its second depression. In the February 13, 2008 edition of the *New York Times*, Robert Reich (Secretary of Labor under Clinton in the 1990s) issued a set of warnings and recommendations in an article titled "Totally Spent." I agree with the warnings and his recommendations, but add what he undoubtedly knows but does not specify; namely, that for either the warnings or the recommendations to be heeded in practice, the US must move onto a road going in a very different direction. We, and other countries, must see to it that our economy will be steered from the bottom and the middle up. The "top" has again shown that it is untrustworthy. Here are some excerpts from Reich, well worth quoting at length:

> We're sliding into recession or worse, and Washington is turning to normal remedies for economic downturns...; but this isn't a normal downturn. The problem lies deeper: It is the culmination of three decades during which American consumers have spent beyond their means. That era is now coming to an end. Consumers have run out of ways to keep the spending binge going. The only lasting remedy, other than for Americans to accept a lower standard of living and for businesses to adjust to a smaller economy,

is to give middle- and lower-income Americans more buying power – and not just temporarily. The underlying problem has been building for decades. America's median hourly wage is barely higher than it was 35 years ago (adjusted for inflation). The income of a man in his 30s is now 12 percent *below* that of a man his age three decades ago. Most of what's been earned in America since then *has gone to the richest 5 percent*... Yet the rich already have most of what they want. Instead of buying, and thus stimulating the American economy the rich are more likely to invest their earnings wherever around the world they can get the highest return. The binge seems to be over; we are reaping the whirlwind of widening inequality and more concentrated wealth.

That is the nature of the problem as Reich sees it. I mostly agree, but will add the critique of Bill Moyers in a recent essay:

We have fallen under the spell of money, faction, and fear, and the great American experience in creating a different future together has been subjugated to individual cunning in pursuit of wealth and power and to the claims of empire, with its ravenous demands and stupefying distractions. A sense of political impotence pervades the country... We hold elections, knowing they are unlikely to bring the corporate state under popular control...; we do not have the political will to address our most intractable challenges. (Moyers, 2008)

So it goes, and so it will keep going unless and until "We the People" take over the steering wheel. The next chapter will show that the US has some lessons to learn from the other rich capitalist countries; while noting that in recent years they too have been dangerously bewitched by the siren calls of US ways and means. Be that as it may, the next chapter will summarily examine the many differences between the US and Western European nations regarding the issues discussed in preceding chapters. The differences are substantial, as are (or, until recently, were) in important ways, their politics and their socio-economic institutions. Although those societies are also rife with social defects, their capitalism was for many decades after World War II somewhat "tamed" as, meanwhile, the US lurched back toward nineteenth-century savagery.

12

COMPARISONS OF INEQUALITY AND ITS TREATMENT BETWEEN THE US AND WESTERN EUROPE

Introduction

"We the people" of the US have long seen our country as the "land of the free and the home of the brave": a model for all other lands to envy and to become. Had we been or were we now such a society, there would be no need for a book such as this criticizing our all too many prejudices, modes of discrimination, and deep inequalities. On the other hand, had the US been unique in its abhorrent ways, we would not have become the land of numberless immigrants who, except for those enslaved, mostly came to our shores with hope for a better life. They did so for many reasons, not least economic; but many also came to escape from the discriminatory "racial" practices and inequalities of their native lands. (See Handlin, 1981.)

However, those who made it here were often inclined to discriminate against – and to be discriminated against by – other immigrants who, like themselves, were called "dirty names." All of us, not least in the US, have lived all too long as though we are better off if we can spit on others. In doing so, we have placed ourselves in still *another* land of institutionalized inequalities; almost all of us targeting almost all others: most severely, "those of color" – "blacks, browns, and yellows." The election of Barack Obama to the presidency of the US undoubtedly shows that some progress has been made; just as certainly, it leaves a long way to go, not least regarding the mistreatment of blacks.

Inequalities and prejudices of all categories exist everywhere: of gender, "race," national origin, religion, income, wealth, power and class; in access to health care, education, housing, nutrition, and opportunity. Moreover, if one is black *and* a woman *and* poor *and* follows the "wrong" religion *and* is a worker…, you're in really *deep* trouble, because each intensifies the difficulties of being one or more of the others.

Earlier chapters have tried to show how the victims are treated in the US. How are they treated in the other rich countries – in Britain, France, Germany, the Netherlands, Italy, in the Scandinavian countries? The short answer is that whatever their many shortcomings and with important exceptions (e.g., Nazi Germany, English vs. Irish), until recently, those countries have dealt with such matters less indecently than in the US. Before going further, it is pertinent to comment briefly with one especially revealing exception; namely, the "racism" of "white" against "white."

I continue to place quotation marks around "race" because, as noted in Chapter 3, there is no basis for it, except in the attitudes of the "racists." There it was pointed out that the "white" English discriminated harshly against the "white" Irish who had emigrated to England because Ireland had been impoverished first by having been invaded and conquered by the English in the seventeenth century, and then by the devastating ideologically-created potato famine of the mid-nineteenth-century (Woodham-Smith, 1962). The Irish "learned" to despise the English as such, and vice versa, each seeing the other as an "inferior race." As though that insanity were not enough, the Irish also developed hatred among themselves: Catholics vs. (Scottish or English) Protestants; often associated with a politics connected with being for or against independence.

Whether as regards the treatment of the Irish by the English or the Irish of other Irish, there is all too much similarity in what is going on today in Europe, whether in Germany (vs. Turks), France (vs. North Africans), in England (vs. Pakistani, and/or others), in Italy (vs. the "Roma" immigrants from "ex-Yugoslavia"), or Ethiopia, or… All of this is intensified as globalization drives always greater numbers of people from the poorer countries to seek jobs in those richer, while, at the same time and related to that, good jobs are disappearing in the rich countries (see Chapters 6 and 10). The European countries now to be considered are all capitalist countries; as such, they cannot function without capitalism's inherent inequalities of class, and thus of income, wealth, and power. But there are also degrees of social abuse from one country to another.

First, a summary look at the situation of the poor in some of those countries. Then comparisons will be made under some of the same headings used earlier for the US regarding health care and education, plus a brief statement concerning the aged and the homeless. The comparisons greatly favor Europe; but it's a gap that has been closing – much to the harm of Europeans.

Poverty in Europe

In Europe as elsewhere, poverty is closely connected with all the other realms of inequality. The US takes the prize for being the richest country in the world with, also, the highest poverty rate *and* the stingiest and *meanest* welfare system. Poor people aren't popular anywhere, but nowhere in the powerful countries are they treated as cruelly as in the US; nowhere are welfare programs run as punitively and inefficiently, whether measured by cost per person or by their success or failure in assisting poor people into self-support and *off* welfare. (See Osberg, 1991.)

In Western Europe in the 1980s, for example, anti-poverty programs pulled from 10 to 60 percent up and out of poverty; the success rate in the US was closer to 1 percent. Lars Osberg's 1991 book, *Inequality and Poverty: International Perspectives*, is both comprehensive and technical with chapters of his own and seven contributors. In Chapter 2, "Cross-National Comparisons of Inequality and Poverty Position," Timothy Smeedling measures the inequality of "disposable income" for ten countries. The US had the highest income inequality, followed by Australia, Canada, Netherlands, Switzerland, United Kingdom, Israel, Germany, Norway, and Sweden in that order; Sweden with the least inequality.

Those data were for the late 1980s; in the OECD (2008) study they were both confirmed and shown as having worsened. A different study, using similar procedures, compares international *poverty* rates in the late 1990s and shows much the same picture; namely, that higher *inequality* rates go hand in hand with higher *poverty* rates (see Mishel et al., 2003–04).

> The United States, with 16.9% of its total population living in poverty, has the highest level of overall poverty among the 19 countries examined here. The next closest is Australia (14.3%) then Italy (14.2%), the United Kingdom (13.4%), and Canada (12.8%). The United States is also unique in that it has the highest rate or child poverty (22.3%).

Those figures are for the rich countries. Those in the poor countries? The World Bank estimated in 2004 that more than a third of the world's 6 billion people live in what they called "plain" or "extreme" poverty. Also, as noted in Chapter 11, while the US economy was booming in the 1990s, globalization was also putting pressure on workers to work more hours for the same or less income (with less or no benefits) or get laid off. Here is some related bad news from Robert Reich, US Secretary of Labor in the Clinton years:

> America's median hourly wage is barely higher than it was 35 years ago (adjusted for inflation). The income of a man in his 30s is now 12 percent *below* that of a man his age 30 years ago. Most of what's been earned in America since then has gone to the richest 5 percent... Inequality can be reversed only through better schools for children in lower- and moderate income communities...; which would require good preschools, fewer students per classroom, and better pay for teachers... (*NYT*, February 13, 2008)

Good suggestion; but the White House and Congress and state governments are not so much deaf and dumb as they are bought and sold. (See Chapters 9 and 10 and the discussions of health care and education below.) Now another statement from Reich:

> America's largest corporations have decoupled from the United States: Their overseas subsidiaries are booming even as their American operations

stagnate. General Electric expects more than half its revenue this year [2007] to come from outside the United States for the first time; more than half of Boeing's new orders are from overseas. Ford is struggling in America, but doing well in Europe. In other words, Bush's supply side tax cuts are great for America's global investors, who have been investing either in foreign companies or in global American-based ones. (Robert Reich, in his weekly commentary on American Public Radio's "Marketplace")

Item: General Motors had several hundred thousands of workers in the 1960s and 1970s; now it has 73,000, moving toward bankruptcy and zero. Once upon a time, its workers' strong union (UAW) achieved a good health care program; but GM has recently forced the now weak union to accept a deal that cuts benefits for past and present workers and that will be unavailable for those hired in the future. A "question": Innumerable large and small companies are going through pending health care disasters like GM's. How long will it take our businesses and workers to see that it is in *their mutual* best interest to demand a universal governmental health care system? Are US capitalists more stupid than those in Europe, where all of the rich countries (and even some of the less rich) have such systems?

Now we turn to a comparison of the US health care system with those countries neither as rich nor as self-destructive of their own people as we are of ours.

Health Care in Western Europe: A Need, Not a Commodity

As we now examine the great differences between the US and European treatment of health care, a note on the critical relationship between poverty and health. One doesn't have to be a genius to comprehend that the poorer you are, the more likely you are to be unhealthy; and the more unhealthy you are... and so on. Here are some relevant excerpts from the article "Poverty is Poison" by Paul Krugman (*NYT*, February 19, 2008):

"Poverty in early childhood poisons the brain." [He is quoting the research presented a week earlier at the meetings of the American Association for the Advancement of Science.] "Many children who grow up in very poor families… experience unhealthy levels of stress hormones, which impair their neural development…", impairing language development and memory…and hence the ability to escape poverty. After Pres. Johnson's 1960s "War on Poverty," the poverty rate for children fell from 23 to 14 percent, in just six years. But progress stalled from the 1970s on… and by 2006, 17.4 percent of all US children were living below the poverty line…which understates the true depth of many children's misery.

The distance between the poor and the rest of us is now much greater than it was 40 years ago, for most American incomes have risen in real terms but the official poverty line has not. To be poor in America today, even more than in the past, is to be an outcast in your own country.

Many relevant comments about our expensive and literally deadly health care system were made earlier, in Chapter 9. A summary of those characteristics shows that "deadly" is the appropriate name for that system:

- More than 45 million US citizens are without *any* health insurance. Medicaid is designed to provide health care for the poor, but only half of those officially classified as "poor" are eligible and those who are covered, are inadequately so. And what about the health insurance program for the old, Medicare? Just look at "Medicare Audits Show Problems in Private Plans" (*NYT*, October 7, 2007):

   Tens of thousands of Medicare recipients have been victims of deceptive sales tactics and had their claims denied by private insurers that run the system's huge new drug benefit program and offer other private options encouraged by the Bush administration… Since March [2007], Medicare has imposed fines of more than $777,000 on 11 companies for market violations and failure to provide timely notice about changes in costs and benefits. The insurance companies include three of the largest participants in the Medicare market, UnitedHealth, Humana, and WellPoint. WellPoint, one of the largest insurers, had "a

> backlog of 354,000 claims"...offered through its UniCare subsidiary. The company's call center took an average of 27 minutes to answer phone calls from its members and 16 minutes...from [its] health care providers. More than half the callers hung up before speaking to a company representative. A spokeswoman for WellPoint had no immediate comment.

- Meanwhile, at least 100 million *with* health insurance have desperately inadequate coverage – and always more so, as hospital costs, always disgustingly high, have risen higher as, at the same time, employer health care benefits are being eliminated as drug costs rise at an average of 10–15 percent every year.

All of that is awful, much of it cruelly so, some of it fatally so, and all of it is getting worse. Those deadly trends will continue so long as the US health care system is run by business and for profit; not just "any old business," but by giant insurance companies, giant drug companies, and giant HMOs (the latter mostly controlled by the insurance companies).

So much for the US. But what about Europe? It is not perfect, but it stands in sharp contrast. From the 1950s on, the politicians of Europe were faced with voters who, aided by strong unions and political parties with social reform and/or socialism as their position, would no longer put up with "It's each for himself and God for all."

In consequence, in Britain and Western Europe, the people receive needed health care, no matter what age, gender, color, religion, income or wealth. Now some details regarding various health issues and problems, keeping in mind that what is said about health in what follows also applies for education, housing and hunger (with appropriate variations). My examples are taken from my years in Italy (by no means the most generous provider in Europe), beginning with access to doctors, hospitalization and prescription drugs:

- All who want one have a (free) "family physician" to whom they go when they need advice or treatment. If special treatment is needed, they are sent to another doctor (or to a hospital). If medicines are needed, they are given a prescription. No money changes hands.

- The other doctor examines you to the degree necessary, may send you to a hospital, and/or give you a prescription. No money changes hands.
- If you are sent to a hospital, they admit you, take care of you (x-rays, surgery, etc.), and send you home, with a prescription, if necessary. No money changes hands.

So, how does all that get paid for? In Italy and elsewhere in countries even more generous, health care expenses are paid for by "health care taxes" in keeping with one's income. In France and Britain those annual health care taxes were, respectively, $1,800 and $1,312 (and about the same elsewhere in Europe). As we saw in Chapter 9, compare that with what I have paid in the US: $9,000–$10,000; *not* for visits, surgery, etc., but for "supplements to my health insurance" plus "deductibles and co-payments" for who knows what?

Just to fill out the story, in Europe there are of course physicians and hospitals and pharmacies where "money changes hands." When and why? Only when those who (for some reason) wish to bypass the governmental health care system. Many, perhaps all, of the doctors who receive payments from individuals also work in the governmental system.

President Obama is seeking to move the US health system toward decency and sanity. It would be useful for him – and the rest of us – to read the article by Amartya Sen on that and the ongoing crisis: "Capitalism Beyond Crisis" (*New York Review of Books*, March 26, 2009).

Education

My direct knowledge of education in Europe is confined to about 20 years of teaching in Italian universities. Italy's overall educational system has many virtues, but I have learned from discussions with many Italian teachers and students that education is as good or better in Germany, the Netherlands, Sweden, et al. I also know that the principles and the practice of education in Italy are very much better than those of the US, although they may not entirely meet the principle argued for decades ago by the distinguished child psychologist Erik Erikson: "Some day, maybe, there will exist a well-informed, well-considered, and yet fervent public conviction that the most deadly of all possible sins is the mutilation of a child's spirit..." (Erikson, 1950).

Traditionally, children's spirits have (or have not) been enriched at home and/or in school. Until the curse of TV, those were the two most potent realms of education for the young; the most vital years for both education and health. In both respects, the "spirit" of a child born, raised and educated in the US is more likely to be "mutilated" in the US than in Western Europe. Simply reading that would anger most in the US. If so, it is more of a reflection of how ignorant we are of what could and should be and the dismal ways in which we fail when set against those others. We are too accustomed at looking in the mirror asking "who's the fairest of them all?": and bowing.

As noted above, most of what follows will be based upon the relevant conditions in Italy since World War II. Before then, the developments which brought about today's conditions were virtually non-existent in almost all of Europe. For them to come into being, two related conditions were needed: a strengthening economy and correspondingly strong political pressures from the political left of center.

When Italy (as elsewhere in Europe) emerged from two wars and decades of fascism, it also entered a period when its people's basic needs could be met for the first time in its history. Its economy by the 1960s was its strongest ever and getting stronger, and its government, as noted above, was answering to strong left-of-center politics; thus, by the end of the 1960s Italy had significantly begun to meet its people's needs for health care, education, housing, and hunger; all seen as the responsibility of its government. (Repeat: Italian achievements were surpassed in several other European nations.)

The "educational" policies in Italy begin with the child's birth. In the US there is much dispute as to how much, if any, "care" should be provided to parents who are unable to provide it themselves (for whatever reason). In Italy, from the moment a child is born until it begins formal schooling, it is entitled to the benefits of the program called "*nido*" (nest): All children are provided (at no cost) with nursing and nutritional care, with "child care" when parents are working and with what else is needed in the post-natal, pre-school, years. That coverage extends from time of birth for six years, after which what we would call "kindergarten" begins; *and* as child care continues. The *nido* service is usually free, with, usually, those who are very well off taking care of their own needs as they wish.

In elementary school, child care is provided for parents who request it because their job keeps them away from home. "Need" is the key word. Schools function Monday through Saturday for both elementary and high schools. That schooling is free, but studying at one of the many "state universities" is not. The yearly tuition (which includes residence if desired) is in the range of $3,000–$4,000. In my many years of teaching in Italy, I have found the students to be excellent.

The foregoing discussions of poverty, health care, and education make the US look pretty awful in comparison. It should not be surprising that as I now turn to the treatment of the aged, of housing, and of hunger, Europe also comes out looking considerably more "civilized" than the richer US. Note that here again the focus will be almost entirely on Italy, with the reminder that Italy, although superior to the US in all these respects, lags behind several other European countries.

The Aged

If the focus is on "social security" the similarities between Italy and the US are greater than the differences; but only at first glance. The guiding principle in the US is that "you get back what you put in": If you had a low income and poor jobs all of your life, and thus paid in very little, then very little is what you will get (except for Medicare). So, if you've been living poorly and your "contributions" were low, your monthly check from Uncle Sam will also be low (if any). You get what you *paid* for, not what you need: the worse your working life has been, the worse – or "worser" – it will be when you can no longer work. That may sound fair to the US ear; it doesn't in Western Europe.

The income of all of the aged *should* provide for their needs for food, clothing, shelter, and health. In some ways the needs of the old are less than those of the young, but in some vital ways they are much greater, not least because the older you are the greater the likelihood of illnesses. However, in Italy that likelihood is less:

- you have been getting good health care all along, even if poor
- you are less likely to be ill
- there are *no* medical or prescription drug costs
- you are likely to be living in good housing if well off, or, if poor, in subsidized (and decent) housing
- and you are likely to be living with or near your family.

"Family" suggests a closer look. In Italy there is a strong connection between a sense of community and a sense of family; both considerably stronger than in the US. Not only does this have great significance for the aged, but it has had a substantial political consequence, not least because it is the basis for a strong sense of community. That in turn serves as a vital and positive basis for those national politics which bear upon social decency and basic needs. Of course, Italy is not "Europe"; but most of Western Europe is more like Italy than like the US. Sadly, it needs adding that in the past few years the gap between the US and Western European policies has narrowed: one of the several damages done by globalization.

Usually in a disparaging way, I have used the term "Americanization" in this book. The key element of that "Americanization" has been the adoption by Europeans (not least the Italians) of *consumerism*. It is a passion well on its way to becoming "a social disease" in Italy. It is of the essence of consumerism that its addicts become habituated to responding to appeals to their "individuality," be it of their appearance and/or status (clothes, cars, cell phones, etc.) and to be easily diverted from considering, even thinking about, their *society's* health and wellbeing, let alone that of others. In such processes one also "learns" *not* to give serious attention to the realities of social existence; or, if and when attention is paid, to accept the messages of those in the seats of political power. Thus it is, for example, that the Prime Minister of Italy (Silvio Berlusconi), whose politics are all too similar to those of Bush II (and more dangerously, for he is – who isn't? – smarter than Bush). In the last election, Berlusconi was voted into that office for the third time, with an always weaker opposition. As I write in early 2009 he is running Italy as though it is his kingdom. And getting away with it.

However, as for the US, over the last 20 years or so globalization has begun to reduce the number of good jobs in Europe. In those same years, US consumerism has taken hold in Western Europe. As that process continued, the political strength that brought Europe decent social policies has steadily weakened, facilitated by the always stronger hold of consumerism, much assisted by the media. Taken together, they have increasingly led workers to think and act more as individual consumers than as members of the working class, muffling or setting aside the earlier "class struggle." Meanwhile, wages and conditions worsen and good jobs disappear.

The foregoing applies not only to the needs of the aged but to the basic needs of all: nutrition, education, health care, housing, and opportunity. In recent years, however, the combination of globalization, Americanization, and economic crisis has significantly reduced budgets in the realms of basic needs in Western Europe.

The Homeless and the Hungry

I live in Bologna and teach in nearby Modena. In their streets and parks I now and then see what are probably homeless persons;

also likely to be hungry. I have seen many, many more in my home town of San Francisco, not just "now and then" but virtually every hour of every day in the central area. But there is a big difference; "big" not only in the numbers but in "the reasons why." To begin with, in Italy many of the poor who are *not* on the streets are living with or near their families; others who are also not in the streets are living in decent apartments by themselves or with their mates, in *public* housing; and at *very* low rents: 300 euro per *year* (just over $400 in spring 2009). The public housing is not in some dingy part of town (of which there are few), but spotted all over Italy's cities and their outskirts. "Low rents"? In San Francisco, a barely decent apartment with one bedroom, kitchen, etc. would rent furnished at a minimum of $500 a *month* = $6,000 a year.

What about *hunger*? Well, there are people begging in the streets of Bologna, hands out, etc. I don't have the relevant data, but my daily observations tell me this: They are few in number, they are either Gypsies or recent immigrants from Africa or ex-Yugoslavia, and/or unemployed musicians, and/or cripples, and/or druggies, and/or they don't know that there is a church nearby where they can eat free every day; and/or I don't know what. The immigrants can get residence by applying but, in this Berlusconi epoch of rising unemployment (and rising racism) might fear to try. Also, sprinkled over the city are specified buildings in which the old can sit and play cards, eat, and talk; which they do (especially talk).

There is much more to consider and say; doing so would be a matter simply of details. But the "big picture" would be the same: in terms of human needs and children's possibilities, the Europeans are considerably more like (or better than) the Italy I have been describing than like the US. That is less true of the poorer European countries of the East and Southeast ("ex-Yugoslavia," Greece, et al.); but they are poor countries: the US is the richest in history.

In sum, the European poor, both in absolute and relative numbers are few by comparison to the US; still, if they are recent immigrants or Gypsies they are victims of a long-standing and now increasing racism. Yet those realities, if inexcusable, are considerably less so than the always terrible realities of the US; all of which were given a second and stronger life since the 1970s.

I now bring this long discourse to a close. I do so as the year 2009 begins, and as the whole world has fallen into a recession which is all too likely to become a depression (see Epilogue). The causal center of that crisis is to be found in the US. Whether or not the Obama presidency will be able to act effectively to prevent such a worsening cannot yet be known; what is certain is that Europe and the US must jointly work toward a solution, for globalization has put all of us "in the same boat."

By the time this work is published in mid 2009 the Obama presidency will be well on its way. It will almost certainly seek to reverse the socially harmful tendencies that took hold from the 1970s on and that provided the basis for today's economic crisis and social deterioration. How much and in which way the Obama White House will seek or be able to direct the US toward a saner and more decent society cannot yet be known; but what could and should be worked for have been discussed in the Preface and will now be discussed in the Epilogue.

EPILOGUE

What has been discussed in this book regarding either domestic or foreign policy has by no means been comprehensive, but it should be sufficient to raise many worrisome questions about the vitality of democracy, especially in the US. In doing so, it also directs attention to where we have been, are now, and where we are headed. It looks scary. In now concluding with an analysis of inequality's meanings for the present and future the emphasis will be upon how recent and current trends in the concentration and uses of socio-economic power point to dangers that go beyond the discussions of earlier chapters:

- an economy caught up in a serious recession, set off and intensified by the worst ever financial crisis
- persisting wars in Iraq and Afghanistan with the distinct possibility of one in Iran
- and, not least in importance, a spreading set of environmental disasters whose prevention is likely to be set aside and allowed to be intensified by economic and military developments.

The accompanying worsening of inequality has been serious enough in itself; but since the 1970s the intensification of the above-noted three tendencies greatly increased the strength and misuse of the ruling "plutocracy." Whether or not the Obama presidency will be inclined seriously to reverse those tendencies is presently unknown. What is certain is that if there is to be a reversal it must be brought about finally by those *not* presently ruling the power structure, to be shoved aside by those now in the middle and on the bottom of the pyramid: that is, by us. The alternative facing us has many elements; most worrisome are:

- a qualitative increase in the already highly-concentrated power structures
- the likelihood of "permanent war"
- an acceleration of already serious environmental damages
- the likelihood of a present-day variation of what was called "fascism" before World War II: that is, a steady evolution toward the "friendly fascism" noted briefly in the Prologue and of which more below (and see Gross, 1980).

It is vital to consider what must be done if today's capitalist societies are not to be pushed further back toward the black hole of authoritarianism (no matter its name). In doing so it is necessary to be clear on just how serious the present crisis is, and to explore the very meaning of "crisis." A word with medical roots, denoting the turning point of a disease, crisis signifies the existence of a serious problem which will move either toward substantial improvement or substantial worsening. How does that apply to today's "financial crisis"? For present purposes the answer has two sides: its causes and nature, and its desirable and undesirable consequences. First, the causes related to the economy.

What Went Wrong?

The misbegotten processes were examined at length in Chapters 6 and 7; here a reminder. The financial crisis was triggered by the "subprime" housing collapse, itself but one of the serious outcomes of a reckless political economy. The financial collapse was itself but the first of what have been and will continue to be disastrous problems not only in the entire US *and* global financial world, but in the *economies* of the entire world. It has been seen as a "blown-up" repetition of the 1929 US stock market crash. By the early 1930s, that "crash" was seen as the first step toward a global depression.

The general view today is that the financial crackup can be restrained and ended within the next year or so. I beg to differ, and that opinion is likely to spread always more rapidly, as present "cures" prove to be not only inadequate but – as regards the "financial bailouts" – rewards to those responsible. Such a view is becoming less unusual by the day. Thus, already in March 2009 the economist Robert Kuttner had taken this position:

> The economic crisis doesn't have to be a second Great Depression – *if* government does nearly everything just right, and soon. But if government doesn't do more, and fast, this could be worse than the 1930s. Why? There are three big reasons: (1) Finance: The financial system is in far worse shape than when the stock market crashed in 1929. It was a "bubble," [but] the banking system was relatively healthy... Today, thanks to the securitization of loans..., the process of sorting it all out and getting banks functioning again is something the markets simply cannot do. We are not even clear who owns what. The wise guys on Wall Street invented a doomsday machine from which there is no market escape; [by comparison] in 1929 the banking system was relatively healthy; today the banking mess is dragging down the real economy with no effective end in sight. (2) Wealth, Deficits, and Demand: The economy now bears all the earmarks of a depression... American households are out several *trillion* dollars. In the 1920s there were no 401(k) [retirement] plans – [or credit cards] – and less than 2 percent of Americans owned stock. Weak demand in one sector is cascading into other sectors... Business sales and profits are down, which causes other layoffs, and the cycle deepens. Roosevelt was said to be a big spender, but his biggest peacetime deficit was 6 percent of GDP. This year the deficit will exceed 11 percent, and the recession will deepen all year. It took the truly massive deficits of World War II – nearly 30 percent of GDP – to finally end the Great Depression. (3) A Debtor Nation: America in 1929 was a major international *creditor*. Today, the US is the world's biggest debtor. The financial bubble created the illusion of prosperity..., and [US] foreign borrowing disguised domestic weaknesses, such as our much-diminished manufacturing sector. For now, foreigners are willing to lend us vast sums, but that may not continue indefinitely. ("Surviving the Great Collapse," *International Herald Tribune*)

Kuttner's article was published March 13, 2009. The very next day this was the headline of a lead article in the *New York Times* (parent newspaper of the *IHT*): "China's Leader Says He Is Worried Over US Treasuries." As well he, and many others, should be. China and Japan alone are owed well over $2 *trillion*.

Meanwhile, on that same day, the *NYT* reported "US trade contracts sharply: The US Department of Commerce said that American imports and exports in January were down 20 percent from a year before." Also: "Those trade numbers [came out] as some of America's largest trading partners were reporting even starker rates of economic contraction and drops in trade levels (e.g., China's exports plummeted over 25 percent in February)..." Not much later, the *IHT* provided the data for this story: "Grim News is Expected in Export Numbers" (April 6, 2009).

Kuttner ends his dour analysis observing that "this crisis doesn't yet have a name. It has all the hallmarks of a depression, but people are understandably reluctant to use the D-word. So let me suggest one. The Great Collapse, since this was both a financial collapse and an ideological one."

The "collapse" can easily go beyond serious recession to serious depression, both broader and deeper than that of the 1930s. That is likely to be so not for primarily economic, but for political/ ideological reasons. But it is not unavoidable. How? A good starting point would be Roosevelt's "Second Bill of Rights" (to be discussed below). But first, here are the main reasons for believing that this might well become a deep and broad depression:

- As was discussed at length in Chapters 6 and 7, the financial sector is considerably more central to the economy today than 80–90 years ago, and the economies of the world are much more tightly interdependent than ever before.
- As was also suggested in earlier chapters, not only has the US economy become the world's largest debtor and consumer ever, in doing so it has also "lost its head and balance" in socio-political terms. Put differently (and to repeat earlier observations), the political lives of an unknowable but high percentage of Americans have become diverted and/or hypnotized by consumerism, often combined with racism, passionate religions, and a passive (or enthusiastic) militarism to the point that its politics, culture, and mentalities have become "easy pickings" for political groups and politicians for whom any reasonably

decent social policies are successfully presented as heresy, or weakness, or "un-American," or...something (including an almost cultivated apathy). As discussed earlier, this has been accompanied by a sharp and dangerous decline in the percentage of unionized workers (and the political strength accompanying it), at a time when greater strength is needed. (See below.)

What Must We Do?

The answers being given in the US in 2008–09 have been worrisome, and disgustingly so in the financial "bailout" for those who created the problem and who appointed or allowed remedial policies to be handled by those responsible (or their friends); for example, Treasury Secretary Paulson (earlier head of Goldman Sachs and a major profiteer of the dangerous process); new Treasury Secretary Geithner, and Rubin (both friends of Paulson and participants in abolishing earlier regulations). The "bailout" will probably amount to handing over more than a *trillion* dollars to the guilty companies to do with as they please. Nor does it help that as of early 2009 Obama had not yet moved in a different direction in the appointment of his financial advisors. (See the note on Summers as hedge fund advisor, Chapter 11.)

There must and can be a better path toward dealing with this disaster *and* with what brought it about, including but going well beyond Wall Street and its fancy games. There is much more that can and must be done if we are to retain even our limited democracy, let alone to have a healthy economy and a thriving democracy. It doesn't have to be invented; some steps in that direction were initiated in response to the depression of the 1930s in the US when Roosevelt was president. The reforms did not begin until 1935 (with Social Security); but "better late than never." FDR was re-elected for the fourth time in 1944. In his State of the Union Address in 1945, just before he died, FDR proposed what he called "A Second Bill of Rights" under which a new basis of security and prosperity can be established for all – regardless of gender, race, or creed. He proposed the *right*

- to a useful and remunerative job
- to earn enough to provide adequate food and clothing and recreation
- of every family to a decent home
- to adequate medical care and good health
- to adequate protection from the economic fears of old age, sickness, accident, and unemployment
- to a good education.

Not all of that was achieved, but at least it got started. FDR was in effect proposing that the "basic needs" of *all* should be met. I read that speech in 1944 (in a foxhole) and it sounded just great. In 2009 it sounds like a fairy tale; but it is at least as necessary and it could be done. With never-ending political involvement a "Third Bill of Rights" could become the very heart of a movement that would attract all sane and decent people, in the US and elsewhere. Without that popular involvement it is unlikely that Obama can or would move in that direction (nor did FDR, for his first few years). As with FDR then, Obama now needs the political demands and support of the people to bring out the best in him. The appropriate pressure and support began to take hold two years before 1935, as employed workers fought for unions on both coasts and in the industrial middle; and he got it from ordinary citizens as they fought for survival and decency. As most who read this will know, steps in those same directions (or, mostly, going beyond) were put in place in the UK and Western Europe beginning in the 1950s and spreading nicely from then on. However, in recent years, those "steps" have been reversed.

It needs emphasizing that when FDR took office in 1933 he was faced with a thoroughly corrupted Congress (as governors were with their legislators – and when they looked in the mirror). It was the mix of depression, "ground up" political organization, and the pressures of World War II which finally (if only temporarily) replaced deep corruption with strengthening democracy. Today's corruption of politics is both broader and deeper than in FDR's day. Even more worrisome is that today's voters have been considerably more brain-weakened by consumerism and a powerful and deceitful media. (See Chapter 5.) The task for us today, in short, is more difficult than in the past; but it is even more important now that we democratize our society. That's saying a lot, considering that the 1930s ended with the worst war ever. But consider also that the next world war, if there is one, could literally be the "war to end all wars" – and us.

The foregoing is not meant only to raise either fears or hopes, but to stir determination and to serve as the preface to a warning. Capitalist societies move *either* toward *or* away from decency and democracy. That was shown all too clearly in the 1920s and 1930s. The powerful were caught up in a deep economic and political crisis, and they stopped at nothing to maintain what they saw as their needs and "rights"; up to and including acceptance of the murderous rule of fascism (beginning with Italy and Mussolini and lurching east, north, and south). For us to avoid that set of developments in these times of an ongoing and worsening crisis, we must come to life politically, taking our needs *and* our ideals seriously and doing something about them.

Most who read this will not have memories of what fascism meant, nor remember that four of the six leading capitalist nations – France, Germany, Japan, and Italy – became fascist. Only the US and the UK – the two wealthiest – did not. (See R. Brady, 1943.) In all fascist countries, utterly ruthless force was normal (up to and including concentration camps and mass murder); as was permanent war; as was deadly racism; as was a deep and enforced poverty for the majority; as were daily horror and legalized social cruelty.

"Friendly fascism"? As will be seen below, there is nothing "friendly" about "friendly fascism"; Bertram Gross used the adjective to distinguish between the massive brutalities of historic fascism and what in the US (and elsewhere) could achieve some of its patterns with only minimal domestic violence within a perverted democracy. How and why? A big part of the answer is that "classic" fascism came into being as a response to two interacting developments: strong anti-capitalist movements and the substantial socio-economic crises following World War I. Those crises strengthened the workers' movements and provided the manpower for the fascist movements provided by disgruntled war veterans and that part of the working class not reached by the anti-capitalist movements. Led by charismatic leaders such as Hitler and Mussolini the above masses became the backbone of fascist strength, even though they were utilized and exploited by the leaders of business, agriculture, the military, and (in Italy) the Church. (Again, see R. Brady, 1943.) The major theme of Gross's *Friendly Fascism* (1980) is that massive brutality is unlikely to be necessary in the future if a threatened capitalism is to maintain its social control; that the costs will be borne by an increasingly hypnotized and/or terrorized public, made passive and vulnerable by consumerism and a cooperative media; that populations can and will be exploited culturally, economically, militarily, and, politically: all of that because of the absence of a popular counter-movement seeking a better life in a decent society. When Gross wrote his book, there was reason to expect that over time there would be always less meaningful opposition to a full loss of democracy. Is there, today? This is how Gross defined his fears:

> A "friendly fascist"' society is one without the need for a charismatic dictator, [for] one-party rule, glorification of the state, dissolution of legislatures, termination of multi-party elections, ultra-nationalism, or attacks on rationality. Rather if and when neo-fascism emerges it may be associated with a relaxation of crude terror and the maturation of more sophisticated, effective and ruthless controls. In my judgment one of the greatest dangers is the slow process through which friendly fascism could come into being. For a large part of the population the changes would be unnoticed. Even those most alive to the danger may see only part of the picture – until it is too late. (Gross, 1980)

As noted earlier at some length, especially but not only in the US, from the 1970s to the present there has been a steady increase in inequalities of income and wealth, in corruption and mismanagement of government, and in almost continuous war. All of that, along with deterioration of jobs from "good" to "awful" to "none" with barely a shrug from more than a slim minority. What is badly lacking is that the "silent majority" become "noisy" for a want of a better world.

In today's world there seems to be little or no likelihood of either classic communist or classic fascist movements: "Communist Russia" has re-joined the capitalist parade, as have Communist China, and Vietnam. So why any fear of fascism of any sort in the US, the land of the free? Absurd! Not quite: Until the 1920s, Italy and Germany, the first two fascist countries, had earlier been seen as the centers of western science and culture; even, in many ways, of democracy. In modern dress, fascism "can happen here."

Where does that leave the capitalist world today and tomorrow? The answer is to be found in what we do (or don't do). For it to be positive, we must hope that crises emerge slowly rather than suddenly, and allow time for a political awakening. In that time, we must also get to work politically sooner rather than later; must change our lives to include working socio-politically a few hours every week, rather than an hour a month (or not at all). We must join existing organizations, try to change them for the better, and/or help to start new ones; seek to be creative and tolerant of our co-workers (as we would hope they would be of us). And we must learn and teach and contribute as much as we can in every way possible. Is such a change in behavior possible?

In 2007, few indeed of us – except Obama and his team – would have thought that Obama *could be* elected. But he *was*. Given Obama's color, and that he ascended to the presidency against all odds, then clearly much more is possible; and just as surely much more is necessary. The hope for his victory was in itself energizing; but that victory has already stirred his opponents and fed the anti-democracy and racism of those who created and/or took us to today's dangerous economic, social, and military situations. It must energize us even more, to prompt him to seek a better society than even he had in mind. It is more than just an interesting fact that Obama's proposals for funding education and housing and health care, in Congress have received actual zero votes from the Republican members of the House of Representatives. That "zero" denotes something in the nature of an organized plan. It must be countered by political energies from the public.

All hell has been on its way for decades, and much of it has arrived. No matter what we do that hell will continue to harm all corners of all our lives; bit by bit. All too likely is a gush of depression and/or war, and/or environmental disaster. It may be both thought and hoped that the numbers of people in the US and elsewhere who yearn for social decency and peace outnumber those who do not. But those in power have habit as well as money on their side; we have only our principles and our numbers. They must be translated into energy and political participation. It is quite possible that no matter what we do we cannot win; it is certain that if we continue to do too little that not only are we leaving open the door to "friendly fascism," but that we will have lost our humanity in "looking the other way" as that set of atrocities evolves.

BIBLIOGRAPHY

Adams, N. and McCoy, A. (1978) *Laos: War and Revolution*

Adams, W. and Brock, J. (1986) *The Bigness Complex: Industry, Labor, and Government*

Albelda, R., et al. (2001) *Unlevel Playing Fields*

Albelda, R. and Withorn, A. (eds.) (2004) *Lost Ground, Poverty, Welfare, and Beyond*

Allen, G. (1946) *A Short Economic History of Modern Japan: 1867–1937*

Alterman, E. (2003) *What Liberal Media?*

Anderson, S., et al. (2000) *Field Guide to the Global Economy*

Ardzroomi, L. (ed.) (1934) *Essays in Our Changing Order*

Arnold, T. (1941) *The Folklore of Capitalism*

Aronson, J. (1970) *The Press and the Cold War*

Ashworth, W. (1987) *A Short History of the World Economy since 1750*

Bacevich, A. (2008) *The Limits of Power: The End of American Exceptionalism*

Bagdikian, B. (1983) *The Media Monopoly*

Balibar, E. and Wallerstein, I. (1991) *Race, Nation, Class: Ambiguous Identities*

Baker, D. and Weisbroit, M. (2000) *Social Security: The Phony Crisis*

Banner, S. (2002) *The Death Penalty: An American History*

Baran, P. (1957) *The Political Economy of Growth*

—— (1969) "Theses on Advertising," in *The Longer View*

Baran, P. and Sweezy, P. (1966) *Monopoly Capital: An Essay on the American Economic and Social Order*

Barber, B. (1996) *Jihad vs. McWorld: How Globalism and Tribalism are Reshaping the World*

Barnet, R. and Cavanagh, J. (1994) *Global Dreams: Imperial Corporations*

Beitel, K. (2008) "Understanding the Subprime Crisis," *Monthly Review*, May

Benaria, L. and Friedman, S. (1992) *Unequal Burden, Economic Crises, Persistent Poverty and Women's Work*

Berle, A. and Means, G. (1932) *The Modern Corporation and Private Property*

Berry, W. (1977) *The Unsettling of American Culture and Agriculture*

271

Bezruchka, S. (2006) "Is America Driving You Crazy?" University of Washington Population Health Forum (October)

Blair, J. (1978) *The Control of Oil*

Blix, H. (2004) *Disarming Iraq*

Block, E. (1977) *The Origin of International Economic Disorder*

Bluestone, B. and Harrison, B. (1982) *The De-industrialization of America*

—— (1988) *The Great U-Turn: Corporate Restructuring and the Polarizing of America*

Blum, W. (2000) *Rogue State: A Guide to the World's Only Superpower*

—— (2004) *Killing Hope: US Military Interventions since World War II*

Boggs, C. (1976) *Gramsci's Marxism*

Boies, J. (1994) *Buying for Armageddon: Business, Society, and Military Spending Since the Cuban Missile Crisis*

Bok, D. (2003) *Universities in the Marketplace: Commercialization of Higher Education*

Bonner, R, (1994) *Weakness and Deceit: US Policy and El Salvador*

Bookchin, M. (1970) "Toward an Ecological Solution," *Ramparts*, May

Boucher, D. (ed.) (1999) *The Paradox of Plenty: Hunger in a Bountiful World*

Bowden, W., et al. (1937) *An Economic History of Europe Since 1750*

Boxer, C. (1965) *The Dutch Seaborne Empire*

Brady, J. (1993) *Theory of War*

Brady, R. (1933) *The Rationalization Movement in German Industry*

—— (1937) *The Spirit and Structure of German Fascism*

—— (1943) *Business as a System of Power*

Braudel, F. (1979) *The Structures of Everyday Life*

Breslow, M., et al. (1999) *The Environment in Crisis*

Brittain, J. (1972) *The Payroll Tax for Social Security*

Bromwich, D. (2008) "Euphemism and American Violence," *New York Review of Books*, March

Bronfenbrenner, K. (2003) "Declining Unionization, Rising Inequality," *Multinational Monitor*, May

Brown, C. (1965) *Manchild in the Promised Land*

Brzezinski, Z. (1985) *Power and Principle: Memoirs of the National Security Adviser, 1977–1991*

Cahill, T. (1995) *How The Irish Saved Civilization*

Cahn, B. (ed.) (2002) *The Affirmative Action Debate*

Cammett, I. (1967) *Antonio Gramsci and the Origins of Italian Communism*

Carson, R. (1962) *Silent Spring*

Cash, W. (1941) *The Mind of the South*

Chang, I. (2003) *The Chinese in America*
Chang, L. and Kornbluh, P. (eds.) (1992) *The Cuban Missile Crisis*
Childe, V. (1951) *Man Makes Himself*
Chomsky, N. (1993) *Year 501: The Conquest Continues*
Chomsky, N. and Herman, E. (1988) *Manufacturing Consent: The Political Economy of Mass Media*
Cirino, R. (1971) *Don't Blame the People*
Clark, G. (1947) The *Seventeenth Century*
Cockroft, J., et al. (1972) *Dependence and Underdevelopment*
Coll, S. (2005) *Global Wars: The Secret History of the CIA, Afghanistan, and Bin Laden*
Conason, J. (2004) *Big Lie: The Right Wing Propaganda Machine and How it Distorts the Truth*
Cumings, B. (1981) *The Origins of the Korean War*
Cumings, B. and Halliday, J. (1988) *Korea: The Unknown War*
Cypher, J. (1987) "Military Spending," *Journal of Economic Issues*, March 3
—— (1991) "The War Dividend," *Dollars & Sense*, May
—— (2001) "Nafta's Lessons: From Economic Mythology to Current Realities," *Labor Studies Journal*, Spring
—— (2002a) "Return of the Iron Triangle," *Dollars & Sense*, Jan/Feb
—— (2002b) "A Prop, Not a Burden: The US Economy Relies on Militarism," *Dollars & Sense*, July/August
Daly, H. (1996) *Beyond Growth: The Economics of Sustained Development*
Daly, H. and Cobb, J. Jr. (1989) *For the Common Good: Redirecting the Economy Toward Community, the Environment, and a Sustainable Future*
Danner, M. (1994) *The Massacre at El Mozote: A Parable of the Cold War*
De Castro, J. (1950) *The Geography of Hunger*
De Zengotita, T. (2002) "The Numbing of the American Mind," *Harper's Magazine*, April
Delany, W. (2001) *The Green and the Red*
Dobb, M. (1937) *Political Economy and Capitalism*
—— (1966) *Soviet Economic Development Since 1917*
Dobson, A. (ed.) (1991) *The Green Reader: Essays Toward a Sustainable Society*
Dollars & Sense (2008) *The Wealth Inequality Reader*
Donovan, J.A. (1970) *Militarism: USA*
Dowd, D. (1989) *The Waste of Nations*
—— (1993) *US Capitalist Development Since 1776: Of, By, and For Which People?*
—— (2004) *Capitalism and Its Economics: A Critical History*

Draper, T. (1991) *A Very Thin Line: The Iran-Contra Affair*

Du Boff, R. (1989) *Accumulation and Power: An Economic History of the USA*

Edwards, R., et al. (1986) *The Capitalist System*

Ehrenreich, B. (2001) *Nickel and Dimed: On (Not) Getting By in America*

—— (2008) *This Land is Their Land: Reports from a Divided Nation*

Ellsberg, D. (2002) *Secrets: A Memoir on Vietnam and the Pentagon Papers*

Engler, R. (1961) *The Politics of Oil*

Ensenzberger, H. (1974) *The Consciousness Industry*

Erikson, E. (1950) *Childhood and Society*

Everest, L. (2004) *Oil, Power, and Empire: Iraq and the US Global Agenda*

Ewen, S. (1976) *Advertising and the Social Roots of Common Culture*

—— (1996) *A Social History of Spin*

Fall, B. (1967) *Last Reflections on a War*

Faulkner, H. (1947) *The Decline of Laissez-faire: 1897–1917*

Feagin, C. and J. (1978) *Discrimination American Style: Institutionalized Racism and Sexism*

Feagin, J. and Sykes, L. (1994) *Living with Racism: The Black Middle Class Experience*

Feis, H. (1930) *Europe, the World's Banker*

Finnegan, W. (1998) *Cold New World: Growing Up in a Harder Country*

Fishman, T. (2004) *China, Inc.: How the Rise of the Next Superpower Challenges America and the World*

Folbre, N., et al. (1995) *The New Field Guide to the American Economy*

—— (1996) *The War on the Poor: A Defense Manual*

Foster, J. (1999) *The Vulnerable Planet*

—— (2008) "The Financialization of Capital and the Crisis," *Monthly Review*, April

Frank, T. (2008) *The Wrecking Crew: How Conservatives Rule*

Fredrickson, G. (2009) *Diverse Nations: Explorations in the History of Racial and Ethnic Pluralism*

Friedman, M. (1962) *Capitalism and Freedom*

Fromm, E. (1997) *The Anatomy of Human Destructiveness*

Frumkin, G. (1951) *Population Changes in Europe Since 1939*

FTC (Federal Trade Commission) (1939) *Report on the Automobile Industry*

Fussell, P. (1975) *The Great War and Modern Memory*

Galbraith, James (2008) *The Predator State: How Conservatism Abandoned the Free Market and Why Liberals Should Too*

Galbraith, John K. (1955) *The Great Crash: 1929*
—— (1958) *The Affluent Society*
Gans, H. (1995) *The War Against the Poor*
Genovese, E. (1966) *The Political Economy of Slavery*
George, S. (1976) *How the Other Half Dies*
—— (1979) *Feeding the Few: Corporate Control of Food*
George, S. and Sabelli, F. (1994) *The World's Secular Empire*
Gershenkron, A. (1943) *Bread and Democracy in Germany*
Gordon, C. (1995) *Dead on Arrival: Clinton Health Care Plan and Why it Failed*
Gordon, D. (1996) *Fat and Mean: The Corporate Squeeze of Working Americans and the Myth of Corporate Downsizing*
Gould, S. (1981) *The Mismeasure of Man*
—— (2003) *The Hedgehog and the Fox and the Magister's Pox: Mending the Gap Between Science and the Humanities*
Greider, W. (1997) *One World, Ready or Not: The Manic Logic of Global Capitalism*
—— (2003) *The Big Fix: How the Pharmaceutical Industry Rips Off the American People*
Gross, B. (1980) *Friendly Fascism: The New Face of Power in America*
Hacker, J. (2003) *The Divided Welfare State: The Battle Over Public and Private Benefits in the United States*
Hahnel, R. (1999) *Panic Rules: Everything You Need to Know About the Global Economy*
Haldeman, H. (1994) *The Haldeman Diaries: Inside the Nixon White House*
Haley, A. (1977) *Roots: The Epic Drama of One Man's Search for His Origins*
Hallinan, A. (2001) *Going Up the River: Travels in a Prison Nation*
Hammond, B. and J. (1924) *The Rise of Modern Industry*
Handlin, O. (1981) *The Uprooted*
Harrington, M. (1962) *The Other America*
Hartman, C. (1983) *America's Housing Crisis: What is to be Done?*
Haynes, H. (1989) *The Recurring Silent Spring*
Heckscher, E. (1935) *Mercantilism* (2 vols.)
Heinberg, R. (2004) *The Party's Over: Oil, War, and the Fate of Industrial Societies*
Henderson, W. (1958) *The State and the Industrial Revolution: 1740–1870*
Henwood, D. (1997) *Wall Street: How it Works and For Whom*
—— (2004) *After the New Economy*
Herman, E. (1981) *Corporate Control, Corporate Power*
—— (1999) *The Myth of the Liberal Media*

Herman, E. and McChesney, R. (1999) *The Global Media: The New Missionaries of Global Capitalism*

Herman, E. and O'Sullivan, G. (1989) *The Terrorism Industry: The Experts and the Institutions That Shape Our View of Terror*

Herman, E. and Peterson, D. (2008) "There is No War on Terror," *Z Magazine*, January 18

Herman, E. and Wuerker, E. (2002) *Beyond Hypocrisy: Decoding the News in an Age of Propaganda*

Hersey, J. (1946) *Hiroshima*

Hersh, S. (1970) *My Lai 4: A Report on the Massacre and its Aftermath*

—— (1983) *The Price of Power: Kissinger in the Nixon White House*

—— (2007) "The Redirection," *The New Yorker*, March 5

Hertsgaard, M. (1988) *On Bended Knee: The Press and the Reagan Presidency*

Himmelstein, D. and Woolhandler, S. (2002) "We Pay for National Health Insurance But Don't Get It," *Journal of Health Affairs*, July

Hoare, Q. and Smith, G. (eds.) *Selections from the Prison Notebooks of Antonio Gramsci*

Hobsbawm, E. (1968) *Industry and Empire*

—— (1990) *Nations and Nationalism Since 1870*

Hochschild, A. (1999) *King Leopold's Ghost: A Story of Greed, Terror, and Heroism in Colonial Africa*

Hoffman, R. (1933) *Great Britain and the German Trade Rivalry*

Huberman, L. and Sweezy, P. (1969) *Socialism in Cuba*

Hunt, E. (1979) *History of Economic Thought: A Critical Perspective*

Ignatieff, M. (1984) *The Needs of Strangers*

Ivins, M. and Dubose, L. (2000) *Shrub: The Short But Happy Political Life of George W. Bush*

Johnson, C. (2000) *Blowback: The Costs and Consequences of American Empire*

—— (2005) "Blowback: The Costs and Consequences of American Empire." In *dispatch* a weblog of *The Nation Magazine*, March 15

Jonas, S. (1991) *The Battle for Guatemala: Rebels, Death Squads, and US Power*

Josephson, M. (1934) *The Robber Barons*

Kahin, G. (1968) *The United States in Vietnam*

—— (1986) *Intervention: How America Became Involved in Vietnam*

Kaiser, R. (2008) *So Damn Much Money: The Triumph of Lobbying and the Corrosion of American Government*

Kapp, K. (1950) *The Social Costs of Private Enterprise*

Keaney, M. (2002) "Unhealthy Accumulation: The Globalization of Health Care Privatization," *Review of Social Economy*, September

Kennan, G. (1998) "Letter from London," *New York Review of Books*, December 3

Kennedy, P. (1989) *The Rise and Fall of the Great Powers*

Keynes, J. (1919) *The Economic Consequences of the Peace*

—— (1931) *Essays in Persuasion*

—— (1936) *The General Theory of Employment, Interest and Money*

Killens, J. (1969) *And Then We Heard the Thunder*

Kinzer, S. and Schlesinger, S. (1982) *Bitter Fruit: The US Coup in Guatemala*

—— (2003) *All the Shah's Men: An American Coup and the Roots of Middle East Terror*

Klare, M. (2001) *Resource Wars: The New Landscape of Global Conflict*

Klein, N. (1999) *No Logo*

—— (2002) *Fences and Windows*

Kolko, J. (1988) *Restructuring the World Economy*

Kornbuhl, J. and Byrne, M. (eds.) (1992) *The Iran-Contra Scandal: The Declassified History*

Kozol, J. (1967) *Death at an Early Age*

—— (1991) *Savage Inequalities: Children in America's Schools*

Krugman, P. (2003) *The Great Unraveling: Losing Our Way in the New Century*

—— (2007) *The Conscience of a Liberal*

Kuttner, R. (1996) *Everything for Sale: The Virtues and Limitation of Markets*

LaFeber, W. (1976) *America, Russia, and the Cold War*

Langer, W. (1966) *An Encyclopedia of World History*

Lapham, L. (1989) *Money and Class in America*

Lappe, F., et al. (1998) *World Hunger: 12 Myths*

Laski, H. (1936) *The Rise of European Liberalism*

—— (1943) *Reflections on the Revolution of Our Time*

Lebowitz, M. (2006) *Build It Now: Socialism for the 21st Century*

Leigh, J. (1995) *Causes of Death in the Workplace*

Lewis, M. (1989) *Liar's Poker*

—— (2008) *Panic: The Story of Modern Financial Insanity*

Lewis, S. (1936) *It Can't Happen Here*

Lewis, W. (1949) *Economic Survey: 1920–1939*

Liebling, J. (1961) *The Press*

Litwack, L. (1980) *Been in the Storm So Long: The Aftermath of Slavery*

McChesney, R. (1999) *Rich Media, Poor Democracy: Political Economy of the Media*

—— (2004) *The Problem of the Media: Communications Politics in the 21st Century*

McCoy, A. (1972) *The Politics of Heroin in Southeast Asia*

McGinnis, J. (1969) *The Selling of the President*

McNamara, R. (1995) *In Retrospect: The Tragedy and Lessons of Vietnam*

Madrick, J. (2008) *The Case for Big Government*

Magdoff, F. (1968) *The Age of Imperialism*

Magdoff, F., et al. (2000) *Hungry for Profit: The Agribusiness Threat to Farmers, Food, and the Environment*

Malraux, A. (1927) *Man's Fate*

—— (1940) *Man's Hope*

Malthus, T. (1798) *An Essay on the Principle of Population*

Mander, J. (1978) *Four Arguments for the Elimination of Television*

—— (1992) *In the Absence of the Sacred: The Failure of Technology and the Survival of Indian Nations*

Mannheim, K. (1936) *Ideology and Utopia*

Mantoux, P. (1906) *The Industrial Revolution in the Eighteenth Century*

Markusen, A. and Yudken, J. (1992) *Dismantling the Cold War Economy*

Marshall, A. (1890) *Principles of Economics*

Marx, K. (1867) *Capital (Vol. I)*

—— (1853) *The German Ideology*

Marx, K. and Engels, F. (1848) *The Communist Manifesto*

Mathias, P. (1987) *The First Industrial Revolution*

Matray, J. (ed.) (1991) *Historical Dictionary of the Korean War*

Mayer, J. (2008) *The Dark Side: The Inside Story of How the War Turned into a War on American Ideals*

Meier, D. (2004) *Many Children Left Behind: How the No Child Left Behind is Damaging Our Children and Our Schools*

Melman, W. (1970) *Pentagon Capitalism*

—— (1974) *The Permanent War Economy*

Miliband, R. (1969) *The State in Capitalist Society*

Mill, J. (1848) *The Political Economy of Capitalism*

Miller, H. (1971) *Rich Man, Poor Man*

Miller, M. (2001) *The Bush Dyslexicon*

Mills, C. (1956) *The Power Elite*

Mishel, L., et al. (various years) *The State of Working America*

Mitchell, B. (1947) *Depression Decade*

Moody, W. (1970) "An Ode in Time of Hesitation," in *From Poems and Plays*

Morris, C.R. (2008) *The Trillion Dollar Meltdown: Easy Money, High Rollers, and the Great Credit Crash*

Moyers, B. (2008) *Moyers on Democracy*

Navarro, V. (2002) *The Political Economy of Social Inequalities: Consequences for Health and Life*

Navasky, V. (1980) *Naming Names*

Naylor, R.T. (1987) *Hot Money and the Politics of Debt*

Nelson, C. (1999) *Manifesto of a Tenured Radical: Higher Education Under Fire*

Newman, K. (1993) *Declining Fortunes: The Withering of the American Dream*

Nordholdt, W. (1970) *The People That Walk in Darkness*

OECD (2008) "Income Inequality and Poverty Rising in Most OECD Countries," October 21. Available from www.oecd.org

Offner, A., et al. (2003) *Real World Macro*

Oglesby, C. and Shaul, R. (1967) *Containment and Change*

Omi, M. and Winant, H. (1994) *Racial Formation in the United State: From the 1960s to the 1990s*

Orwell, G. (1938) *Homage to Catalonia*

—— (1948) *Nineteen Eighty-Four*

—— (1970) "Politics and the English Language," in *The Collected Essays, Journalism, and the Letters of George Orwell* (Vol. 1940–50)

Osberg, L. (ed.) (1991) *Inequality and Poverty: International Perspectives*

Oz, A. (1995) *Israel, Palestine, and Peace*

Peckman, J. (1989) *Tax Reform: The Rich and the Poor*

Perry, J. (1965) *The Spanish Seaborne Empire*

Phillips, K. (1993) *Boiling Point: Democrats, Republicans and the Decline of Middle Class Prosperity*

—— (1994) *Arrogant Capital*

—— (2002) *Wealth and Democracy: A Political History of the American Rich*

—— (2006) *American Theocracy: The Peril and Politics of Radical Religion, Oil, and Borrowed Money*

—— (2008) *Bad Money: Reckless Finance, Failed Politics, and the Global Crisis of American Capitalism*

Pitt, W. and Ritter, S. (2002) *War on Iraq: What Team Bush Doesn't Want You to Know*

Piven, F. and Cloward, R. (1971) *Regulating the Poor*

Pizzo, S., et al. (1989) *Inside Job: The Looting of America's Savings and Loans*

Postman, N. (1985) *Amusing Ourselves to Death: Public Discourse in the Age of Show Business*

Potter, D. (1958) *People of Plenty*

Powers, T. (2002) *Intelligence Wars: American Secret History from Hitler to al Qaeda*

Rashid, A. (2008) *Descent into Chaos: The United States and the Failure of Nation Building in Pakistan, Afghanistan and Central Asia*

Ravenscroft, D. and Sherer, M. (1987) *Mergers, Sell-Offs and Economic Efficiency*

Reed, J. (1917) *The Ten Days that Shook the World*

Ricardo, D. (1817) *Principles of Political Economy and Taxation*

Rodman, S. (1938) *A New Anthology of Modern Poetry*

Roediger, D. (1991) *The Wages of Whiteness: Racism and the Making of the American Working Class*

Rogin, Leo (1956) *The Meaning and Validity of Economic Theory*

Ross, A., et al. (2005) *Real World Globalization*

Russell, E. (1993) "A Bad Bargain: Why US Health Care Costs So Much and Covers So Few," *Dollars & Sense*, May

Ryan, W. (1976) *Blaming the Victim*

Salvemini, G. (1936) *Under the Axe of Fascism*

Sampson, A. (1975) *The Seven Sisters*

Sandburg, C. (1936) *The People, Yes*

Saviano, R. (2006) *Gomorra*

Schiller, H. (1971) *Mass Communications and American Empire*

—— (1973) *The Mind Managers*

—— (1989) *Culture, Inc.: The Corporate Takeover of Public Expression*

Schlesinger, A. (1959) *The Age of Jackson*

Schmidt, C. (1939) *The Corporate State in Action*

Schor, J. (1998) *The Overspent American*

Scitovsky, T. (1976) *The Joyless Economy*

Sen, A. (1981) *Poverty and Famine: An Essay on Entitlement and Deprivation*

—— (2009) "Capitalism Beyond Crisis," *New York Review of Books*, March 26

Shawcross, W. (1979) *Sideshow: Kissinger, Nixon, and the Destruction of Cambodia*

Sherman, H. (1977) *Stagflation*

Sherwin, M. (1987) *A World Destroyed: Hiroshima and the Origins of the Arms Race*

Shiller, R. (2008) *The Subprime Solution*

Silone, I. (1934) *Fontamara*

Sinclair, U. (1906) *The Jungle*

—— (1920) *The Brass Check*

—— (1926) *Oil!*

Singer, P. (2003) *Corporate Warriors: The Rise of the Privatized Military Industry*

Slatter, P. (1971) *The Pursuit of Loneliness*

Smith, A. (1776) *An Inquiry Into the Nature and Causes of the Wealth of Nations*

Snell, B. (1939) "American Ground Transport," in *US Senate Hearings on Antitrust and Monopoly, 93rd Congress, 2nd Session*

Soros, G. (2008) *The New Paradigm for Financial Markets*

Soule, G. (1947) *Prosperity Decade*

Starr, P. (1982) *The Social Transformation of American Medicine: The Making of a Sovereign Profession and the Making of a Vast Industry*

Steffens, L. (1904) *The Shame of the Cities*

Steinbererg, S. (1981) *The Ethnic Myth: Race, Ethnicity, and Class in America*

Stiglitz, J. (2003) *Globalization and Its Discontents*

—— (2006) *Making Globalization Work*

—— (2008) *The Three Trillion Dollar War*

Stockdale, J. and S. (1984) *Love and War*

Stone, I. (1952) *The Hidden History of the Korean War*

Streeten, P. (1984) "Basic Needs: Some Unsettled Questions," *World Development* (Vol. 12)

Stretton, H. (1999) *Economics: A New Introduction*

Sullivan, J. (1889) *Manifest Destiny*

Sullivan, K. (2004) "Healthcare: The Medical Drug Mill is Bad News for the Seniors," *Z Magazine*, December

Sward, K. (1948) *The Legend of Henry Ford*

Tanzer, M. (1961) *The Political Economy of Oil and the Underdeveloped Countries*

Tawney, R. (1912) *The Agrarian Problem in the 16th Century*

—— (1920) *The Acquisitive Society*

—— (1926) *Religion and the Rise of Capitalism*

—— (1931) *Equality*

Taylor, A. (1961) *The Course of German History Since 1815*

Terkel, S. (1974) *Working People Talk About What They Do All Day and How They Feel About It*

—— (1984) *The Good War: An Oral History of World War II*

Thompson, E. (1968) *The Making of the English Working Class*

Tucker, R. (1978) *The Marx–Engels Reader*

Turgeon, L. (1996) *Bastard Keynesianism: Economic Thinking and Policymaking Since World War II*

Tye, L. (1998) *The Father of Spin: Edward L. Bernays and the Birth of Public Relations*

Ullman, J. (ed.) (1983) *Social Costs in Modern Society*

UNICEF (1986) *United Nations Report on the World's Children*

—— (1990) *Human Development Report*

US Senate Intelligence Committee (1975) *Report on Covert Action in Chile, 1963–73*

Uribe, A. (1975) *The Black Book on American Intervention in Chile*

Veblen, T. (1899) *The Theory of the Leisure Class*
—— (1904) *The Theory of Business Enterprise*
—— (1914) *The Instinct of Workmanship*
—— (1915) *Imperial Germany and the Industrial Revolution*
—— (1918) *The Higher Learning in America: The Conduct of Universities by Businessmen*
—— (1919) *The Place of Science in Modern Civilization*
—— (1923) *Absentee Ownership and Business Enterprise*
—— (1925) *The Laxdaela Saga*
—— (1948) *The Portable Veblen* (edited by Max Lerner)
Wang Hui (2003) *China's New Order: Society, Politics, and Economy in Transition*
Wharton, E. (1892) *The Age of Innocence*
—— (1904) *House of Mirth*
White, J. (1995) *Competing Solutions: American Health Care Proposals and International Experience*
Wilcox, C. (1969) *Toward Social Welfare*
Williams, E. (1944) *Capitalism and Slavery*
—— (1984) *From Columbus to Castro: The History of the Caribbean (1492–1959)*
Williams, W. (1966) *The Contours of American History*
—— (1969) *The Roots of Modern American History*
—— (1980) *Empire as a Way of Life*
Wills, G. (1969) *Nixon Agonistes: The Crisis of the Self-Made Man*
—— (1988) *Reagan's America*
Winant, H. (2001) *The World is a Ghetto*
Wittner, L. (1978) *Cold War America: From Hiroshima to Watergate*
Wolff, E. (1987) *Growth, Accumulation, and Unproductive Activity*
—— (1995) *Top Heavy: A Study of Increasing of Wealth in America*
Woodham-Smith, C. (1962) *The Great Hunger*
Woodward, C. (1956) *Reunion and Reaction*
Wright, R. (1992) *Stolen Continents: The Americas Through Indian Eyes Ever Since 1492*
Yates, M. (1994) *Longer Hours, Fewer Jobs: Employment and Unemployment in the United States*
—— (1998) *Why Unions Matter*
—— (2003) *Naming the System: Inequality and Work in the Global Economy*
—— (2007) *More Unequal: Aspects of Class in the USA*
Young, M. (1991) *The Vietnam Wars: 1945–1990*
Zinn, H. (2000) *A People's History of the United States*
Zweig, M. (2000) *The Working Class Majority: America's Best Kept Secret*

INDEX

Compiled by Sue Carlton